Staff Ride Handbook for the Battle of Perryville, 8 October 1862

Dr. Robert S. Cameron
Office of the Armor Historian
US Army Armor Center
Fort Knox, Kentucky

Cover photo: The author took this photo during an annual public reenactment at the Perryville Battlefield, Perryville, Kentucky.

Published by Books Express Publishing
Copyright © Books Express, 2012
ISBN 978-1-78039-793-1

Books Express publications are available from all good retail and online booksellers. For publishing proposals and direct ordering please contact us at: info@books-express.com

Contents

Figures

Maps

Stands

Foreword

In August and September 1862 Confederate armies were on the move northward. Robert E. Lee was invading Maryland, Earl Van Dorn and Sterling Price were moving into Tennessee, and Braxton Bragg and Edmund Kirby Smith were advancing into Kentucky. James McPherson, in his acclaimed *Battle Cry of Freedom,* cites this period as the first of the four major turning points of the American Civil War. The Confederate counteroffensive defeated Union hopes to end the war in 1862. However, by mid-October, hard on the heels of the broad Confederate advance the Union forces had regained the strategic and operational advantage, cited by McPherson as the second turning point of the war. Union victories at Antietam in the east and Perryville in the west carried significant weight in determining the final outcome of the conflict. While vast literature surrounds the former battle Perryville has been somewhat neglected. This work seeks to alleviate that lacuna. The US Army has used Civil War and other battlefields as "outdoor classrooms" to educate and train its officers. Since 1983 the Combat Studies Institute has produced a series of staff ride guides to assist units and classes in this training. The most recent volume in that series, Dr. Robert Cameron's *Staff Ride Handbook for the Battle of Perryville, 8 October 1862*, is a valuable study that examines the key considerations in planning and executing the September-October campaign and battle. Modern tacticians and operational planners will find themes that still resonate. Cameron demonstrates that Civil War leaders met their challenging responsibilities with planning, discipline, ingenuity, leadership, and persistence—themes that are well worth continued reflection by today's officers.

Thomas T. Smith
Colonel, Infantry
Director, Combat Studies Institute

Preface

Handbook Purpose

The staff ride remains an important tool for teaching military history and promoting leadership development. It links historical events with the actual ground upon which they occurred, providing an emotional as well as intellectual experience. The staff ride thus offers a vehicle for analyzing the human experience of combat. From this analysis emerge insights that are applicable to modern battle command. Technology and doctrine change over time, but the human dimension provides a connection between past and present. By concentrating on the actual ground upon which armies fought, the staff ride combines the formal study of the schoolhouse environment with the more visceral experience of the battlefield. By merging the analysis of command, doctrine, and weaponry with the terrain on which they were employed, the staff ride immerses students in the dynamics of combat.

This handbook serves to facilitate military staff rides to Perryville Battlefield State Historic Site in Kentucky. It is a tool to assist in applying the US Army's staff ride methodology to this battlefield. It provides a means of interpreting and understanding the battle of Perryville. In particular, this handbook assists small-group instructors in organizing and conducting a staff ride that focuses on relevant training objectives. In the process, awareness of the national military heritage is promoted.

Perryville Battlefield Attributes

The battle of Perryville symbolized the high-water mark of the Confederacy in the western theater of operations. In August 1862 General Braxton Bragg and Major General (MG) Edmund Kirby Smith led separate armies into Kentucky to wrest the state from the Union and install a Confederate governor. They initially met success and captured the state capital, simultaneously shifting the war in the west from northern Mississippi and Alabama to Kentucky. In response the North raised additional forces to protect Cincinnati and Louisville while MG Don Carlos Buell halted his offensive against Chattanooga and marched his Army of the Ohio back to Kentucky. On 8 October 1862 Buell's army clashed with Bragg's at Perryville. The Confederates achieved a tactical success in a hard-fought engagement that generated more than 7,000 casualties. Of the regiments engaged, 10 suffered losses between 40 and 60 percent. However, outnumbered by three to one, Bragg's army could not sustain its victory and withdrew. Within days of the battle, all of the invading Southern forces retired from the state. Kentucky remained firmly in the Union and secure from Confederate invasion for the war's duration.

Despite its importance to the course of the war in the west, Perryville does not benefit from the high visibility accorded the better-known Civil War sites such as Manassas, Gettysburg, Antietam, and Chickamauga. Although more than 70,000 Union and Confederate soldiers deployed in and around Perryville, understanding of the battle and its significance to the overall course of the war remains poor. For staff ride purposes this unfamiliarity can be a benefit. It forces the participants to study and think about the situation facing their Civil War counterparts without the preconceived notions that surround the more popular sites.

Perryville does not face the threat of encroaching development. The terrain on the battlefield looks today as it did in 1862. One of the most attractive features of the park for a staff ride is the ability to analyze the terrain and understand how the Civil War soldier saw and used it. The terrain has not been altered through modern construction and development. In addition, the surrounding landscape remains undeveloped farmland that adds to the area's feel of historicity. The park, itself, has also expanded considerably over the last decade. Where much of the most intensive fighting occurred now lies within the park's boundaries. Following the course of the battle no longer requires special arrangements with private property owners. Further land acquisitions are planned, permitting the scope of the staff ride to expand in tandem with the park.

The battle provides an excellent vehicle for studying brigade and below operations. This fight was not dominated from corps and division headquarters. Initial dispositions made by both army commanders, coupled with the nature of the terrain, ensured that individual brigade and regimental commanders' actions had a disproportionate influence on the battle's outcome. Focus on these command echelons encourages analysis of the tactical command climate and the influence of personality upon battlefield operations. The nature of the battle also facilitates studying brigade and regimental organization, internal command structure, and maneuver. Moreover, the smaller scale of the multiple engagements that comprised the fighting at Perryville permits detailed study of basic troop-leading procedures, soldier training, and small-unit leadership, including the noncommissioned officer's role.

Situational awareness proved just as important in 1862 as it is on today's battlefield. The battle of Perryville was a confused affair in which neither army possessed a clear sense of its opponent's intent or disposition. At the unit level, the rolling terrain often made it difficult for attacking regiments to know what lay behind the next hill. Command decisions were made with imperfect knowledge of enemy and sometimes friendly forces. In several instances, fratricide resulted. Poor situational awareness, friendly fire, unexpected developments, and mass casualties from enemy fire created a chaotic battlefield environment that challenged the abilities of leaders at all levels. Some commanders nevertheless achieved success. Thus, Perryville offers the opportunity to study these different dimensions of combat in detail, extracting insights that are applicable to current and future operations.

To be practical in today's military training environment, staff rides need to be cost and time effective. Perryville's small size and its close proximity to a major Army installation permit the conduct of a thorough staff ride in a single day, including transportation time. The park lies 1.5 hours from Fort Knox. Depending on the training objectives desired and the amount of prior preparation, time actually at the park will vary from 3 to 6 hours. Ample picnic areas exist on site to support large groups, and fuel should constitute the principal expense of the staff ride.

What This Handbook Provides

This handbook is modeled on the series of staff ride guides developed by the Combat Studies Institute (CSI), Fort Leavenworth, Kansas. It includes information concerning the nature of Civil War armies, the 1862 Kentucky campaign, maps, and more specialized material detailing the Armies of the Ohio and the Mississippi. A variety of instructional information helps readers to understand the flow of the battle; its participants; and related doctrinal, materiel, command, and organizational issues. The handbook is based on the latest interpretations of the battle that the park staff, recent publications, and archaeological findings have compiled. The heart of this guide, however, lies in chapter 3, which outlines a recommended route through the park based on the sequence of actual battle events. Specific stops have been identified for instruction, beginning with an orientation of the situation facing each army commander. Each subsequent stop includes background on the general situation, a vignette, and recommended teaching points for discussion. Where appropriate, additional information has been provided, detailing command, terrain, and unit information. The route concludes with a stop devoted to medical care and the problems the battle created for the local community. The bibliography provides a roadmap to sources related to Perryville. It is intended to facilitate supplemental study of the campaign and battle before the actual staff ride. Much detail regarding unit movements on the battlefield has been included in this handbook to facilitate its use by small-group leaders who may lack the time for an extended, formal study of the battle.

What This Handbook Does Not Offer

This guide offers a general sense of the flow of the battle of Perryville, punctuated by select snapshots of specific units and events for study and discussion. It does not provide a detailed description of all aspects of the battle. Its focus lies on those actions that occurred within the park's boundaries and can be accessed without special private property usage arrangements. However, using the offices identified in the administrative support chapter, it is possible to broaden the scope of the staff ride to include troop movements and operations that preceded the battle. Potential expansions include the Army of the Ohio's advance from Louisville to Perryville, the related Confederate cavalry rear guard actions, and the skirmishing that occurred on Peters Hill. Time and interest will be the principal constraints upon such an expanded staff ride.

This handbook is not a definitive work on Perryville. Group leaders conducting staff rides will need to supplement the information provided with some additional study. However, this guide is intended to reduce greatly the volume of such work. While teaching points are recommended, the group leader will need to determine how best to discuss them and maximize their training value for each audience. The success or failure of the staff ride as a training event will depend less on the volume of historical input and more on the manner of presentation. Group leaders need to identify their objectives and determine the best means of execution, relying on this handbook as an enabler to their success.

Acknowledgments

The author would like to acknowledge the support that several people and organizations offered in compiling this handbook. The park manager at Perryville Battlefield State Historical Site, Kurt Holman, provided insights and materials that proved invaluable to a work of this nature. His knowledge of Perryville stems from a lifetime spent studying the Civil War era in general and the battle for Kentucky in particular. Through his labors the park office now includes an extensive collection of primary-source material devoted to the soldiers who fought and died in this engagement. Further understanding of the battlefield and the surrounding area came from the Perryville Battlefield Preservation Association and its director, Stuart W. Sanders. This organization actively seeks to purchase additional properties with historical links to the battle, and it has accumulated its own reference collection for the battle of Perryville. The latter includes many of the research notes compiled by Kenneth W. Noe for his book *Perryville: This Grand Havoc of Battle* (Lexington, KY: University Press of Kentucky, 2001).

Information regarding the experiences of units and individuals during the campaign and during the battle drew heavily on the excellent and extensive Civil War source material available at the US Army Military History Institute, Carlisle, Pennsylvania. Dr. Richard Sommers, assistant director, Patron Services Division, provided research and editorial guidance that helped this handbook to evolve into a coherent product. Additional content and editorial feedback came from Doctors Russell F. Weigley, Anne W. Chapman, and J. Britt McCarley. The author is also indebted to Colonel (COL) Paul Jussel for his insights regarding what type of information to include and how to present so that it is useful to military personnel. Special thanks also to the many other soldiers, Department of Army civilians, and scholars who offered suggestions and advice throughout the course of this handbook's development. Responsibility for errors and inaccuracies, however, remains solely with the author.

Chapter 1. The Armies

Organization

The US Army in 1861

The US Regular Army on the eve of the Civil War served primarily in a frontier constabulary role. It comprised 16,000 officers and men, organized into 198 companies and scattered across the nation in 79 different posts. At the war's start, 183 companies were either on frontier duty or in transit. The remaining 15, mostly coastal artillery batteries, guarded the Canadian border, the Atlantic coast, or the nation's 23 arsenals. In 1861 Lieutenant General Winfield Scott commanded this army. A 75-year-old hero of the Mexican-American War, his position as general in chief was traditional, not statutory. Since 1821 Secretaries of War designated a general to be in charge of the field forces without formal congressional approval. The field forces were controlled through a series of geographic departments whose commanders reported directly to the general in chief. With modification this department system characterized Union and Confederate administration of regions under military control.

By 1860 a system of bureaus whose senior officers were in the twilight of long careers in their technical fields handled Army administration. Six of the 10 bureau chiefs were more than 70 years old. These bureaus, modeled after the British system, answered directly to the War Department. They were not subject to the general in chief's orders. Predecessors of many of today's combat support and combat service support branches, the following bureaus had been established by 1861:

> Quartermaster
> Medical
> Ordnance
> Adjutant General
> Subsistence
> Paymaster
> Engineer
> Inspector General
> Topographic Engineer (merged with the Engineer
>   Bureau in 1863)
> Judge Advocate General

During the war, Congress elevated the Office of the Provost Marshal and the Signal Corps to bureau status. It also created a Cavalry Bureau. No operational planning or intelligence staff existed since no such structure had been required before the Civil War.

This system provided suitable civilian control and administrative support to the small field army in the years before 1861. However, the bureau system also responded effectively, if not always efficiently, to the mass mobilization required over the next four years. Indeed, it would remain essentially intact until the early 20th century. In forming its own army and administrative structure, the Confederate government modeled its efforts on the US Army. In fact, many important figures in Confederate bureaus had served in one of the prewar bureaus.

Raising the Armies

With the outbreak of war in April 1861, both sides faced the monumental task of organizing and equipping armies much larger than the prewar force structure. The North retained control of the Regular Army, leaving the South to create its own regular force, although the latter existed primarily on paper. However, a large portion of the prewar officer corps joined the newly formed Confederate Army, including many of exceptional talent. Of 1,108 Regular officers serving as of 1 January 1861, 270 ultimately resigned to join the South. Only a few hundred of the 15,135 enlisted men left the ranks.

The North considered two options for employing the Regular Army: dispersing the existing units to train a newly raised volunteer force and committing them to the field without disruption. Initially, Scott envisioned a relatively small force to defeat the rebellion. He therefore insisted that the Regulars fight as units. Although some Regular units fought well in the war's early battles, this decision ultimately limited their impact on the war. Battle losses and disease soon thinned their ranks. Officials seeking replacements found themselves in competition with state organizations raising volunteer regiments. Many Regular units became so depleted that they were withdrawn from frontline service in November 1864. The commitment and wastage of Regulars in field deployments ensured their absence from the training base. Consequently, volunteer officers and men with little or no prior military service comprised most of the Union war effort.

Neither side had difficulty in recruiting the numbers initially required to fill the expanding ranks. In April 1861 President Abraham Lincoln called for 75,000 men from the states' militias for a three-month period. This figure represented an estimate of the number of soldiers required to quell the rebellion. The states first recruited their already existent militia companies and secured nearly 92,000. However, many of these soldiers lacked effective training and leadership. The war's continuation and expansion generated additional demands for manpower. In the North the federal government established quotas for local districts to fill. Similarly, the Confederate Congress authorized the acceptance of 100,000 one-year volunteers in March 1861. One-third of these men were under arms within a month. The Southern spirit of voluntarism was so strong that possibly twice that number could have been enlisted had sufficient arms and equipment been available.

In 1861 the US War Department considered making recruitment a federal responsibility, but this proposal seemed unnecessary for the short war then envisioned. Therefore, responsibility for recruiting remained with the states. Northern and Southern state governors continually encouraged local constituents to form new volunteer regiments. This practice strengthened support for local, state, and national politicians and provided an opportunity for glory and high rank for ambitious men. Such local recruiting created regiments with strong bonds among the men, but it hindered the flow of replacements to existing regiments. The Confederates attempted to funnel replacements into units from their same state or region, but the North continued to create new regiments. Existing Union regiments detailed men back home to recruit replacements, but their efforts could not compete with the allure of joining a new, local unit. New regiments thus lacked seasoned veterans to train the recruits while the battle-tested regiments lost men faster than they could replace them. Indeed, many regiments on both sides were reduced to combat ineffectiveness as the war progressed. Seasoned regiments were therefore often disbanded or consolidated, usually against the wishes of the men assigned.

As the war continued and casualty lists grew, the glory of volunteering faded. Both sides resorted to conscription to secure more soldiers. The Confederates enacted the first conscription law in American history in April 1862. The North followed suit in March 1863. These first experiments in American conscription proved inefficient and suffered from flawed administration. Conscription laws tended to exempt wealthier citizens, and numerous draftees hired substitutes or paid commutation fees. As a result, the average conscript's health, capability, and morale proved poor. Many eligible men, particularly in the South, enlisted to avoid the onus of being considered a conscript. Still, conscription, or the threat of conscription, helped to fill the ranks of both Union and Confederate armies.

Conscription was never a popular program. The North tried several approaches to limit conscription requirements. These efforts included offering lucrative bounties, or fees paid to induce volunteers to fill required quotas. The federal government also offered a series of reenlistment bonuses, including money, 30-day furloughs, and the opportunity for long-serving regiments to maintain their colors and receive the designation "veteran" volunteer infantry regiments. The Invalid Corps, later renamed the Veteran Reserve Corps, comprised men unfit for frontline service who performed essential rear-area duties. The North also recruited almost 179,000 African-Americans for service in separately organized volunteer regiments. This source of manpower soon became subject to conscription as well. In the South the recruitment or conscription of slaves remained a sensitive subject. It was not attempted until March 1865, too late to influence the war.

The imperfect mobilization machinery nevertheless provided large numbers of soldiers to feed the war's demands. Approximately 2 million men enlisted in the Union Army between 1861 and 1865. Nearly half were under arms at war's end. An estimated 750,000 to 800,000 men served in the Confederate military over the course of the war; however, peak strength never exceeded 460,000. The methods of manpower mobilization found expression in World Wars I and II. The lessons learned from the Civil War experience directly influenced the Selective Service System crafted and implemented in both of the later conflicts.

Tactical Organizations

Union and Confederate armies followed similar organizational patterns that reflected their common roots. In the North each of the 10 prewar Regular Army regiments consisted of 10 87-man companies with a maximum authorized strength of 878. At the war's start nine more infantry regiments were established, each following an organizational structure adopted from the French. These "French model" regiments comprised 2,452 officers and men organized into three battalions. Each of the latter included eight 100-man companies. In effect, these new battalions resembled the prewar Regular Army regiments. The new structure sought to reduce staff officer slots, but it proved unfamiliar to most commanders. Consequently, the smaller, prewar regiments were the models for volunteer units in the North and South. The US War Department set the authorized strength for volunteer regiments at between 866 and 1,046 officers and men. The Confederate Congress fixed the size of its 10-company regiments at 1,045. However, only newer units had numbers approximating these authorizations. Combat casualties, sickness, leave, details, desertion, and straggling quickly reduced actual field strength.

The battery remained the basic artillery unit, although battalion and larger formal groupings of artillery emerged later in the war. The US Army included 60 batteries in 1861, organized into five regiments. At war's start, however, the regiments performed largely administrative and personnel functions. In the field, batteries of the same regiment often did not serve together. Instead they were assigned to different infantry formations. Demands for additional artillery were met by creating volunteer batteries. By war's end volunteer batteries constituted most of the artillery among the Union and Confederate armies. Union batteries often included six guns, an authorized strength that varied between 80 and 156 men, and up to 130 horses. Confederate batteries frequently included only four cannon due to limitations on available manpower and ordnance. Indeed, many batteries included a mix of cannon types.

Before the Civil War the Regular Army included five mounted regiments. They consisted of two dragoon, two cavalry, and one mounted rifle regiment. Another cavalry regiment was established shortly after the war's outbreak. In August, all of these units were redesignated cavalry regiments and renumbered based on their date of organization. In July 1862 a common 12-company structure was applied. Authorized company strength varied from 79 to 95 men. Although the term "troop" was also introduced, most cavalrymen continued to use the more familiar term "company" to describe their units throughout the war. Union cavalry generally grouped two companies into a squadron and six squadrons into a regiment. Confederate cavalry regiments were authorized 10 76-man companies. Organizations larger than regiments tended to evolve throughout the war, but Union and Confederate armies gradually organized their mounted regiments into cavalry brigades, divisions, and corps.

		Union		Confederate
Infantry	19	regular regiments	642	regiments
	2,125	volunteer regiments	9	legions*
	60	volunteer battalions	163	separate battalions
	351	separate companies	62	separate companies
Artillery	5	regular regiments	16	regiments
	61	volunteer regiments	25	battalions
	17	volunteer battalions	227	batteries
	408	separate batteries		
Cavalry	6	regular regiments	137	regiments
	266	volunteer regiments	1	legion*
	45	battalions	143	separate battalions
	78	separate companies	101	separate companies

*Legions included infantry, artillery, and cavalry under a single command. Their strength approximated that of a large regiment. Sustained operations usually resulted in the loss of the legions' combined arms nature long before the war's end.

Figure 1. Organized forces.

For both infantry and cavalry, brigades comprised three to five regiments. Union brigades generally contained regiments from more than one state, while the Confederates often grouped regiments from the same state. Division structures varied, including two or more brigades. In the Confederate Army a brigadier general usually commanded a brigade and a major general commanded a division. The Union Army possessed no rank higher than an major general until 1864. Thus, colonels often commanded brigades, and brigadier generals led divisions.

Leaders

How units performed in battle often depended on the quality of their individual leaders. The respective central governments appointed general officers. At the start of the war, most of the senior officers in the Union and Confederate armies had attended the US Military Academy (USMA), West Point, New York, or another military school. In 1861 Lincoln appointed 126 general officers, of which 82 were, or had been, professional officers. Jefferson Davis appointed 89, of which 44 had received professional training. The rest were political appointees, but of these only 16 Federal and seven Confederate generals had no military experience.

Much has been made of the West Point backgrounds of the men who ultimately dominated the senior leadership positions of both armies, but such institutions did not prepare their graduates to command divisions, corps, or armies. Moreover, although many leaders had some combat experience from the Mexican War era, very few had experience above the company or battery level in the peacetime years before 1861. As a result, "professional" officers, in today's terminology, did not initially conduct the war at any level. Leaders became more professional through experience and at the expense of their soldiers' lives. General William T. Sherman would later note that the war did not enter its "professional stage" until 1863.

Of the volunteer officers who composed most of the leadership for both armies, state governors normally appointed colonels (regimental commanders). States appointed other field grade officers, although many were initially elected within their units. Company grade officers were usually elected by their men. This long-established militia tradition, which seldom made military leadership and capability a primary consideration, was largely an extension of the states' rights philosophy and sustained political patronage in both the Union and the Confederacy.

Civil War Staffs

In the Civil War, large military organizations' success often depended on the effectiveness of the commanders' staffs. Modern staff procedures had evolved only gradually with the increased complexity of military operations. This evolution was far from complete in 1861, and throughout the war, commanders personally handled many vital staff functions, most notably operations and intelligence. The nature of American warfare up to the mid-19th century had not yet clearly overwhelmed single commanders' capabilities.

Civil War staffs were divided into a general staff and a staff corps. This terminology, defined by Winfield Scott in 1855, differs from modern definitions. Table 2 lists typical staff positions at army level, although key functions are represented down to regimental level. The chief of staff and aides-de-camp formed a commander's personal staff. Hand-picked by the commander, their tenure changed with each turnover in army leadership. The remaining staff officers included representatives from the various bureaus. Logistics functions were particularly well represented. Collectively, staffs reflected the commander's personality, work ethic, and philosophy. In an environment in which staff officers and commanders struggled to discover and master their responsibilities, micromanagement flourished, particularly among those commanders who considered themselves professional soldiers. Experience bred competence among commanders and staffs as the war continued. Consequently, the general effectiveness of army management and leadership tended to improve. However, neither the North nor the South provided a mechanism within which to train competent staff officers.

General Staff

Chief of staff
Aides
Assistant adjutant general
Assistant inspector general

Staff Corps

Engineer
Ordnance
Quartermaster
Subsistence
Medical
Pay
Signal
Provost marshal
Chief of artillery
Chief of cavalry

Figure 2. Typical Army staff.

George B. McClellan, when he appointed his father-in-law as his chief of staff, was the first to use this title officially. Even though many senior commanders had a chief of staff, this position was not used in any uniform way. Seldom did the man in this role achieve the central coordinating authority of a modern chief of staff. This position, along with most other staff positions, was used as each commander saw fit. Hence staff functions and duties varied with each army commander. Inadequate use of the chief of staff was among the most important shortcomings of Civil War staffs. An equally important weakness was the lack of any formal operations or intelligence staff. Liaison procedures were also ill defined, and various staff officers or soldiers performed this function with little formal guidance. Miscommunication and lack of knowledge of friendly units repeatedly proved disastrous in combat.

The Army of the Ohio

In 1862 Major General (MG) Don Carlos Buell commanded the Army of the Ohio in its abortive movement against the Confederate railway hub at Chattanooga, Tennessee. The Union commander commenced operations in June, but as he neared the city, a combination of logistics and rear area security problems reduced his advance to a crawl. Buell commanded some 40,000 soldiers, most concentrated in his army's seven infantry divisions. His area of responsibility comprised northern Alabama, Tennessee, and Kentucky. It included a 400-mile frontage stretching from Battle Ground, Alabama, to Piketon, Kentucky. The rear area spanned a depth of some 350 miles and included his principal supply base at Louisville, Kentucky, the Louisville and Nashville Railroad, and his forward depots at Bridgeport and Stevenson, Alabama.

Moreover, Buell was charged with rebuilding and protecting the Memphis-Charleston Railroad from Corinth, Mississippi, to Chattanooga. Following repeated attacks on his lines of communication and supply, Buell ordered that garrisoned strong points be created at key points in Tennessee and northern Alabama. However, rear area security threatened to sap the Army of the Ohio's strength and make it incapable of further offensive actions against Chattanooga. Therefore, Buell limited the diversion of combat forces to rear area security. He left Kentucky to fend for itself with only 4,000 soldiers scattered across the state.

In August a Confederate force commanded by MG Edmund Kirby Smith invaded Kentucky, isolating one of Buell's divisions at the Cumberland Gap and moving into the central part of the state. The movement created panic among the North's leaders, and within days of the Confederate advance into

Kentucky, a reorganization of the Union command structure occurred.

On 19 August the War Department created a new Department of the Ohio commanded by MG Horatio G. Wright. Headquartered in Cincinnati, Wright assumed authority for Ohio, Illinois, Indiana, Michigan, Wisconsin, and Kentucky east of the Tennessee River. The Cumberland Gap fell within the department's boundaries. Buell remained in charge of the forces under his direct command and those in Tennessee reporting directly to MG Henry W. Halleck, general in chief of all Union armies. This restructuring relieved Buell from a host of administrative and command responsibilities that were unrelated to his operations near Chattanooga, but it also removed Brigadier General (BG) George W. Morgan's 7th Division at the Cumberland Gap from his command. Buell's line of supply and communications now stretched across his own area of responsibility and that of the Department of the Ohio. Moreover, his principal supply base at Louisville lay within Wright's command.

Formation	Status
1st Division BG Albin Schoepf	Pelham, Tennessee
2d Division MG Alexander M. McCook	Altamont, Tennessee
3d Division BG Lovell H. Rousseau	Huntsville, Alabama
4th Division BG Jacob Ammen 6th Division BG Thomas J. Wood	McMinnville, Tennessee Temporarily grouped under command of MG George H. Thomas
5th Division MG Thomas L. Crittenden	Hillsboro, Tennessee
1st Division, Army of the Mississippi BG John M. Palmer	En route. Arrives in Nashville, Tennessee, on 12 September
4th Division, Army of the Mississippi BG Jefferson C. Davis	En route. Arrives in Murfreesboro, Tennessee, on 1 September
8th Division BG James S. Negley	Organized 14 September at Nashville from unassigned railroad security forces

Figure 3. Army of the Ohio status, 30 August 1862.

When General Bragg moved north from Chattanooga in the last days of August, Buell's forces were dispersed across the principal routes leading to Nashville. Uncertainty regarding the true location and objective of the Confederate force led Buell on 30 August to concentrate his forces at Murfreesboro. In early September two additional infantry divisions joined Buell. These forces came from MG William S. Rosecrans' Union Army of the Mississippi in response to a request from Buell for reinforcements to secure his line of communications.

During the long march from Murfreesboro to Louisville, Buell directly commanded six infantry divisions with supporting cavalry. Upon reaching Louisville, however, Buell also assumed command of the new regiments that had been raised to defend the city against an expected Confederate attack. He now commanded some 80,000 soldiers. However, many of the new regiments he acquired lacked training and experience. In April 1862 the War Department had believed the war was nearly won and stopped accepting volunteers. By July it was clear that hostilities would continue, and President Lincoln called for an additional 300,000 volunteers. Between July and September many of these volunteers formed regiments in Ohio, Indiana, and Illinois. They were hurriedly raised and mustered into service to defend Cincinnati and Louisville. Those units sent to Louisville became part of the Army of the Ohio, but digging entrenchments around the city comprised most of their military experience. With minimal training and led by equally inexperienced officers, these units proved to be little more than a uniformed mob.

Buell restructured his army to permit the new units to learn from experienced ones. Green regiments were brigaded with veteran ones while divisions likewise comprised a collection of brigades with mixed experience levels. This restructuring generally benefited the new regiments at the expense of brigade integrity. Regiments that had served together in the same brigade since their organization now found themselves reshuffled alongside new units with whom they had no common bonds. State affiliation could not replace the ties born of shared experience. To reduce the meddling of state politicians, Buell previously had ensured that his brigades comprised regiments of different states. Thus, integrating the new regiments into the Army of the Ohio came at the cost of reduced cohesion at the brigade and division levels. For the individual soldier, his primary loyalties lay with the company and regiment where men from the same county and state served. Little encouragement existed for the soldier to identify with his brigade or his division.

In an order issued on 29 September Buell formally reorganized the

Army of the Ohio. He formed three new infantry divisions from the new regiments gathered in Louisville and from additional units sent from western Tennessee. He also implemented a corps structure, creating three corps, each of three divisions. Previously Buell had either issued orders directly to each of his division commanders, or he had assigned a senior division commander responsibility over a two-division grouping. The new corps organization rationalized his senior command structure and aligned it with similar changes already implemented in other Union armies.

To fill the new corps command slots Buell selected his senior division commanders. MG Alexander M. McCook and MG Thomas L. Crittenden became the I and II Corps commanders, respectively. McCook graduated from the USMA in 1852. He served in the West until 1858 when he became a tactics instructor at West Point. Upon the outbreak of war in 1861, he was commissioned a colonel in the volunteers and commanded the 1st Ohio Infantry at Bull Run. At Shiloh he commanded a division as a BG, rising thereafter to MG. Crittenden had no formal military education. He saw active service in the Mexican War as an aide to MG Zachary Taylor and later as a colonel commanding a volunteer regiment. Professionally educated as a lawyer, he maintained a law practice in Kentucky, and he had risen to the rank of MG in that state's militia by 1860. Following the outbreak of war, Crittenden assumed overall command of the Kentucky State Guard before being commissioned a BG in the Union Army in September 1861. Like McCook he had already attained division command before the battle of Shiloh. Both commanders had considerable experience as division commanders before assuming corps command.

Buell intended for BG William Nelson to command III Corps. Although his brusque manner made him unpopular, Nelson had proven himself to be an aggressive fighter. He commanded a division at Shiloh and during the subsequent campaigns against Corinth and Chattanooga. In August Buell dispatched Nelson along with several officers and cannon to Louisville to organize Kentucky's defenses and restore his supply line between Nashville and Louisville. Upon arrival in Louisville, he was instead designated to command the newly raised Army of Kentucky, responsible for defending the Commonwealth from Confederate invasion. Wounded at the battle of Richmond on 30 August, he returned to Louisville to recover. There he assumed command of the city's defenses. On 29 September BG Jefferson C. Davis shot and killed him following an altercation. Davis commanded one of the divisions sent to reinforce the Army of the Ohio. With Nelson dead and Davis under house arrest, Buell appointed Charles C. Gilbert to command III Corps.

Formation	Status
I Corps	Louisville, Kentucky
2d Division	
BG Joshua W. Sill	
3d Division	
BG Lovell H. Rousseau	
10th Division	Organized from new
BG James S. Jackson	regiments in Louisville
II Corps	Louisville, Kentucky
4th Division	
BG William S. Smith	
5th Division	
BG Horatio P. Van Cleve	
6th Division	
BG Thomas J. Wood	
III Corps	Louisville, Kentucky
1st Division	
BG Albin Schoepf	
9th Division	Previously 4th Division,
BG Robert D. Mitchell	Army of the Mississippi, commanded by BG Jefferson C. Davis
11th Division	Organized from elements of
BG Philip H. Sheridan	5th Division, Army of the Mississippi and new regiments
Unattached	
12th Division	Louisville, Kentucky
BG Ebenezer Dumont	
8th Division	Nashville, Tennessee
BG James S. Negley	Organized 14 September
13th Division	Nashville, Tennessee
BG John M. Palmer	Previously 1st Division, Army of the Mississippi
Cavalry	
Cavalry Division	Elizabethtown, Kentucky
COL John Kennett	Organized 5 September

Figure 4. Army of the Ohio status, 30 September 1862.

Gilbert graduated from the USMA and served with distinction during the Mexican War. Afterward he served on the frontier and taught at

West Point. Promoted to captain in 1855, he commanded a company at the outbreak of the Civil War. Wounded at Wilson's Creek in 1861, he subsequently served as an inspector general for the Army of the Ohio. In August 1862 he accompanied Nelson to Louisville and became the inspector general for the ill-fated Army of Kentucky. Following the battle of Richmond, efforts to organize Kentucky's defenses suffered from a lack of general officers. Gilbert's combat record and military education led to his recommended appointment as MG, although he lacked command experience beyond the company level. The US Senate never confirmed this rank, but in the chaos that characterized the Union command structure in Kentucky, Gilbert remained a de facto general. After the Army of the Ohio's arrival in Louisville and Nelson's death, Buell assigned Gilbert to command III Corps. As a corps commander Gilbert proved ineffective and unpopular. Following the battle of Perryville he was relieved of his command, and his general officer rank was revoked. He saw no further field service, and he ended the war as a major.

Command of III Corps might have passed to MG George H. Thomas, but Buell designated him to serve as his second in command. A Virginian, Thomas opted to fight for the North. A graduate of the USMA and a veteran of both the Seminole Indian Wars and the Mexican War, Thomas was a major in the 2d Cavalry when the Civil War began. Assigned to the Army of the Ohio, he defeated a Confederate force at Mill Springs early in 1862. He participated in the Shiloh, Corinth, and Chattanooga campaigns as a division commander and remained one of the most effective senior officers within the Army of the Ohio. However, his appointment to second in command left him without any effective control or direct influence upon field operations.

The appointment of corps commanders opened vacancies at the division level. Senior brigade commanders assumed these positions. BG Albin Schoepf replaced Thomas as the 1st Division commander, despite his well-known animosity toward Buell. Indeed, Schoepf considered the army commander a traitor for his soft war policies. However, Schoepf had previously commanded the division in Thomas' absence. BG Joshua W. Sill replaced McCook in charge of the 2d Division. BG Lovell H. Rousseau commanded the 3d Division, having assumed this position the previous July following MG Ormsby M. Mitchel's recall to Washington. BG William S. Smith and BG Horatio P. Van Cleve assumed command of the 4th and 5th Divisions, respectively. Of the seven divisions that initially comprised the Army of the Ohio four underwent changes in division leadership during Buell's reorganization at Louisville less than two weeks before the battle of Perryville. Only the 6th Division, led by BG Thomas J. Wood, remained free from this reshuffling. The 7th Division had been isolated at the Cumberland Gap and removed from Buell's command.

New division leaders were also appointed to command the 9th, 10th, and 11th Divisions. BG Jefferson C. Davis commanded the 9th Division, but he remained under temporary house arrest in Louisville after Nelson's murder. In his stead BG Robert B. Mitchell commanded. BG James S. Jackson commanded the 10th Division. Lacking a formal military education, he had served as a private and later an officer in the 1st Kentucky Cavalry during the Mexican War. His military service ended when he resigned to avoid a court-martial for fighting a duel with another officer. He ran for and was elected to Congress in 1858. He remained a politician until his resignation from office in 1861 when he was commissioned a colonel of volunteers and assumed command of the 3d Kentucky Cavalry. Although present at the battle of Shiloh, his regiment was not engaged there. He briefly led the Army of Kentucky's cavalry regiments before assuming command of the 10th Division. BG Philip Sheridan received command of the 11th Division, and the battle of Perryville marked his debut as a division commander.

The restructured Army of the Ohio lacked time for its new corps and division commanders to learn their responsibilities. Buell's reorganization in the last days of September occurred simultaneously with preparations to march on Confederate forces at Bardstown and Frankfort. Lack of senior command experience compounded the challenges already facing those regiments raised during summer 1862. With insufficient training and led by regimental officers struggling to understand their roles and responsibilities, these green units now found themselves assigned to divisions and corps undergoing similar leadership challenges. In a singular departure from Buell's otherwise consistent mixing of green and veteran troops, Jackson's 10th Division comprised entirely new regiments. It had no leavening of experienced soldiers, commanders, or staffs. At Perryville this division would find itself in the forefront of the fighting.

At the army level, Buell possessed a well-organized and capable staff. It performed the functions demanded of it, but the staff did not represent an extension of command authority. Instead it remained focused on precisely executing the duties Buell prescribed. The chief of staff, for example, did not exercise authority in the absence of the army commander. Oriented on Buell, the army commander's staff thus offered little support to the new corps and division leaders. Corps and division staffs did exist, but they, too, focused on implementing instructions as given rather than providing input to their respective commanders.

The Army of the Mississippi

General Braxton Bragg commanded the Army of the Mississippi, often called the Army of Mississippi, during its invasion of Kentucky in 1862. In the aftermath of Shiloh, Bragg became the fifth most senior ranking general in the Confederacy, responsible for the Western Department. This department encompassed a large geographic area ranging from the Mississippi River to eastern Tennessee and from the Gulf of Mexico to the Tennessee-Kentucky border. Bragg further subdivided the department into several military districts, each with a separate commander. The most important of these districts included the Gulf, Mississippi, and Tennessee. The first bore responsibility for defending the Gulf Coast in general and Mobile, Alabama, in particular. MG Earl Van Dorn commanded the District of Mississippi, charged with defending much of that state, especially Vicksburg, the principal obstacle to further Union operations on the Mississippi River. MG Sterling Price was responsible for the District of Tennessee. His mission lay in preventing any further Union advance into northern Mississippi.

During the Kentucky campaign Van Dorn and Price's armies were to support Bragg's operations. Their mission was to prevent the dispatch of Union reinforcements from western Tennessee and to advance on Nashville. Although Bragg intended these forces to act independently, Van Dorn subordinated Price to his own command with the support of the Confederate War Department. The resultant unified leadership, however, did little to improve the cooperation of Van Dorn's army with Bragg's. Van Dorn favored an attack on Corinth, Mississippi, rather than an advance into Tennessee. Moreover, he also interfered with the operations of MG John C. Breckinridge and his division. Breckinridge was intended to follow in the wake of Bragg's advance and reinforce the Army of the Mississippi. As the campaign unfolded, Van Dorn delayed the northward movement of Breckinridge's division until it could no longer influence events in Kentucky.

Bragg retained most of his department's strength under his personal command. In preparation for the Kentucky campaign, he moved this force via rail to Chattanooga. The latter town lay in the Department of Eastern Tennessee, commanded by MG Edmund Kirby Smith. His primary responsibility was to protect eastern Tennessee and secure the last direct rail link between the Western Department and northern Virginia. For the invasion of Kentucky, Smith was to secure the Cumberland Gap and support Bragg's movements. However, Smith planned an independent invasion of Kentucky. Smith successfully lobbied for additional forces on the pretext of defending his department. He also received additional soldiers from Bragg following Bragg's decision to redeploy to Chattanooga.

On the eve of the Kentucky campaign, Smith's Army of Eastern Tennessee comprised the infantry divisions of BG Carter Stevenson, BG Henry Heth, BG Thomas J. Churchill, and BG Patrick R. Cleburne. The last formation comprised two infantry brigades temporarily attached to Smith's army from Bragg to support operations against the Cumberland Gap. The Army of Eastern Tennessee included some 19,000 infantry and cavalry troops. In addition, Smith received indirect support from the mounted force commanded by Colonel (COL) John H. Morgan whose raids into Kentucky and Tennessee helped set the stage for the entire Kentucky campaign. Smith also arranged for additional support from the Department of Western Virginia. From there BG Humphrey Marshall would lead a small army of some 4,500 troops into eastern Kentucky.

Despite the planned contributions of Marshall, Smith, Price, Van Dorn, and Breckinridge, Bragg considered his Army of the Mississippi to be the main effort for invading Kentucky. Concentrated at Chattanooga, this army included some 27,000 soldiers, not including the reinforcements sent to Smith. Before commencing operations, Bragg reorganized his army into two wings, each comprising two divisions and a cavalry brigade. Each infantry division included four brigades of infantry, but the number of regiments in these brigades varied. One artillery battery was also assigned to each brigade to provide fire support. At the start of the campaign additional cavalry units also reported directly to Bragg.

To coordinate the army's actions, Bragg relied on a less than ideal staff. Despite the importance of the coming invasion of Kentucky, many of his staff officers lacked experience. Bragg unsuccessfully lobbied the Confederate War Department for more qualified personnel. He lacked a chief of cavalry to centrally oversee cavalry operations and provide administrative support to the mounted units. The Army of the Mississippi also had no chief of staff when it began its march toward Kentucky. The incumbent for this position considered himself physically unfit for the rigors of a major campaign and requested relief from this responsibility. Unable to secure another experienced officer for this position, Bragg opted to perform the duties of both army commander and chief of staff himself. Although he possessed an extraordinary penchant for work, especially administrative and organizational, merging these responsibilities in one person threatened to overtax the army commander. With critical positions vacant and others held by officers who were new to their responsibilities, the ability of Bragg's staff to properly execute the commander's intent remained limited.

The wing commanders proved a contrast in military expertise. MG Leonidas Polk commanded the right wing. He also served as Bragg's second in command. Despite the importance of these positions, Bragg had little faith in Polk's military abilities. Polk graduated from the USMA in 1827 only to resign his commission shortly thereafter to join the Episcopalian ministry. A personal friend of Jefferson Davis, upon the outbreak of the Civil War Polk received the rank of MG and command of the Western Department, despite his lack of military experience. He helped organize the Army of the Mississippi, but he also was responsible for the Confederacy violating Kentucky's neutrality.

Replaced by General Albert Sydney Johnston as department commander, Polk continued to serve in the Army of the Mississippi as a corps commander. In this capacity he fought at Shiloh and remained with the army during the siege of Corinth and later its retreat to Tupelo. Bragg requested he be removed from command, but Davis refused. Unable to avoid appointing him to a senior leadership position, Bragg made Polk his second in command, a position with little responsibility. However, when the army adopted a wing organization, Bragg had little choice but to assign Polk as wing commander.

William J. Hardee graduated from the USMA in 1838. He saw action during the Mexican War and later served as Commandant of Cadets at his alma mater. He was author of *Rifle and Light Infantry Tactics*, a manual that both Union and Confederate armies later used for training. When the Civil War began, Hardee joined the Southern cause and became a BG. He served in the West and was promoted to MG. At Shiloh he commanded a corps. When Bragg reorganized his army Hardee assumed command of the left wing, an appointment that reflected his own abilities and the army commander's confidence.

At the division level Bragg's commanders represented a similar mix of abilities. MG Benjamin F. Cheatham and MG Jones M. Withers had the most command experience. Cheatham had no formal military education, but he had seen extensive service during the Mexican War, first commanding a company, then a regiment, and finally a brigade. In the Civil War he led a division at Shiloh and became an MG shortly thereafter. He also proved popular among the Tennesseans he commanded. Withers began the war commanding the 3d Alabama Infantry. Promoted to BG he assumed responsibility for Alabama's state guard and defending the state's coastline. He, too, had risen to division command before Shiloh and afterward received promotion to MG. He ranked among Bragg's most trusted subordinates.

BG Simon B. Buckner and BG J. Patton Anderson lacked Cheatham's and Withers' experience. Buckner graduated from the USMA in 1844, served in the Mexican War, and remained with the Army until he resigned in 1855. He remained connected to military affairs in his home state of Kentucky. In 1860 he commanded the state guard. Shortly after the Civil War began, he accepted a commission as a BG in the Confederate Army. However, in February 1862 Buckner surrendered at Fort Donelson. He remained a prisoner until being exchanged the following summer. He assumed division command in Hardee's left wing shortly before Bragg's army left Chattanooga. Anderson's background included medicine, politics, and service in the Mexican War with a Mississippi volunteer regiment. Appointed to command the 1st Florida Infantry at the Civil War's start, he rose to BG and led a brigade at Shiloh. His tenure as division commander began in the weeks before the Kentucky campaign.

At the brigade level the Army of the Mississippi was generally well served. Several commanders led brigades at Shiloh, and unlike their Union counterparts all of them gained experience by campaigning with their units in the weeks before the battle of Perryville. Cleburne numbered among the most capable of these brigade commanders, having risen on the basis of merit from an enlisted soldier to the rank of BG before the campaign opened. He had also served as a temporary division commander during MG Edmund Smith's initial invasion of Kentucky. Indeed, Cleburne's leadership contributed considerably to the decisive victory at Richmond that opened the way for Smith's army to seize the state capital.

The brigades generally comprised regiments from the same state. Whereas the Army of the Ohio mixed regiments from different states in the same brigade, the Army of the Mississippi built upon state loyalties to improve brigade cohesion. Confederate brigades represented their home states on the battlefield, a symbolic relationship that helped seal each soldier's loyalty to his regiment and parent brigade. Moreover, even new regiments served together throughout the campaign, and they generally performed better than those Northern units organized almost on the eve of battle.

The battle of Perryville was not a planned event. Buell's aggressive pursuit of the Confederate columns withdrawing toward Harrodsburg forced the Confederates to deploy or risk being attacked while on the march. A belated effort to concentrate in preparation for the attack at Perryville proved only partially successful. The brigades previously attached to Smith's army returned to Bragg's control, but only three infantry divisions and two cavalry brigades participated in the battle. Artillery support included those batteries assigned to the infantry brigades. No effort was made to create larger groupings of cannon under a separate commander for massed fire support.

Force	Status
Army of Eastern Tennessee MG Edmund Kirby Smith	Estimated 19,000 men at Jacksboro, TN
Army of the Mississippi General Braxton Bragg	Estimated 27,000 men concentrated at Chattanooga, TN
Army of the Mississippi MG Earl Van Dorn	Estimated 16,000 men at Tupelo, MS
Army of the Mississippi MG Sterling Price	Estimated 16,000 men in central and western Mississippi with headquarters at Vicksburg
Army of Western Virginia BG Humphrey Marshall	Estimated 4,500 men at Abingdon, VA
Breckinridge's Division MG John C. Breckinridge	Rest and recuperation following 4 August attack on Baton Rouge, LA

Figure 5. Confederate dispositions for the Kentucky campaign, August 1862.

Weapons

Infantry

In the 1850s the rifle musket began to supplant the smoothbore musket as the principal infantry weapon in Europe and America. During the Civil War it became the standard firearm for both Union and Confederate armies. Nevertheless, smoothbore muskets continued to see service throughout the conflict. The initial mobilization of soldiers in both the North and South quickly outstripped stocks of rifle muskets. Over time, however, foreign purchases, production, and battlefield captures ensured that both sides possessed sufficient quantities of rifle muskets.

The predominance of the rifle musket marked a significant shift in infantry firearms. Previously rifled weapons tended to be reserved for select units that employed light infantry and skirmishing tactics. The rifle was not the foot soldier's primary weapon because it proved slow to load and often could not carry a bayonet. The smoothbore musket did not share these drawbacks. Moreover, the close-order drill and linear tactics of the late 18th and early 19th centuries emphasized volume of fire over

19

accuracy. This emphasis reflected the close range firefights characteristic of this period.

Technological development, however, triggered a change in the relative status of the rifle and the smoothbore musket. In particular, the emergence of new ammunition types helped to decrease the time necessary to load the rifle. In 1854 the US Army adopted with some refinement the Minié ball designed by French Army Captain Claude Minié. Unlike the spherical ball used in smoothbore muskets the Minié ball was actually a cylindrical-conoidal projectile with a hollow base. Intentionally made smaller than the rifle's bore, the bullet could be loaded with ease. When the weapon fired, the hollow base expanded to fit the rifling inside the gun barrel. The resultant ballistic spin gave the rifle its accuracy. Previous generations of rifles used ammunition exactly fitted to match the grooves inside the gun barrel. Loading required the round to be forced down the gun barrel, a process requiring considerable energy and time. In contrast, the ball ammunition that many smoothbore muskets used could be dropped into the gun barrel, simplifying and speeding the loading process. The Minié ball, however, permitted the rifle's accuracy to be combined with the smoothbore's ease of loading and higher rate of fire.

In the United States, the model 1855 Springfield rifle musket became the first regulation arm to use the .58-caliber Minié bullet. This weapon combined the outward appearance of the smoothbore musket with the rifle's accuracy and longer range. Hence, the Army adopted this weapon to replace both the .69-caliber smoothbore musket and the .54-caliber rifle. Minor changes to the base design resulted in the model 1861 and model 1863. In terms of its production and use, the model 1861 became one of the most common shoulder weapons found on the Civil War battlefield. It was 56 inches long overall, had a 40-inch barrel, and weighed 8.75 pounds. It could be fitted with a 21-inch socket bayonet (with an 18-inch blade, 3- inch socket). The weapon featured a rear sight graduated to its maximum effective range of 500 yards. At 1,000 yards it still retained killing power, albeit much reduced. The Minié ball fired could penetrate 11 inches of white pine board at 200 yards and 3 ¼ inches at 1,000 yards. Penetration of one inch was considered the equivalent of killing or seriously wounding a person.

In addition to the Springfields, more than 100 types of muskets, rifles, rifle muskets, and rifled muskets found employment during the Civil War. Their calibers similarly varied to a maximum of .79-caliber. The numerous American-made weapons were supplemented early in the conflict by a variety of imported models. The British .577-caliber Enfield rifle, model

1853, proved among the most popular and numerous of the foreign weapons. It stood 54 inches long (with a 39-inch barrel), weighed 8.7 pounds (9.2 pounds with bayonet), could be fitted with a socket bayonet with an 18-inch blade, and had a rear sight graduated to a range of 900 yards. The Enfield design was produced in a variety of forms, both long and short barreled, by several British manufacturers and at least one American company. Of all the foreign designs the Enfield most closely resembled the Springfield in characteristics and capabilities. Indeed, their ammunition could be used interchangeably, providing each weapon's barrel was clean. The United States purchased more than 436,000 Enfield pattern weapons during the war. Statistics on Confederate purchases are more problematic, but according to a February 1863 report, deliveries since the war's start totaled 70,980 long Enfields and 9,715 short Enfields. Another 23,000 awaited delivery.

While the quality of imported weapons varied, experts considered the Enfields and the Austrian Lorenz rifle muskets to be very good. Some foreign governments and manufacturers took advantage of the huge initial demand for weapons by dumping their obsolete weapons on the American market. This practice was especially prevalent with some of the older smoothbore muskets and converted flintlocks. The greatest challenge, however, lay in maintaining these weapons and supplying ammunition and replacement parts for calibers ranging from .44 to .79. The quality of the imported weapons eventually improved as the purchasers' procedures, standards, and astuteness improved. For the most part, the European suppliers provided needed weapons, and the newer foreign weapons were highly regarded.

The United States purchased about 1,165,000 European rifles and muskets during the war, nearly all within the first two years. Of those 110,853 were smoothbores. The rest were primarily the French Minié rifles (44,250), Austrian model 1854s (266,294), Prussian rifles (59,918), Austrian Jagers (29,850), and Austrian Bokers (187,533). Estimates of total Confederate purchases range from 340,000 to 400,000. In addition to Enfields the Confederacy also received 27,000 Austrian rifles and 21,040 British muskets. It also purchased an additional 2,020 Brunswick rifles and 30,000 Austrian rifles, which were awaiting shipment when the war ended.

At Perryville the Army of the Ohio included a number of new regiments. These units were outfitted with whatever firearms were available in military stocks. Many of the weapons were American smoothbore muskets—some modified into rifles—and a variety of foreign rifles. Nor was it uncommon for a single regiment to possess multiple weapon types. Their quality varied, and many soldiers complained of entering combat with defective muskets. Consequently the effectiveness of Union infantry fire tended to vary, depending not only on experience but also on the weaponry used. The Confederate regiments had a smaller variety of smoothbore and rifle muskets, and most units were equipped with a single weapon type. Moreover, several units benefited from the capture of large numbers of modern Springfields at the earlier battle of Richmond.

The smoothbore and rifle muskets used at Perryville and most Civil War battlefields were muzzleloaders that required a similar loading process. First the soldier took a paper cartridge in hand and tore the end of the paper with his teeth. He poured the powder down the barrel and placed the bullet in the muzzle. Then, using a metal ramrod, he pushed the bullet firmly down the barrel until seated. He then cocked the hammer and placed a percussion cap on the cone or nipple that, when struck by the hammer, ignited the gunpowder. Green soldiers became notorious for forgetting to remove their ramrods before firing. The ramrod became a dangerous projectile, whirling through the air. Its loss, however, rendered the weapon useless as a firearm. The black powder used tended to wreath the weapon and its user in smoke that reduced visibility. The powder also tended to foul a weapon quickly, reducing its accuracy and increasing the chance of a misfire. In the latter case, failure to clear the weapon before reloading increased the possibility of the weapon exploding.

Repetitive training in loading and firing the rifle musket thus became critical to its proper use in combat. Drills at the individual and unit levels focused on enabling soldiers to load and fire regardless of their circumstances. In this manner, they would be less likely to misuse their weapon even when under fire. However, unit training focused on rapid loading and firing rather than accuracy. Engaging targets at longer ranges required a collective proficiency that most Civil War units did not possess. The rise and fall of the rifled musket's trajectory required careful estimation of range and a corresponding precision in aiming the piece. However few units ever practiced live-fire training to master these skills. Instead companies and regiments learned to fire as part of a prescribed drill that emphasized the repetition of loading and firing as an individual and as a team. In field conditions a seasoned soldier generally achieved a rate of fire of two to three rounds per minute.

Breech-loading weapons suited the training emphasis given to a sustained volume of fire over long-range accuracy. A variety of breech-loading guns and repeating rifles became available before 1861. When the

Civil War began, individual soldiers often purchased limited quantities for military use; however, they were generally not issued to soldiers in large numbers. Many guns had technical problems such as faulty ammunition, complicated mechanisms, and poor breech seals. The Ordnance Department also feared that such weapons would result in a prodigious consumption of ammunition that could not be supplied or sustained. Moreover, the ability of breechloaders to deliver large volumes of fire was not universally considered an asset because it discouraged soldiers from relying on offensive action to close with the enemy. In an age in which the psychology of the offensive predominated, weapons that discouraged decisive, tactical movements did not merit favor or support. The comparatively high cost of the breechloader further discouraged its widespread military use.

The war's duration and demands from the field for rapid-firing weapons only partially overcame these obstacles. In the North the War Department fielded a large number of breechloaders, but most of these went to cavalry units. Few reached foot soldiers except for a few select units. In some instances infantry regiments purchased these weapons directly from the manufacturer. Overall, however, the rifle musket remained the standard and most common weapon. Confederate infantry fared little better, relying more on battlefield captures rather than on production and imports to secure the small number of breechloaders actually used.

Cavalry

Cavalry weaponry made significant changes during the course of the war. Union cavalry initially suffered from a number of shortages, including firearms. In particular the mounted regiments serving in the west suffered initially from insufficient firearms of any kind. Some units began operations armed only with sabers. Although this situation quickly changed to include pistols, securing large numbers of carbines and rifles proved to be more difficult. At the war's start no single office within the War Department represented or oversaw cavalry needs. Fielding priorities for new weapons invariably favored the eastern theater. Hence, throughout 1861 and 1862, Union cavalry in the west was forced to use whatever firearms could be secured. The uneven state of cavalry arms directly contributed to their varied effectiveness.

When available, mounted soldiers preferred easier-handling carbines, particularly breechloaders, to the more cumbersome muzzle-loading muskets and rifles. Several different types were used, including the Hall .52-caliber, the Merrill .54-caliber, the Maynard .52-caliber, the Gallager

.53-caliber, the Smith .52-caliber, and the Burnside .56 caliber. Together these models totaled over 240,000 carbines produced. The Sharps .52-caliber proved the most famous of the single-shot carbines the Union cavalry used. It used a linen cartridge and a pellet primer feed mechanism.

Mounted regiments also employed several multishot weapons. Before the war the model 1855 Colt repeating rifle offered a larger version of Colt's popular series of revolvers. This weapon was manufactured in several different lengths and calibers, ranging from 32 to 42 ½-inches and from .36 to .56 calibers. Most versions featured six chambers, but the .56-caliber held only five. The sturdy and reliable nature of Colt's revolvers made them popular, but the repeating rifle lacked these qualities. It used a conical bullet with a paper cartridge attached. With each chamber loaded, its rate of fire depended solely on the speed with which the hammer was cocked and the trigger was squeezed. However, it proved slower than other multishot weapons to reload. Its most notorious drawback was in its tendency to fire all chambers at once without warning. The resultant explosion often caused severe injury, including the loss of fingers, to the operator.

Despite this defect Union cavalry in the west sought this weapon for its rapid firepower. In the Army of the Ohio, the 2d Michigan achieved considerable success with it. Buell sought large numbers of the rifle with which to equip his cavalry. His efforts proved unsuccessful. The War Department purchased less than 5,000 during the war before more reliable multishot weapons became available. The seven-shot Spencer repeater was the best known of these later models. It came in rifle and carbine versions, both .52-caliber. The rifle weighed 10 pounds and stood 47 inches. The carbine weighed 8 ¼ pounds and was 39 inches long. The Spencer became the first weapon the US Army adopted to fire a metallic rim-fire, self-contained cartridge. Soldiers loaded rounds through an opening in the butt of the stock, which fed into the chamber through a tubular magazine by the action of the trigger guard. The hammer still had to be cocked manually before each shot. By war's end more than 94,000 Spencers had been produced, and it had become a favorite among the Union cavalry.

Confederate cavalry suffered from the restraints imposed by the South's limited industrial capacity. Domestic production of firearms suitable for cavalry use remained low. Consequently, cavalry regiments found themselves armed with an array of different weapon types, including personal weapons that soldiers brought to their units. Many regiments lacked uniformity in their muskets, rifles, revolvers, shotguns, and sabers. Revolvers and shotguns proved common and popular because they provided considerable firepower at short range and they could be fired while mounted or dismounted. Battlefield salvage and capturing Union weapons provided another means of securing sufficient firearms. Indeed these means offered the principal source of breech-loading carbines. While conducting rearguard actions, COL Joseph Wheeler's cavalry captured a number of Colt revolving rifles the day before the battle of Perryville. However, in general, the South's difficulty in producing metallic-rimmed cartridges limited the utility of weapons that required them, including the Spencer repeater.

Artillery

Civil War artillery comprised four general weapon types: guns, howitzers, mortars, and columbiads. Long-barreled cannon constituted the first category. They delivered flat-trajectory, long-range fire. Howitzers had a shorter barrel and lighter carriage. Their function was to fire explosive projectiles over short distances. Mortars used a small powder charge to lob a large projectile at a high angle. Columbiads combined characteristics of all three. They had relatively long barrels, a large caliber, and used a large powder charge to fire a heavy projectile over a great distance.

These weapons were further grouped according to their employment. Field artillery, the lightest and most mobile, operated within infantry and cavalry formations. Siege and seacoast artillery operated more or less independently of the combat arms. Siege artillery units normally formed siege trains that were called to the front only under special circumstances. Seacoast artillery, the heaviest Civil War ordnance, was emplaced in fixed positions. Buell's Army of the Ohio and Bragg's Army of the Mississippi relied exclusively on field artillery, whose organization and weaponry bore the influence of pre-Civil War trends.

In 1841 the US Army selected bronze as the standard material for fieldpieces. The same year witnessed the adoption of a standard system for artillery organization and weaponry. Under this setup field artillery comprised a mix of smoothbore muzzleloaders and howitzers. The former included 6- and 12-pound guns; the latter 12-, 24-, and 32-pound howitzers. Batteries before the Civil War normally included six cannon—four guns and two howitzers. The 6-pounder battery proved to be the most common. It comprised four 6-pound guns and two 12-pound howitzers. A heavier battery built around the 12-pound gun included four 12-pound guns and two 24-pound howitzers. Both battery types employed similar ammunition. The guns and howitzers both fired shell, spherical case, grapeshot, and canister rounds. For longer ranges the guns also relied on solid shot.

The 6-pound gun proved a reliable and popular field piece from the Mexican War until the Civil War. The adoption of the 12-pound gun-howitzer, model 1857, however, began to replace the lighter weapon. Popularly known as the Napoleon, the 12-pound gun-howitzer combined gun and howitzer functions into a single weapon, giving it greater versatility in combat. It also fired the full range of ammunition available to both guns and howitzers. The Napoleon was a bronze muzzle-loading smoothbore with an effective range of 1,500 yards with solid shot. With a nine-man crew the piece could fire at a sustained rate of two aimed shots per minute. At closer ranges a seasoned crew could fire up to four canister rounds in the same time.

The Napoleon became one of the most common field pieces to see service in the Civil War. However, when the war began, few of these cannon were available. As a result, both Union and Confederate armies relied on a variety of other gun and howitzer types. Until sufficient quantities of Napoleons became available to replace them, the lighter 6-pound gun remained in service. The lower fielding priority given to the western theater by both the North and South ensured the 6-pounders' continued use there long after more powerful cannon had become available. This condition proved particularly true for the Confederates armies because of the slower rate of cannon production in the South.

In addition to the development of the smoothbore gun-howitzer, field artillery also benefited from the emergence of rifled cannon. Projectiles fired from the latter did not suffer from the windage and irregular flight pattern associated with smoothbores. Hence, the rifled cannon had greater range and accuracy. Despite these advantages the US Army had few rifled cannon available when the Civil War began. Therefore an effort began almost immediately to convert older smoothbores into rifled pieces, particularly the 6-pound smoothbore. Many of these weapons underwent conversion with the James rifling system named for MG Charles T. James. This process entailed re-boring the gun before adding rifling grooves. It converted the weapon and permitted it to fire a larger round that James specially designed. The anticipated benefits, however, did not materialize. Marginal improvements in performance resulted, but the rapid erosion of the rifling grooves shortened the gun's overall service life. In addition, the larger powder charge required to fire the James ammunition generated a powerful recoil that the gun carriage was not designed to withstand.

Rifled cannon, however, proved less reliable and required longer to load. Compared to the Napoleon they were generally less effective against personnel targets. At longer ranges the lighter round the rifled piece fired reduced its killing power. At close range its ability to deliver deadly canister fire proved inferior. Hence, the 12-pound smoothbore became the weapon of choice for defensive operations and against enemy personnel. Throughout the war, however, no consensus emerged regarding the optimum mix of smoothbores and rifles. Field commanders varied in their opinions, and most Civil War armies retained a combination of both weapon types.

The most common rifled guns were the 10-pound Parrott and the 3-inch Ordnance rifle, also know as the Rodman rifle. The Parrott rifle was a cast-iron piece, easily identified by the wrought-iron band reinforcing the breech. The 10-pound Parrott was made in two models. The model 1861 had a 2.9-inch rifled bore with three lands and grooves and a slight muzzle swell, while the Model 1863 had a 3-inch bore and no muzzle swell. The Rodman, or Ordnance, rifle was a long-tube, wrought- iron piece with a 3-inch bore. Ordnance rifles were sturdier than the 10-pound Parrott and displayed superior accuracy and reliability. However, the common bore of the 1863 Parrott and the Ordnance rifle permitted them to use the same ammunition.

The Army of the Ohio and the Army of the Mississippi each made a deliberate effort to standardize the number and type of cannon assigned to each battery. Following the battle of Shiloh the latter adopted a four-gun battery, and the former opted for six-gun organizations. However, many deviations existed, reflecting the actual types and numbers of cannon available for service. The mix of cannon types required an equally diverse set of ammunition requirements, complicating resupply efforts. At Perryville the 12-pound howitzer and the 6-pound smoothbore proved the most common fieldpieces for the Confederates. The Army of the Ohio had a greater variety of cannon types, but the 12-pound howitzer, 10-pound Parrot, 12-pound Napoleon, and rifled 6-pounders predominated. The more modern Union Napoleons and Parrot rifles outranged the Confederate 6-pounders, but the shortage of newer cannon forced the Army of the Mississippi to continue their use.

Battlefield recovery of captured artillery, however, did provide Confederate batteries with opportunities to secure more modern fieldpieces. Battery commanders often simply exchanged their lighter pieces for more effective ones they captured in combat. This practice was followed at Perryville. However, the failure to secure cannon captured during the first day's fighting at Shiloh resulted in their loss when the Confederates retreated from the field on the second day. Consequently more detailed preparations were often made to remove captured cannon quickly from the field before every major battle. At the battle of Stones River special teams were designated to perform this task even while the fighting continued.

Rifled and smoothbore cannon fired the same ammunition types: solid shot, shell, case, and canister. Solid shot, with its smashing or battering effect, was used against buildings, enemy artillery, and massed troop formations. Smoothbores fired a cast-iron ball, while rifled cannon used an elongated projectile known as a bolt. The latter's tendency to bury itself into the ground reduced its effectiveness against troop targets. Shell comprised a hollow projectile filled with black powder and ignited by a fuse. Upon detonation it burst, showering the target with projectile fragments. However, the small size of the detonation limited the number of fragments produced and, hence, the shell's killing power. It could, however, be used to obtain an air burst effect upon formed troops and artillery.

Case shot comprised a hollow projectile filled with round lead or iron balls set in a mix of sulfur surrounding a small bursting charge. A fuse ignited the charge that broke apart the thin sides of the round and spewed its contents over the burst area. Ideally, timed to explode directly over a body of soldiers, case shot originated with Henry Shrapnel, a British artillery officer who invented this type of exploding projectile. Canister included a tin can filled with iron balls packed in sawdust. When fired the can disintegrated and the balls flew forward in a widening swath. Canister effectively transformed a cannon into a giant shotgun. While it did not have the airburst effect of case or shell, canister proved devastating against large troop concentrations at close range or under 400 yards. When circumstances required gunners resorted to double charges of canister to increase further its killing power.

Effective use of these ammunition types, however, required trained gun crews. Crude gun sights, the absence of any recoil mechanism, and unreliable fuses reduced the artillery's ability to dominate the battlefield. Unskilled crews often engaged targets for extended periods with no appreciable effect. However, gunnery effectiveness was not simply a matter of luck. The artillery constituted one of the most technical branches of service. Experienced gunners learned how to compensate for the effects of wind, cant, and temperature. They made ready use of the gunnery tables provided with each limber to accurately determine elevation setting, fuse length, and powder charge. Indeed the combination of training and experience, and the emergence of the rifled cannon permitted gunners to reach unprecedented levels of accuracy in battle.

Battery	Brigade	12-pd Howitzer	6-pd Smoothbore	12-pd Napoleon	6-pd James Rifling	3-inch Bronze	3.3-inch Bronze	Battery Total
Barrett	Powell	2	2					4
Calvert (Section)	Wheeler		2					2
Calvert (Section)	Cleburne	2						2
Carnes	Donelson		4					4
Darden	Johnson	2	2					4
Lumsden	Jones			4				4
Palmer	Brown	3	3					6
Scott	Smith	2	2					4
Semples	Wood			4	2			6
Slocomb	Adams	2	2				2	6
Stanford	Stewart					4		4
Swett	Liddell	2	6					8
Turner	Maney	2	2					4
Totals		17	25	8	2	4	2	58

Figure 6. Confederate artillery at Perryville.

29

Battery	Brigade or (Division)	12-lb Howitzer	6-lb Smoothbore	10-lb Parrot Rifle	12-lb Napoleon	6-lb James Rifling	3-inch Ordnance Rifle	24-lb Howitzer	12-lb Mountain Howitzer	Battery Total
Barnett	(Sheridan)			2	2	2				6
Bradley	Harker	2		4						6
Bush	Starkweather	2	2			2				6
Canby	Grose			2	4					6
Carpenter	Caldwell				2		4			6
Church	Walker	2				2				4
Cockrill	Hazen	6				5				11
Cox	Wagner	2		4						6
Dawley	Carlin	4								4
Drury	Matthews	2		4						6
Estep	Hascall	2	4							6
Harris	Webster	4					2			6
Hescock	(Sheridan)			2	4					6
Hotchkiss	Gay	2								2
Huntington	McCook				2					2
Loomis	Lytle			6						6
Mendenhall	Grose				2			2		4
Parsons	Terrill	2		1	5					8
Pinney	Gooding	2		2					2	6
Simonson	Harris	2	2			2				6
Smith	Steedman	4								4
Southwick	Fry	2				4				6
Standart	Cruft		2			4				6
Stevens	Hawkins		8							8
Stone	Starkweather		2	2		2				6
Swallow	Beatty	2		4						6
Totals		42	18	33	21	23	6	2	2	147

Figure 7. Union artillery at Perryville.

Tactics

The 1846-1848 Mexican War strongly influenced American tactics in the early phases of the Civil War. It also reinforced the Napoleonic concepts taught in the nation's military schools. The wars of Napoleon offered a wealth of lessons regarding the conduct of war to which the Mexican War provided a more recent addendum. The success of American arms encouraged the study and application of the tactics employed in the latter conflict. Moreover, aside from periodic encounters with the Plains Indians, the Mexican War constituted the US Army's principal source of firsthand combat experience until the Civil War.

In Mexico, the US Army relied on formations and weapons similar to those employed since the start of the 19th century. Infantry moved in close-order formations, principally the line and column. The latter facilitated movement, but in several instances, attack columns were successfully employed. More often, however, infantry regiments fought in lines, screened by one or two companies of skirmishers. The unit advanced deliberately on the enemy, carefully maintaining its formation. Once within close range of its intended target the unit fired a volley and charged with bayonets. The American regiments' better training, élan, and cohesion compared with their Mexican counterparts normally ensured the latter's withdrawal or surrender.

Artillery provided direct support to these attacks. Indeed, fast-moving batteries of 6-pound guns often advanced ahead of the infantry. Deployed just beyond effective musket range the cannons unleashed canister that disrupted the close-order Mexican formations. Infantry attacks followed and the defenders generally fled. Alternatively the batteries provided a forward defense against attacking formations. They fired into the ranks of the advancing enemy and withdrew when directly threatened. Mexican assaults that actually reached the ranks of waiting American infantry then received volleys while in a disorganized state. In this manner, artillery provided effective, mobile firepower that facilitated offensive and defensive infantry actions.

Cavalry was not employed in large concentrations. Instead it operated in small detachments that were primarily responsible for reconnaissance and direct support to infantry units. It also provided flank and rear area security. In battle cavalry exploited the effects created by American infantry and artillery fire to transform orderly Mexican retreats into panic-stricken routs. However, due to their dispersal and conservative employment, mounted units lacked the means and the command structure necessary to undertake aggressive, independent operations. Instead they supported the infantry-artillery team.

America's Mexican War experience tended to reinforce the Napoleonic emphasis on the offensive to achieve victory in battle. American soldiers took the offensive with considerable success. They suffered relatively light casualties, even against fortified positions. Consequently the war tended to confirm existing concepts of warfare rather than to offer new ones. In battle commanders continued to rely on close-order formations. Doing so preserved unit cohesion and simplified command and control. Massed troop concentrations also provided a volume of fire that offset the smoothbore musket's inherent inaccuracy and short range. The successful use of assault to overcome enemy positions built confidence in the bayonet. This weapon suited American offensive tactics since bayonet charges by formed bodies of troops generally followed the delivery of close-range volley fire. Napoleon's aggressive use of artillery to shatter enemy formations resonated in the forward battlefield presence of American cannon in Mexico. Relying on small cavalry detachments rather than masses, however, constituted the principal deviation between American tactics in the 1840s and the Napoleonic model.

However, the Mexican experience proved misleading. The titanic clash of national armies that characterized the Napoleonic battles found no parallel in the small-scale engagements of the Mexican War. Consequently the lessons learned from the latter conflict tended to apply to regiment and battery operations. The war offered few insights into properly handling and employing brigades, divisions, and corps, although these organizations became the principal elements of maneuver in the Civil War. Hence, while many Civil War leaders received their baptism of fire in Mexico, the experience did not prepare them for command beyond the regiment.

Mexican War tactics validated Napoleonic concepts due to the similarities in the weaponry used. The standard infantry firearm remained the smoothbore musket. It proved effective and reasonably accurate at ranges below 100 yards. Accuracy rapidly diminished at longer distances. Armed with this weapon the infantry's inability to disrupt attacking formations beyond close range encouraged the continued application of Napoleonic-era shock tactics. With only a short killing zone to cross advancing infantry could rely on the bayonet to drive the enemy from his position. Similarly, the smoothbore musket's short range permitted the aggressive artillery tactics employed in Mexico. Batteries engaged infantry with canister, deploying just beyond the musket's effective range. Moreover, the mobility of the light 6-pounder permitted it to retire quickly if threatened by an enemy advance.

In the 1850s, however, the rifle musket's emergence changed the dynamics of the battlefield. This weapon merged the rifle's accuracy with the musket's rapid loading. Moreover, it extended the line infantry's effective engagement range. Artillery that deployed within canister range of an infantry target also placed itself within reach of the rifle musket. It risked losing gunners and horses, directly affecting its firepower and mobility. In the United States reaction to the new weapon found expression in drill manuals. General Winfield Scott's three-volume work, *Infantry Tactics* (1835), based on French tactical models of the Napoleonic Wars, stressed close-order, linear formations in two or three ranks advancing at "quick time" of 110 steps per minute.

In 1855, to accompany the introduction of the new rifle musket, Major William J. Hardee published a two-volume tactical manual, *Rifle and Light Infantry Tactics*. Hardee's work contained few significant revisions of Scott's manual. His major innovation was to increase the speed of the advance to a "double-quick time" of 165 steps per minute. In effect, the doctrinal response to the rifle-musket's greater range lay in a faster pace intended to reduce the time spent in the enemy's killing zone. Close-order formations and tactics continued to predominate. Hardee's *Tactics* was the standard infantry manual both sides used at the outbreak of war in 1861. The following year, however, the Union Army adopted BG Silas Casey's *Infantry Tactics*. This publication offered few changes, but it did eliminate the paradox of Union soldiers training for war with a Southern general's manual.

While infantry doctrine provided a limited recognition of the rifle musket's battlefield influence, Napoleonic concepts continued to influence cavalry and artillery tactics. Published in 1841 the principal cavalry manual predated the Mexican War and relied largely on French sources. It placed great emphasis on the mounted attack with sabers or lances. It did not anticipate improvements to infantry firepower, and it offered no solutions for dealing with formed bodies of troops equipped with rifle muskets. The artillery had a drill book delineating individual crew actions, but it had no tactical manual. In practice artillery training continued to emphasize close-range attacks without reference to the new firearm that was increasingly common among its intended infantry targets.

Regular Army infantry, cavalry, and artillery practiced and became proficient in the tactics that brought success in Mexico. As the first volunteers drilled and readied themselves for the battles of 1861, officers and noncommissioned officers trained them in the Napoleonic tactics that had been validated in Mexico. Thus, the two armies entered the Civil War ready to apply the lessons of the Mexican War. Prepared to rely on the bayonet and close-range firepower, the Confederate and Union soldiers were ill prepared for the broader killing fields the rifle-musket engendered.

Commanders on both sides soon discovered that the rifle musket improved the effect of the defender's firepower. This weapon's longer range forced the attacker to cover a greater distance under fire to assault the enemy. Moreover, the rifle musket's range permitted more defenders to engage an advancing force, usually through destructive enfilade fires. Attacks pressed soon resulted in a loss of cohesion, momentum, and casualties. Bayonet charges rarely reached the enemy line, particularly if the defender remained unbroken and had sufficient ammunition. Attacks tended to stop short of their objective, and a firefight ensued, continuing until one side broke. The infantry's action still determined a battle's outcome, but in the Civil War the firefight replaced close assault as its principal form.

Artillery that attempted the Mexican War's aggressive tactics suffered. During the first major battle of the war at Bull Run two Union batteries deployed forward to engage Confederate lines with canister. Instead they suffered heavy losses among their crews and horses before being overrun by Confederate infantry. Consequently, artillery tactics changed. The longer range of the rifle musket forced batteries to deploy farther from enemy infantry. The destructive power of close-range canister fire ceased to be a dominant, offensive influence. Instead artillery supported attacking infantry from a distance, relying on the less deadly shell and case shot against enemy troop formations.

Neither did massed fires offer a means for offsetting this loss in offensive lethality. At the war's start Union and Confederate armies tended to assign each battery to an infantry brigade. This dispersion and subordination to infantry commanders confirmed the artillery's support role. It also discouraged the concentration of large numbers of cannon to shatter enemy formations before the attack of friendly infantry. Ironically, decentralizing fire support did not guarantee its availability at the brigade level. Batteries often became separated from their parent brigade on the battlefield. The cannon had difficulty keeping pace with infantry moving cross-country, particularly through hilly or wooded terrain. Topography also often required artillery to move away from the infantry's path of advance to find suitable firing positions with unobstructed fields of fire.

Separating a battery from its parent brigade eroded the latter's offensive combat power. Batteries required infantry support to protect them from sudden attacks on their positions. Brigade commanders normally designated one or two infantry regiments for this role. When the entire brigade remained in close proximity these regiments could be recalled to support an attack. In the event of the battery's separation, however, the brigade commander effectively lost his fire support and the combat power represented by those regiments assigned to battery security. At Perryville these circumstances reduced the scale of the initial Confederate attack and removed its fire support. During defensive actions, however, the frequency of battery separation diminished. The brigade's infantry and artillery usually deployed together and remained in close proximity to protect a designated position.

In most Confederate and Union armies artillery decentralization soon gave way to centralized control and organization. Batteries were grouped together to form artillery battalions and assigned to divisions. An artillery officer commanded each battalion, which comprised three or four batteries. Additional batteries formed an independent artillery reserve whose commander had at least nominal command over all cannon within the army. This arrangement provided flexibility. Within the division it permitted the concentration of fires to support the formation's main effort. It allowed the independent action of infantry brigades and batteries toward a common objective. Massing fires no longer required the division command chain and each brigade commander to coordinate. Similarly, at the army level, the reserve batteries could support an offensive movement or defend a critical sector without disrupting divisional fire support. However, the artillery commander's authority empowered him to control the operations of **all** batteries when the tactical situation warranted, although doing so created friction with the corps and division commanders whose batteries were affected.

The rate at which centralized organizations emerged varied. It appeared first in the Union and Confederate armies operating in Virginia. In the west the dispersal of batteries to infantry brigades persisted. Before Perryville Buell fundamentally reshaped the Army of the Ohio, but he did not change the organization of his artillery. His successor, MG William S. Rosecrans, assigned groupings of batteries to each division. Routinely associating each battery with a particular brigade, however, partially nullified the potential advantages of this arrangement. He also organized several batteries into an army reserve. At Stones River massed cannon from a single corps shattered the final Confederate attack. Nevertheless Union artillery still retained a loose brigade association and proved slow to develop into an independent force capable of massed fires to support division- and corps-level attacks.

Similarly, Bragg failed to reorganize his artillery. He, too, remained wedded to battery assignments to infantry brigades. Unfortunately many Confederate cannon were outdated or were light smoothbores. In general they proved inferior in quality and quantity. In combat they found themselves outranged and outshot by Union artillery. A centralized organization that permitted massed fires might have offset these disadvantages. In fact, ad hoc battlefield concentrations occurred at Shiloh, Perryville, and Stones River, but the complexity of coordinating the actions of batteries drawn from multiple command chains proved expensive in time. In April 1863 Bragg reorganized his artillery into battalions assigned at division level. The continued association of individual batteries with particular brigades, however, largely nullified the potential advantages of the artillery battalion organization. At Chickamauga, Confederate batteries remained dispersed and operated independently of one another. Only in 1864 after General Joseph E. Johnston replaced Bragg's, did the artillery effectively apply a more centralized control and organization.

The difficulties that afflicted the effective use of artillery as an offensive weapon did not mar its defensive utility. The combination of close-range canister from cannon and rifle muskets proved deadly. Attacks against infantry with artillery support disintegrated in a killing zone dominated by canister and Minié balls. When multiple batteries were employed in the defense, the impact on attacking formations proved catastrophic. Malvern Hill and the final day of fighting at both Stones River and Gettysburg offered compelling testimony to the cannon's defensive power. As the war continued, infantry tended to rely increasingly on rifle pits or more elaborate entrenchments. Their vulnerability to enemy fire consequently lessened. When supported by artillery, their position became almost impossible to overcome unless the attacker was much superior in numbers, attacked through a flank, or discovered a unique local condition to exploit.

Similarly, mounted cavalry charges against formed, undisrupted infantry proved suicidal. Consequently the cavalry's role on the Civil War battlefield remained limited. When two armies collided in battle, mounted forces generally withdrew to provide flank security. They took little part in the numerous firefights that ensued between infantry formations unless forced to by circumstances. Limitations on the battlefield employment of cavalry changed, however, with increased reliance on breech-loading weapons and dismounted operations. Both Union and Confederate cavalry relied on horses for rapid mobility but increasingly fought dismounted. As breechloaders became available in Union regiments their firepower proved superior to infantry units of the same size.

For the Confederates, the assortment of weaponry used, ranging from pistols and shotguns to rifle muskets, directly correlated with the volume of fire provided. In general, however, the cavalry's greatest influence lay outside the battlefield. Its combination of firepower and mobility proved ideal for raids, delaying actions, and blocking movements. Such actions often influenced campaigns and shaped the nature of battles. Once battle was joined, however, cavalry—whether mounted or dismounted—proved little better than infantry at overcoming the power of the defense. Canister and rifle muskets shattered cavalry formations with equal destructive force.

Despite the heightened power of the defense Civil War commanders adhered to the philosophy of the offense. Tradition and training reinforced the belief that only an offensive strategy and tactical attacks could achieve decisive results. The legacy of the Napoleonic Wars and the nation's experience in Mexico encouraged this notion. Few Civil War generals advocated combining strategic offense and tactical defense. Although such an approach exploited the great defensive strength of the armies of the period, it found little favor in the respective political climates of the North and South. It also contradicted commonly held views of warfare. Nations did not win wars by being passive on the battlefield, awaiting the enemy's actions. Instead, they aggressively attacked and drove the enemy from the field. Commanders acting otherwise quickly found themselves out of favor and the target of public criticism. Indeed, the perception of being too cautious on campaign or in battle terminated careers. Removing MG George B. McClellan and MG Don Carlos Buell from army commands underscored the professional imperative to achieve results.

On the battlefield the determination to attack frequently resulted in frontal assaults and heavy casualties. This end state contradicted the intent of corps- and army-level commanders who often attempted envelopments. However, such actions proved difficult to execute. Translating this intent into clear orders required trained staff officers who were familiar with the complexities associated with rapidly moving large troop masses. Such officers were invariably in short supply, especially in the early stages of a war. The small scale of the Mexican War did not serve as a training ground for conducting corps- and army-level operations. Those officers who did accrue staff experience, even at lower command echelons, often found themselves elevated to senior command positions during the Civil War. The shortage of capable staff officers forced commanders to devote more of their own time to overseeing headquarters functions or accepting confusion in executing orders. Most army commanders experienced a mixture of both. Bragg, for example, undertook the Kentucky campaign without a chief of staff, and his headquarters included several officers debuting in staff functions.

Staff inadequacies and the complexities inherent to large troop movements imposed delays on the preparation of a major envelopment. This time lag increased the likelihood that the flanking effort would be discovered before it could begin. Consequently commanders threatened with envelopment gained an opportunity to react. When the attack finally began, too often it fell on the front of a reinforced and refaced battle line instead of on an open flank. At Chancellorsville, Confederate forces executed a successful large-scale envelopment. This success, however, owed as much to its capable preparation and execution as it did to the Union command chain's failure to react quickly to reports of the pending attack.

Battlefield envelopment also required accurate information on the disposition of enemy forces that many Civil War commanders rarely possessed. Cavalry often provided the primary means of reconnaissance on campaign. However, once contending armies came into close proximity and prepared for battle the cavalry generally retired to the flanks. Detailed reconnaissance of enemy positions thus fell to commanders' personal observations, skirmisher reports, and perhaps news from local civilians. None of these means provided a comprehensive view of the enemy's deployment, particularly in wooded or hilly terrain. More deliberate reconnaissance required time, which the enemy could use to alter his dispositions. Commanders faced the choice of acting quickly with inadequate information or losing the initiative while awaiting clarification of the enemy's status. At Stones River both armies prepared flanking movements, but the Confederates struck first, enjoying initial success and forcing the abandonment of the planned Union attack.

Without accurate knowledge of enemy dispositions, finding an enemy flank to attack became problematic. Forces committed to attack under such circumstances advanced until they encountered the enemy. They continued to feed additional troops into the fray until they were successful. The tendency of these engagements to draw units from both sides quickly reduced the intended envelopment into a protracted firefight between battle lines. Such "pile-on" tactics rarely achieved the anticipated results. They tended to erode formation cohesion and waste manpower in an escalating battle of attrition. Unless rapidly concluded, these engagements effectively ended the original flanking effort. At Perryville Bragg attempted a flanking attack on the Union left. His failure to locate the end of the Union line accurately resulted in the initial advance plunging into the center of a Union corps. The Confederate plan unraveled amid a series of frontal attacks on hill positions defended by infantry and artillery that eventually broke the momentum of Bragg's forces and prevented a more complete victory.

The difficulties inherent to large-scale envelopments encouraged reliance on simpler direct assaults on the enemy. Against experienced soldiers supported by artillery, heavy casualties invariably resulted, and the attack disintegrated as exemplified by the Union attacks at Fredericksburg and Cold Harbor. However, wooded or hilly terrain such as that found at Shiloh, Perryville, or Chickamauga often provided a covered approach for attacking units, reducing their exposure to fire and the defender's reaction time. Unit offensive tactics thus sought to close rapidly with the enemy before engaging in a short-range exchange of fire.

Although the rifle musket had a much longer effective range than the smoothbore musket, soldiers rarely exploited the full potential of the weapon. Unit and soldier training focused on loading and firing according to drill, not long-range accuracy. The latter entailed the ability to judge distances, understand bullet trajectory, and practice marksmanship. Yet units rarely conducted the live-fire training necessary to develop these skills, and many soldiers tended to fire too high or low. Ammunition limits further restricted rifle muskets' effectiveness. Each soldier carried between 40 and 60 rounds into combat and could generally fire three shots per minute. A sustained firefight rapidly exhausted this supply and necessitated that the unit withdraw to obtain more. Fire discipline thus became an important factor. Rather than to expend ammunition engaging distant targets unit commanders preferred to hold their fire for the close fight. Firefights at less than 100 yards proved common. At this distance a unit's morale state, experience, and training became critical determinants of success. Smaller veteran units tended to be victorious over larger but less experienced ones, although entrenchments and artillery could shift the balance in favor of the latter.

Unit formations used to conduct operations on the battlefield remained unchanged throughout the war. The line and the column predominated. Several variations of the latter facilitated movement onto and across the battlefield. As the probability of enemy contact rose the regiment formed a two-rank battle line. This formation proved less vulnerable to enemy fire than the column and maximized firepower to the front. Brigades often deployed in two lines, each comprising two or three regiments. Doctrine stressed the importance of separating these lines when advancing to minimize casualties.

Unfortunately, it proved difficult to do so in combat. Too often enemy fire halted the front line while the second line continued forward. The brigade's regiments became intermingled, and a loss of cohesion resulted. Defensively the regiments of the second line represented a reserve. They were normally employed individually to replace units in the front line that had been forced to retire or were out of ammunition. They also provided a counterattack force and provided flank support as necessary.

Two or more brigades constituted a division. When a division attacked, its brigades often advanced in sequence, from left to right or vice versa, depending on terrain, suspected enemy location, and the number of brigades available to attack. At times divisions attacked with two or more brigades leading, followed by one or more brigades ready to reinforce the lead brigades or maneuver to the flanks. Two or more divisions constituted a corps that might conduct an attack as part of a larger plan the army commander controlled. More often groups of divisions attacked under a corps-level commander's control. Division and corps commanders generally took a position to the rear of the main line to control the flow of reinforcements into the battle, but they often rode forward into the battle lines to influence or observe the action.

A critical command decision for brigade, division, and corps/wing commanders lay in committing fresh troops to sustain an attack's momentum. Civil War commanders often developed viable plans to assault enemy positions only to watch their regiments become mired through a combination of terrain, enemy fire, losses, and morale erosion that collectively sapped their ability to advance. Those regiments that became engaged in firefights with the enemy often quickly consumed much of the basic ammunition load, necessitating a temporary withdrawal to resupply.

To prevent these commonplace battlefield developments from extinguishing offensive action, commanders worked to introduce fresh troops into battle at the proper place and time. However, simply pushing uncommitted regiments forward often created more confusion without appreciable gain. An attacking force that became pinned by an obstacle or enemy fire degenerated into a formless mass if more troops simply surged forward. To sustain momentum fresh troops needed to move around those in front of them without losing their formation or organizational integrity. Such a passage of lines, however, required skill since enemy fire added to the confusion inherent in moving one mass of soldiers through another. Not all commanders or units were able to perform this action successfully in combat.

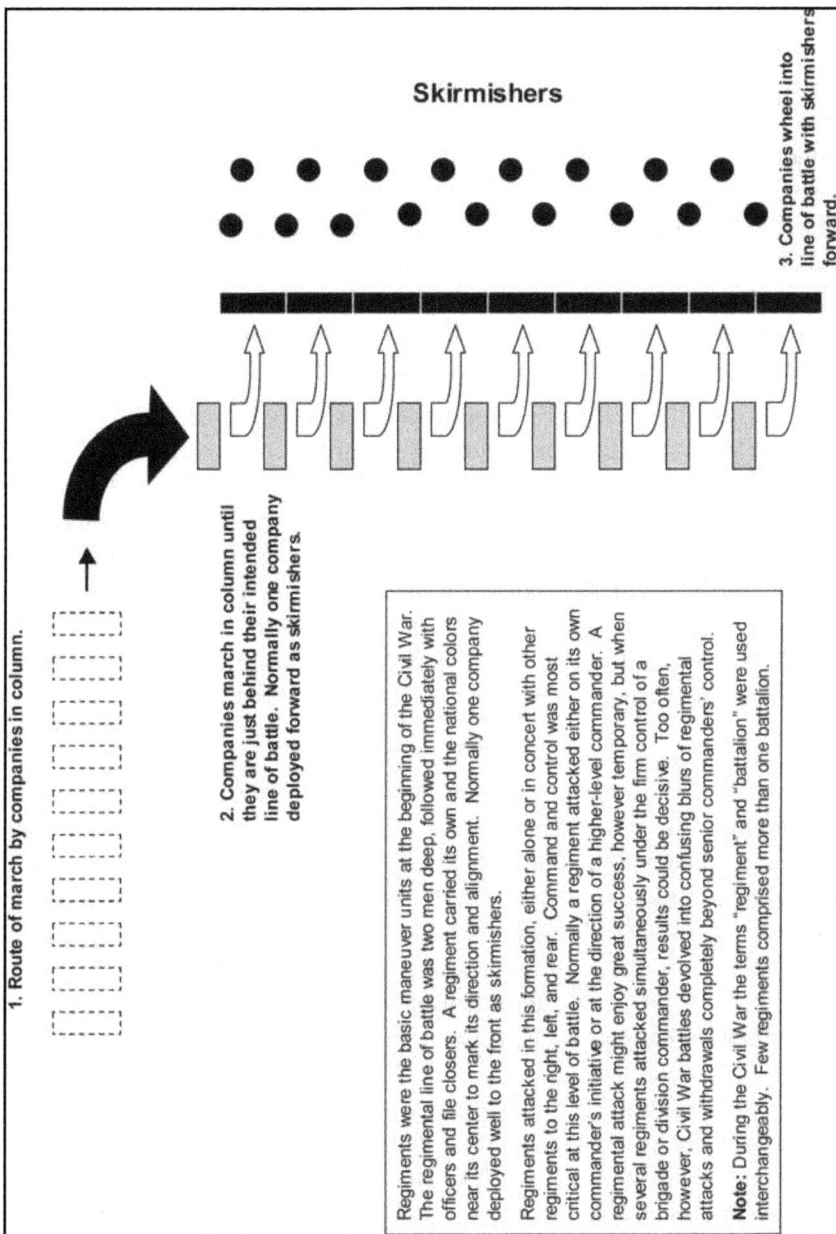

Skirmishers

1. Route of march by companies in column.

2. Companies march in column until they are just behind their intended line of battle. Normally one company deployed forward as skirmishers.

3. Companies wheel into line of battle with skirmishers forward.

Regiments were the basic maneuver units at the beginning of the Civil War. The regimental line of battle was two men deep, followed immediately with officers and file closers. A regiment carried its own and the national colors near its center to mark its direction and alignment. Normally one company deployed well to the front as skirmishers.

Regiments attacked in this formation, either alone or in concert with other regiments to the right, left, and rear. Command and control was most critical at this level of battle. Normally a regiment attacked either on its own commander's initiative or at the direction of a higher-level commander. A regimental attack might enjoy great success, however temporary, but when several regiments attacked simultaneously under the firm control of a brigade or division commander, results could be decisive. Too often, however, Civil War battles devolved into confusing blurs of regimental attacks and withdrawals completely beyond senior commanders' control.

Note: During the Civil War the terms "regiment" and "battalion" were used interchangeably. Few regiments comprised more than one battalion.

Figure 8. Changing from march column to battle line.

41

After 1861 the brigade constituted the principal tactical maneuver element. The brigade commander personally directed its actions. His instructions directly influenced all subordinate regiments' formation and disposition. Whether each brigade fought an independent action or supported a larger plan depended on the controlling division commander. The latter managed his brigades, determining general deployment, sequence of attack, and the commitment of reserves. Division commanders who maintained communications with their subordinate elements and personally checked on the latter's situation tended to be the most effective. Commanders who remained to the rear awaiting information before rendering decisions soon found themselves unable to influence events in a timely fashion. Conversely, those leaders continuously present on the front lines were more prone to becoming casualties or immersed in the details of a brigade, regiment, or battery fight at the division's expense.

Corps commanders set the conditions for division and brigade action. They bore responsibility for executing the army commander's intent and directed major attacks or the defense of a critical sector. They also influenced the ebb and flow of battle by timely inserting reserves or triggering a formation maneuver. The army commander shaped the overall battle and planned its conduct. The details of implementation, however, were generally left to the corps and division commanders. Neither the corps nor army commander needed to be among the forward battle lines, but their presence there, especially at a critical moment, could bolster morale.

Logistics Support

Logistics considerations shaped the planning and execution of Civil War campaigns. The North had an advantage in its ability to supply, equip, clothe, and sustain its soldiers that only increased over time. America's financial, industrial, commercial, and shipping centers were in the North. There, too, lay much of the organizational and managerial talent necessary to harness this industrial and economic power to the war effort. The successful ability to do so made the Union soldiers among the best equipped and supplied in the world. The South struggled to build its own war industries but with much less success. Lack of crucial raw materials and effective management hindered progress. Moreover, the poor state and disorganization of the South's railroads slowed deliveries of necessary supplies and equipment to the field armies. The North established a special War Department Bureau to oversee the operation of its military railroads. In the South overuse, disrepair, mismanagement, and Union cavalry raids ultimately severed the few rail links that connected the Confederate states. The difficulties associated with acquiring and distributing equipment and supplies often resulted in Southern soldiers lacking basic uniform items and food.

At the war's start, however, infantry and artillery weapons constituted the most important needs. Although large quantities of smoothbore muskets were available, the newer rifle muskets proved to be less common. The North had nearly 35,000 of them, and the Confederates secured 10,000. Purchasing agents rushed to Europe to buy existing stocks or contract for future production. This led to an influx of outmoded weapons that resulted in many soldiers going into battle with Mexican War-era smoothbore muskets. Some Union and Confederate soldiers still carried smoothbore muskets in late 1863, particularly in the west. In the east modern artillery proved generally available, but in the west Confederate armies continued to employ older, less effective cannon. Although breech-loading technology was available, muzzle-loading smoothbore or rifled cannon predominated among the Northern and Southern field armies.

With most of the government arsenals and private manufacturing capability located in the New England states, the North ultimately produced sufficient modern firearms for their armies. The Confederates also accumulated adequate quantities, primarily through battlefield recovery and imports. In addition, exceptional management within the Confederate Ordnance Bureau led to creating a series of arsenals throughout the South that produced large quantities of munitions and weapons.

The Northern manufacturing capability permitted the Federals eventually to produce and outfit their forces with repeating arms, the best of which had been patented before 1861. Initially, however, the North's conservative Ordnance Bureau would not risk switching to a new, unproved standard weapon that could lead to soldiers wasting huge quantities of ammunition in the midst of an expanding war. By 1864, after the retirement of Chief of Ordnance James Ripley and with President Lincoln's urging, Federal cavalry received seven-shot Spencer repeating carbines, which greatly increased their combat power.

Both sides initially relied on the states and local districts to provide equipment, supplies, animals, and foodstuffs. As the war progressed, more centralized control over production and purchasing emerged. However, embezzlement and fraud remained common problems throughout the war. The North, with its preponderance of railroads and developed waterways, had ample supply and adequate distribution systems. The South's major supply problem was subsistence. Arguably, the Confederacy produced enough food during the war to provide for military and civilian needs, but mismanagement, parochial local interests, and the relatively underdeveloped transportation network often created havoc with distribution.

In both armies the Quartermaster, Ordnance, Subsistence, and Medical Bureaus procured and distributed equipment, food, and supplies. The items for which these bureaus were responsible were not dissimilar to the classes of supply used today. Some needs overlapped, such as the Quartermaster Bureau procuring wagons for medical ambulances, but conflicts of interest usually were manageable. Department and army commanders requested needed resources directly from the bureaus, and bureau chiefs wielded considerable power as they parceled out occasionally limited resources.

When essential equipment and supplies could not be obtained through normal channels some commanders used their own resources to procure them. One example of this practice was COL John T. Wilder who personally contracted for Spencer rifles for his mounted brigade in the Army of the Cumberland. Wilder obtained an unsecured personal loan to purchase the weapons, and his men reimbursed him from their pay. The Federal government picked up the cost after the rifles' worth was demonstrated in the Tullahoma and Chickamauga campaigns.

Typically materiel flowed from the factory to base depots as the responsible bureaus directed. Supplies were then shipped to advance depots, generally a city on a major transportation artery safely within a department's rear area. During campaigns the armies established temporary advance depots that were served by rail or river transportation. From these points wagons carried the supplies forward to the field units. This principle is somewhat similar to more modern theater sustainment organization.

Managing this logistics system was complex and crucial. A corps wagon train, if drawn by standard six-mule teams, would be spread out from 5 to 8 miles, based on the difficulty of terrain, weather, and road conditions. The wagons, which could haul 4,000 pounds in optimal conditions, could carry only half that load in difficult terrain. Sustenance for the animals was a major restriction because each animal required up to 26 pounds of hay and grain a day to stay healthy and productive. Bulky and hard to handle, this forage was a major consideration in campaign planning. Wagons delivering supplies more than one day's distance from the depot could be forced to carry excessive amounts of animal forage. If full animal forage was to be carried the required number of wagons to support a corps increased dramatically with each subsequent day's distance from the forward depot. Herds of cattle that often accompanied the trains or were appropriated en route created another problem. They provided fresh (though tough) meat for the troops but slowed and complicated movement.

The bulk supply problems were alleviated somewhat by the practice of foraging, which, in the proper season, supplied much of the food for animals and men. Foraging was practiced with and without command sanction wherever an army went. As the war progressed it became a command policy for several army commanders. However, in the early stages of the war, the US Congress sought to minimize the war's impact on Southern civilians. Hence Union armies were restricted in their foraging. This restraint gradually disappeared as the war lengthened. Widespread destruction of civilian property ensued.

Item	Packing	Weight (lbs)
Bulk ammunition		
.58 caliber, expanding ball (500-grain bullet)	1,000 rounds per box	98
12-pound Napoleon canister (14.8 lb per round)	8 rounds per box	161
"Marching" ration (per man per day)		2
1 lb hard bread (hardtack)		
¾ lb salt pork or ¼ lb fresh meat		
1 oz coffee		
3 oz sugar and salt		
Forage (per horse per day)		26
14 lb hay and 12 lb grain		
Personal equipment		50-60
Includes rifle, bayonet, 60 rounds of ammunition, haversack, 3 days' rations, blanket, shelter half, canteen, personal items		

Figure 9. Sample of Union logistics data.

Army of the Ohio

Logistics considerations played a key role in Buell's generalship. A career soldier with considerable field and staff experience, he understood the importance of proper logistics support to military operations. Moreover the myriad calculations necessary to successfully supply and sustain an army suited his view of war as methodical and governed by fundamental principles. Training and temperament encouraged in Buell the direct correlation between maintaining an adequate supply flow and campaign success. Consequently extensive logistical preparations preceded every operation the Army of the Ohio undertook during his command tenure. Once a campaign began logistics issues continued to influence his decisions nearly as much as enemy action.

During his advance on Chattanooga Buell faced a particularly challenging supply situation. He was directed to advance from Corinth to Chattanooga, following the Memphis and Charleston Railroad, which he also was responsible for repairing and securing. Between Corinth and Decatur much of this line lay in a state of disrepair. During the siege of Corinth large sections had been damaged. Indeed many of the trestles and bridges that spanned the numerous creeks and rivers along the entire stretch to Chattanooga had been destroyed. In this condition the railroad could not sustain troop or supply movements. Thus, while Buell's army undertook the repairs necessary to restore the line to running order, wagons carried supplies between the many breaks. Ferries were established at Florence and Decatur to expedite troop movements eastward.

Despite these efforts the Memphis and Charleston Railroad remained an unreliable supply route. Security remained a continuous problem. Confederate raids on the line required time-consuming repair work. Moreover the raiders sometimes seized control of entire sections of the railroad, denying Union access and use for several days at a time. Repair teams and the soldiers assigned to guard them too often became targets themselves, resulting in their periodic removal to safer havens. Ironically, despite the effort expended to open the railroad, a lack of rolling stock and locomotives limited its utility. Among the latter in working order all suffered from excessive wear. The Union capture of Corinth netted several additional locomotives, but they required extensive repairs before being ready for service. Personnel capable of performing this work, however, were not readily available. Efforts to secure additional rolling stock similarly proved unproductive.

These problems encouraged Buell to develop alternate supply routes. His ultimate supply source was in Louisville, Kentucky. The Louisville and Nashville Railroad provided an efficient way to move supplies to central Tennessee, but from there the absence of functioning rail links with Buell's army in northern Alabama forced it to rely on wagon train shuttles. The demands for supply wagons to support the advance on Chattanooga and sustain the supply flow in the rear placed further demands on an already stretched wagon fleet. The shallow depth of the Tennessee River during the summer months, coupled with the prevalence of shoals and rocks, precluded the river's use as a supply route.

Buell attempted to accomplish his mission and resolve his supply problems methodically. He continued bridge construction and railroad repair along the Memphis and Charleston Railroad as directed. He also simultaneously began improving the road net between Nashville and northern Alabama. As his army advanced toward Chattanooga, railroad repairs began on the railroads linking Nashville with Decatur and Stevenson. At the latter location he established a forward depot to sustain his forces once they had secured Chattanooga. Through these actions Buell sought to construct a reliable and efficient logistics architecture largely based on railroads rather than wagon trains.

However, his line of supply still stretched over 300 miles from northern Alabama to northern Kentucky. Buell faced the dilemma of how best to balance his forces between rear area security and his primary objective of Chattanooga. He understood that scattering his army to protect his link with Louisville effectively prevented any direct move on Chattanooga. Therefore he kept most of his forces gradually moving toward the eastern Tennessee town while he implemented minor improvements to his supply line's security.

The Confederates responded with cavalry and partisan attacks on Union railroads and supplies in Kentucky, Tennessee, and northern Alabama. North of Gallatin, Tennessee, along the Louisville and Nashville Railroad, Confederate cavalry blocked a railroad tunnel that effectively stopped all rail traffic for weeks. Mounted raiders also broke the rail link between Nashville and Stevenson only one day after it had been established. These and related actions successfully disrupted Buell's effort to rebuild railroads and supply his army. The advance on Chattanooga slowed to a crawl, and the Army of the Ohio went on half rations.

Buell remained convinced that capturing Chattanooga meant little if the army could not be sustained afterward. He reacted to Confederate depredations by relying on his own cavalry, establishing blockhouses for railroad security, and dispersing some combat elements to protect his rear areas. He refused, however, to permit his soldiers to live off the land at the expense of Southern civilians, even those who openly supported the Confederacy. Buell believed that protecting civilians' rights, regardless of their political sympathies, would ease the task of reconciling the North and South once the war ended. This soft war philosophy, however, antagonized his hungry soldiers. Many took matters into their own hands, often with the tacit support of their commanders. Buell punished those soldiers found plundering civilian property or terrorizing the local populace. In so doing he alienated many of his officers and men. Many began to see Buell as a Southern sympathizer who was concerned more with hostile civilians than with his own men's welfare.

This view hardened following the army's retreat from northern Alabama, first toward Nashville and then to Louisville. Buell was dubbed a traitor by elements within his own command and in the press. His failure to take Chattanooga and his seemingly precipitate retreat into northern Kentucky reinforced this perception. In fact Buell's actions were driven by the arrival of Bragg's army in Chattanooga and the latter's subsequent invasion of Kentucky. Buell reasoned that a retreat toward his supply base in Louisville would permit him to secure the city and exert a measure of constraint on Bragg's operations. Retiring along his own line of supply would further eliminate the food shortages encountered outside Chattanooga. In Louisville the army would receive additional reinforcements, permitting it to assume the offensive. However Bragg's head start into Kentucky required Buell's army to move quickly, lest Louisville fall before its arrival. Consequently the Union army left much of its train and baggage in Nashville and force-marched northward, sustaining itself largely on the limited supplies it carried.

Logistics support improved once the army arrived in Louisville. There it rested for a few days, benefiting from the city's ample stores. Hence the army that Buell led to Perryville was well equipped and had sufficient food supplies. However a severe drought over much of north central Kentucky resulted in shortages of water. This deficiency caused considerable hardship for the newly raised regiments that joined Buell's command in Louisville. The men in these units were not acclimated to the rigors of field operations, and the shortage of water only increased an already high fatigue rate.

Efforts to secure water influenced the actions of all three of Buell's corps at Perryville. As they drew near the town where Confederate forces deployed for battle, the I and II Corps deviated from their respective lines of march in search of water. These movements delayed their arrival in the vicinity of Perryville and led Buell to delay his planned attack. He intended 8 October to be spent on concentrating his army without triggering a general engagement. Instead, after a night of aggressive skirmishing, III Corps launched a dawn attack on forward Confederate positions to secure water flowing in the creeks west of Perryville. In the afternoon the Confederates launched their own attack before Buell completed his offensive preparations. The general shortage of water made the ensuing battle particularly grueling on the soldiers of both sides, many of whom suffered from dehydration. For the wounded, insufficient water increased their misery and adversely affected the medical care that was available.

The battle of Perryville, however, did not immediately end the Kentucky campaign. Bragg retreated to seek a junction with Smith's army. Buell undertook a cautious pursuit, following the Confederates as they headed toward the Cumberland Gap and Tennessee. The pursuit's initial slow pace stemmed from Buell's concern that too rapid an advance would again make his line of supply vulnerable to a rapid Confederate thrust. When Bragg's intent to leave Kentucky via the Cumberland Gap became clear Buell proved reluctant to follow aggressively with his entire army. Although pressed by the War Department and the president to carry the war into eastern Tennessee, he did not believe he could sustain all three corps over the few roads that led into the mountainous region. Moreover the terrain and approaching inclement weather discouraged a rapid advance, particularly if opposed. Instead, leaving a single corps to monitor Bragg's return to Tennessee, he began moving the rest of his command toward Nashville where he intended to resume operations against Chattanooga. This movement effectively ended the Kentucky campaign and directly led to MG William S. Rosecrans replacing Buell.

Army of the Mississippi

The army that General Bragg led into Kentucky had no fixed line of supply. Nor did it rely on railroads since the principal lines connecting Kentucky and Tennessee lay in Union hands and did not link the eastern parts of those states. Consequently the Army of the Mississippi carried its own supplies. However Bragg did not intend his army to sustain itself throughout the campaign with what it could transport from Tennessee. Such a feat would have been impossible due to the size of the army and the broken-down state of its wagon fleet. The latter had seen continuous service since Shiloh, and it required extensive replacement and repair. Instead Bragg intended his army to live off the land once in Kentucky. The Commonwealth was reported to have abundant foodstuffs available. Moreover the Confederates perceived themselves as liberators rather than invaders. They expected to receive a warm welcome and support from Kentucky's inhabitants. Therefore the army's logistics requirements remained limited to those supplies necessary to ensure its arrival in the Commonwealth.

In effect Bragg's supply base moved with his army. He had a freedom of maneuver that Buell's reliance on railroads precluded. However, this independence lasted only as long as the supplies. While the army marched consumption steadily depleted the fixed amount of provisions. Wagon train security thus became critical. On 16 September Buell nearly captured

49

the Confederate wagons at Glasgow when he prepared to attack Glasgow in the mistaken belief that Bragg's army was in the vicinity. Only the successful rear guard and Confederate cavalry's delaying actions averted what might have been a calamity for Bragg.

Hence, Bragg's decisions regarding the route and activities of his army reflected his supply levels. His movement into Barren County and the subsequent seizure of Munfordville stemmed in part from the mistaken belief that the county could support his army's needs. Instead he discovered that prior military operations had already consumed much of the area's food and forage. His army had sufficient rations for only three days' operations. This condition contributed to Bragg's decision to march to Bardstown rather than to fight Buell near Munfordville. At Bardstown the Confederates were able to live off the land. Nevertheless the army commander directed the establishment of a string of depots to sustain his soldiers should a retreat from Kentucky become necessary.

Following the battle of Perryville Bragg effected a juncture with Smith's army. However, he proved unwilling to risk another battle, opting instead to return to Tennessee. Several factors influenced Bragg's decision, including a worsening supply situation. In the rush to concentrate the Confederate armies, following the advance of Buell's army from Louisville, the depots previously created had not been stockpiled with food and forage. Their provisions were sufficient for only a few days. Uncertain whether the available supplies would sustain his army throughout its retreat, Bragg believed any further delay in Kentucky would only make this situation worse. In fact his soldiers consumed their last food supplies while still en route to Tennessee. Hunger and starvation accompanied them, and they arrived at their destination exhausted and temporarily unfit for combat. However, the army also brought its spoils from the Kentucky campaign, including an assortment of weapons and equipment. The most significant capture, however, was a fleet of new supply wagons initially intended for the US Army.

Engineer Support

Military engineers performed tasks that were essential to every campaign in the Civil War. Demands for these highly skilled technical soldiers remained high throughout the war. Union and Confederate armies, in particular, sought USMA-trained engineers. However, the small number of such men resulted in using alternative talent pools. Many civil engineers, once commissioned as volunteers, supplemented the work done by professional engineer officers. The Confederates, in particular, relied on civilian expertise since many of their trained engineer officers preferred serving in combat units. In some cases civilian engineers working for state or local governments planned and supervised fortification work.

Before the Civil War the US Army Corps of Engineers contained a handful of staff officers and one company of trained engineers. After the war's outbreak, this cadre expanded to a four-company Regular engineer battalion. In addition the US Congress established a single company of topographic engineers. Several volunteer pioneer regiments supported the various field armies. The US Army Corps of Engineers also initially controlled the Balloon Corps that was used for aerial reconnaissance. The Confederate Corps of Engineers was formed in 1861. It began as a small staff and one company of sappers, miners, and pontoniers. During the war it grew slowly and generally relied on soldier details and contract labor to perform its duties rather than established military units composed of trained engineers and craftsmen.

Engineer missions included constructing fortifications; repairing and constructing roads, bridges, and railroads; demolition; limited construction of obstacles; and erecting or reducing siege works. For the North the Federal Topographic Engineers performed reconnaissance and produced maps. In practice, however, engineer officers performed the full range of engineering functions, including mapping and reconnaissance. Consequently the Corps of Engineers and Topographic Engineers merged into a single organization in 1863. The Confederates avoided this midwar reorganization by initially consolidating all of its engineer functions.

In 1861 army commanders found maps to be in short supply. In some areas they were nonexistent. However, as the war progressed, the North developed a sophisticated mapping capability. Federal topographic engineers performed personal reconnaissance to develop base maps, reproduced them by several processes, and distributed them to field commanders. Photography, lithographic presses, and eventually photochemical processes enabled Union engineers to reproduce maps quickly. Western armies, which usually operated far from cities, carried their own equipment to reproduce maps on campaigns at army headquarters. By 1864 annual map production exceeded 21,000 copies. Confederate topographic work never approached the Federal effort in quantity or quality. Confederate topographers initially used tracing paper to reproduce maps. Not until 1864 did using photographic methods become widespread in the South.

Military bridging assets included wagon-mounted pontoon trains that carried wooden, canvas-covered, or inflatable rubber pontoon boats. Using this equipment trained engineer troops could bridge even large rivers in a matter of hours. The most remarkable pontoon bridge of the war was the 2,200-foot bridge that Army of the Potomac engineers built in 1864 over the James River, one of over three dozen pontoon bridges built to support campaigns in the east that year. In 1862 the Confederates began developing pontoon trains after they had observed their effectiveness. In fact, during the Atlanta campaign of 1864, General Joseph E. Johnston had four pontoon trains available to support his army.

Both armies in every campaign of the war traveled over roads and bridges that their engineers built or repaired. Union engineers also helped clear waterways by dredging, removing trees, or digging canals. Fixed fortifications laid out under engineer supervision played critical roles in the Vicksburg campaign and in actions around Richmond and Petersburg. Engineers also supervised the creation and development of works used by the besieging Union armies in both instances.

While the Northern engineer effort expanded in both men and materiel as the war progressed major problems confronted the Confederate engineer corps. The relatively small number of organized engineer units available forced Confederate engineers to rely heavily on unskilled soldier details and contract labor. Finding adequate manpower, however, proved difficult due to competing demands. Local slave owners were reluctant to provide work details for the Confederate Army because slaves were crucial to their economic survival. The Confederate congress authorized the conscription of a 20,000-slave labor force, but state government and local opposition largely nullified the measure. The Confederate dollar's declining value also posed a financial hurdle. Engineering projects often required large quantities of building materials whose cost rose throughout the war. Hence the combination of rising costs and declining purchasing power forced the Confederate government to either curtail projects or authorize large-scale expenditures that it could ill afford. The lack of iron resources further hindered the production of iron tools and railroad track, directly impacting Confederate engineers' ability to undertake major fortification projects and repair railroads.

Engineers in the Kentucky Campaign

The Army of the Ohio included a single engineer unit, the 1st Michigan Engineers and Mechanics. Mustered into service in December 1861 this unit participated in all of the Army's principal campaigns. It generally served as a collection of company detachments simultaneously supporting several different infantry divisions and projects. Before the battle of

Shiloh the 1st Michigan facilitated Buell's army's linkup with MG Ulysses S. Grant's army at Pittsburg Landing by building bridges over Tennessee's rain-swollen rivers. During the subsequent advance to and siege of Corinth the engineers operated trains, built corduroy roads, and oversaw artillery emplacement.

When Buell embarked on his advance toward Chattanooga he relied on his engineers to build and maintain his line of communications and supplies. The 1st Michigan helped complete railroad repairs along the Memphis and Charleston Railroad east to Decatur, Alabama. It also built bridges and trestles as it advanced. By July the regiment was concentrated at Huntsville, continuing to repair track and running trains. Its accomplishments included constructing 2,500 feet of bridging, laying 3 miles of track, and opening a tunnel on the Nashville and Decatur line. The 1st Michigan received additional support in its railroad repairs from hired mechanics who operated under the Military Superintendent of Railroads. By month's end the status of the railroads had improved sufficiently for Buell to begin preparing forward depots to support a direct advance on Chattanooga.

Confederate raids, however, forced continuous railroad maintenance and interrupted the flow of rail traffic. Consequently the 1st Michigan spent August building fortifications at key points along Buell's supply line and repairing damaged bridges and track. The 1st Michigan accompanied the Army of the Ohio on its retreat toward Louisville and its subsequent march to Perryville. During the battle fought there, regimental elements were assigned to different divisions. Three companies were thrown into the battle as it neared its climax in a desperate attempt to prevent the Union's left flank from collapsing. Afterward the engineers remained with the army during its return to Nashville.

In contrast, the army that Bragg led into Kentucky included no formal engineer units, although the Army Staff would likely have included an engineer officer. The absence of such special units meant that engineering operations were either not conducted or they were performed with improvised work details of soldiers or slaves where available. During the advance into Kentucky soldiers manhandled cannon and wagons through the mountain passes. They performed similar roles during their retreat back to Tennessee. Although the Confederates crossed several rivers during the course of the campaign, they relied on existing bridges or fords to cross them. Similarly, the lack of reliance upon railroads to transport troops and supplies into Kentucky removed the need to maintain track and bridges.

Communications Support

Communications systems used during the Civil War comprised a variety of systems. Line-of-sight means included semaphores, torches, and rockets. They provided operational and some tactical communications support. The telegraph proved ideal for transmitting information over long distances and therefore proved well suited to strategic and operational communications. On the battlefield, however, the most common means of communication was by courier or personal interaction among commanders. Couriers required no special training and did not rely on relay stations or special equipment. Commanders generally relied on their own aides-de-camp and staff officers, but any junior line officer might find himself pressed into this service. Couriers were effective means of tactical communication, but they were subject to capture, injury, and delays. Moreover, delivering a message did not ensure its timeliness or prevent its misinterpretation. Hence, relying on couriers tended to compound the effects of a commander's misjudgment or poor decision.

In the 1850s the US Army included no organization dedicated to military communications. However, in 1856 Albert J. Myer, an assistant surgeon in the Army, proposed a signaling system. The system used five separate numbered movements of a single flag. Four-number groups represented letters of the alphabet and several common words and phrases. For night use kerosene torches replaced the flags. Known as the "wigwag" system, it was patented in 1858. The following year the Army approved the system for possible military use, and Myer continued to refine and improve it. In 1860 he became a major, and the Army appointed him its first signal officer. He oversaw the first operational employment of his signaling process during the 1860-1861 military expedition in the New Mexico Territory. When the Civil War began Myer directed a small signal organization. Not until 1863 was it officially recognized as the Signal Corps and given bureau status within the War Department. Myer unsuccessfully sought to create a permanent corps of specialists. Consequently, signal elements were largely staffed with temporary detachments of soldiers, despite the specialized nature of the equipment and service. The Signal Corps' maximum strength reached just 1,500 officers and men.

As the US Army's chief signal officer Myer also worked to develop a field telegraph service. He favored using the Beardslee device, a magneto-powered machine operated by turning a wheel to a specific point that sent an electrical impulse that keyed the machine at the other end to the same letter. Although less reliable than the standard Morse code telegraph key, an operator could use the Beardslee with only several hours' training, and it did not require bulky batteries as a power source. Myer's field telegraph units carried equipment on wagons that enabled its operators to establish lines between field headquarters. The insulated wire used could also be hooked into existing trunk lines, thus offering the potential to extend the civilian telegraph network's reach. Myer believed the Signal Corps should be responsible for telegraphic communication. However, his view was not universally shared within the War Department. In November 1863 Secretary of War Edwin M. Stanton relieved Myer as the signal chief and consolidated all telegraphic activity under the separate Military Telegraph Service.

In the South the initial creation of a military force structure included a Signal Service. This organization was influenced by Edward P. Alexander who, as a second lieutenant before the war, had assisted Myer in developing his wigwag signaling system. Alexander demonstrated the system's utility during the war's first major engagement at Bull Run in 1861. There he provided early warning of the Union flanking movement and directly influenced the course of the battle. Later he organized the Confederate Signal Corps, officially established in April 1862. Like its Northern counterpart the Confederate Signal Corps also achieved a maximum strength of 1,500 men.

Attached to the Adjutant General and Inspector General Department the Confederate Signal Corps also controlled the military's telegraph service. However, field telegraph operations remained too limited to be of operational significance. The Confederates' existing telegraph lines provided strategic communications capabilities similar to the North's, but lack of resources and factories in the South for producing wire precluded extending the prewar telegraph networks.

The Signal Corps in the Kentucky Campaign

The Army of the Ohio benefited from a signal element's services. Organized in January 1862 it initially comprised five officers and 10 enlisted men. These soldiers served on detached service from their regiments and required special training in using communications equipment. When Buell marched on Nashville in February this signal party lacked sufficient equipment, and some of its sections remained untrained. Therefore, it remained at Munfordville, but it helped to coordinate boat movement on the Barren River and enabled communications between ground units across the river. Upon completion of training the signal party accompanied Buell's army as it marched across Tennessee to join MG Grant's force at Pittsburg Landing. There the signal sections established a communications link across the Tennessee River that was used to coordinate troop movements on both sides and across the river.

Despite the signal party's potential utility, personnel turbulence routinely interfered with its effective operation. Officers served with it on detached service from a regiment or brigade. Commanders of these regiments or brigades often recalled their officers on short notice, stripping the signal party of its trained leadership. Continuous service also resulted in personnel losses through attrition. Consequently, signal sections underwent training and gained proficiency only to lose qualified personnel, and replacements were not guaranteed because signal units depended on detachments. Creating a signal training facility in Nashville after its capture partially offset the worst effects of this recurring personnel loss, but it could not ensure that qualified signal personnel would be readily available.

During the advance on Chattanooga signal elements created communication links across the Tennessee River. They also established a series of semaphore stations in the wake of Buell's advance from Huntsville to Bridgeport, Alabama. Unfortunately, enlisted personnel's misuse of these stations generated false message traffic that created confusion and alarm in the army's rear area, heightening the general insecurity that Confederate cavalry and partisans caused. The establishment of a cipher system, properly secured, eliminated this problem. Its use represented an early effort at communications security.

The value of signal support was recognized during the Kentucky campaign. It helped to share information among different commands and became a useful tool in coordinating troop movements. When the first Confederate soldiers marched into Kentucky Union officials requested an additional signal party to help track the invaders and better coordinate the Union forces organized in response. The War Department approved this measure and dispatched a second unit to the state. Outside Chattanooga Buell dispersed his forces to cover the principal routes that Bragg might follow toward Nashville. To rapidly concentrate the Union forces once Bragg's path had been determined Buell relied upon signal rockets firing predesignated color patterns to alert his scattered command. Automatic fallback orders to Murfreesboro buttressed these signal preparations.

During Buell's retreat to Louisville the signal party with his army did not play a significant role. However, at Perryville the early creation of semaphore stations connecting Buell's headquarters with those of his corps commanders provided a means of rapid communication in the field.

Unfortunately these stations were not used to alert Buell when the Confederates attacked. He remained unaware that a battle was under way until an exhausted courier arrived in person. By then the battle had nearly ended. Ironically, station operators maintained steady communication among themselves and noted battlefield developments. Nevertheless, the system was not used to apprise the army commander of the enemy attack. After the battle Buell used the stations to prepare to resume fighting the following day. By then, however, the Confederates had withdrawn. During the pursuit of Bragg's army into eastern Kentucky the signal party remained with the army, ready to establish battlefield communications whenever combat appeared imminent.

Bragg's army did not include a Confederate Signal Corps element when it marched from Chattanooga. During the campaign communications occurred via courier. Consequently, it proved difficult for Bragg to communicate with those forces that were not under his direct command. Information was usually outdated by the time it reached its intended recipient. Once Bragg departed Chattanooga his ability to coordinate the movements of all Confederate forces participating in the campaign dropped to naught. On the battlefield the Confederates relied upon couriers and personal interaction as the principal means of communication—similar to their Union counterparts.

Medical Support

Wartime medical organizations bore the imprint of their prewar roots. Union and Confederate surgeons general and medical directors generally had served in the US Army Medical Department before the Civil War. However, this common experience did not prepare them to handle large numbers of casualties administratively. Nor was the state of medicine in the mid-19th century sufficiently advanced for them to accurately understand the cause of disease. The combination of inadequate knowledge and ill preparedness for high battlefield casualty rates proved deadly. Despite considerable improvements in caring for the wounded during the war, far more soldiers died from disease and infection than from direct battlefield action.

The war's first major battle at Bull Run overtaxed the limited medical support available. Indeed, for the routed Union forces, it broke down completely. The Medical Department responded by creating a casualty evacuation and treatment system that surgeon Jonathan Letterman developed. It consolidated field hospitals at the division level, centralized ambulance control, and decentralized medical supplies down to the regiment.

Under this system a casualty recovered from the battlefield first went to a regimental holding area directly to the rear for initial treatment. Here ambulances or impressed wagons transported the wounded to a division field hospital, normally within a mile of the battle lines. The most seriously injured were then removed to general hospitals via ambulances, railroad, or steamboat. These facilities lay in towns along the army's line of communications.

Confederate medical support quickly adopted the same general principles with some variation. Field hospitals were consolidated at brigade rather than division level, and Confederate medical directors did not possess the same span of influence as their Union counterparts. Whereas the latter controlled all medical activities within an army area, Confederate directors' authority ended with their parent brigade or division hospitals. A separate director was responsible for the larger hospitals in an army's rear area. Cooperation was required between the different levels of directors to ensure the smooth flow and proper handling of wounded soldiers.

Commanders discouraged soldiers from leaving the battle lines to escort wounded men to the rear. This practice eroded combat power, but it proved common among new or less-disciplined units. Proper casualty evacuation required the prior selection of men for litter and ambulance duty. Bandsmen frequently found themselves thus employed. A wounded soldier was expected to make his way rearward with assistance as necessary. There litter bearers collected them and transported them to field hospitals in ambulances or available supply wagons. Ambulances were specially designed two- or four-wheel carts with springs to limit jolts. However, rough roads made even short trips agonizing for wounded men, especially in supply wagons that lacked wheel springs. The precise location of the target hospital varied with the battlefield. Generally sites were selected that used existing buildings to supplement hospital tents, provided access to water, and offered protection from battle.

Most operations performed at field hospitals were amputations. Approximately 70 percent of Civil War wounds occurred in the arm or leg. Once it entered the body the Minié ball shattered bones with which it came in contact. Amputation proved to be the best technique available to limit the chance of serious infection. Chloroform, morphine, and other drugs were used to help patients cope with the pain of these operations. Union hospitals were generally well supplied with these supplies, but battlefield shortages still occurred. Confederate surgeons, however, often lacked important medical supplies and drugs.

Despite efforts to provide an effective medical support structure a wounded soldier still faced a series of trials to overcome before his chance for long-term recovery improved. Once wounded the soldier needed to live long enough to be evacuated. If not immediately transferred to the regimental holding area the wounded who were unable to walk might remain without aid for hours or days. Movement via litter or ambulance, however, tended to be painful and could trigger shock. Arrival at a medical facility then exposed the soldier to the overcrowded and unsanitary conditions that were prevalent there. Too often the wounded waited for treatment amid other injured and dying soldiers with the refuse of recent surgeries in plain view. The effectiveness of medical attention varied considerably, depending on the availability of medical supplies and the medical staff's competency. Yet surviving surgery still did not guarantee recovery. A wounded soldier still needed to remain free from infection for about two more weeks before his chances for recovery significantly improved. Many soldiers survived their wounds and surgery only to succumb to infection.

Medical Support in the Kentucky Campaign

Neither the Army of the Ohio nor the Army of the Mississippi received adequate medical support during operations in Kentucky. When Buell decided to retire to Louisville from Nashville, he desired rapid movement. Consequently he reduced the number of wagons available to each brigade and limited their baggage. The number of ambulances available to each brigade fell to one, and the wagon space available for medical supplies similarly became restricted. At Perryville Union medical personnel received little guidance regarding establishing hospitals or how best to organize to prepare for the coming battle. Consequently the surgeons and medical staffs of several brigades opted to pool their resources on their own initiative. Confederate arrangements and resource availability proved little better. For both North and South, the organization of medical support deviated sharply from the orderly structure inherent to the Letterman system.

When the fighting began Union soldiers did not have a clear sense of where the hospitals or casualty stations were. In several instances wounded soldiers wandered the battlefield seeking these facilities or simply congregated at locations out of enemy fire. Casualty evacuation proved to be a significant problem for both armies. While the wounded lay for extended periods on the battlefield, heat and lack of water worsened their plight. Some remained untended until the day after the battle. Confederate wounded left in this situation generally became prisoners because Bragg retreated after the battle. For both sides the number of casualties generated by the fighting overwhelmed the available medical personnel and make-shift hospitals.

Soldiers killed during the battle were left where they fell. The army's retreat disrupted Confederate efforts to collect, identify, and bury their dead. Although Buell's army remained near Perryville the day after the battle, burial efforts focused on Union soldiers. Local residents thus assumed responsibility for collecting and burying the Confederate dead. One such gravesite became the site of the Confederate memorial, which also became the first landmark commemorating the battle. The current park grew over time from this memorial site.

As the armies moved away from Perryville the local community faced a major health crisis. The town was overwhelmed by the needs of the wounded. Injured soldiers occupied nearly every building in a 10-mile radius. Food supplies proved insufficient to sustain both the wounded and the local residents. Nor could the small town provide adequate medical attention. Local families assumed responsibility for caring for soldiers, often sacrificing their own needs. Union soldiers who were able to do so endeavored to walk or beg rides to Louisville, some 80 miles away. They reasoned that better medical facilities would be available there. The US Sanitary Commission's intervention helped to avert disaster. It provided medical personnel and more than 10 tons of supplies to Perryville. This support prevented the outbreak of disease and helped the town to recover in the aftermath of battle.

Chapter 2. Campaign Overview

Introduction

In 1862 the South strove to end the Civil War on terms that were favorable to the Confederacy. From New Mexico to Maryland Southern armies embarked on a series of offensives to ensure the Confederacy's survival. Southern leaders believed that an aggressive military strategy would demonstrate the viability of an independent Confederate States of America and trigger European intervention on its behalf. Central to this strategy was invading and seizing the border states. The populations and land of Missouri, Kentucky, and Maryland represented significant potential resources for the South. Hence Northern armies contested every move into the border states, but the Union's industrial might and larger population had yet to be harnessed effectively to its war effort. The South needed to achieve political and military victories before the North's greater resources crushed the Confederacy into submission. The North struggled to ensure the border states remained loyal to the United States.

Early efforts to do so in Missouri nearly came to ruin at Wilson's Creek in August 1861. There the Confederates won a victory and proceeded to overrun much of the state. However, the victorious Southern militia soon melted away, and the Union hold on the state strengthened. MG Earl Van Dorn's subsequent effort to lead a Confederate invasion into Missouri ended with his army's defeat at Pea Ridge in March 1862. Maryland's proximity to Washington minimized the likelihood of its secession, despite many of its inhabitants' Confederate sympathies and its invasion by General Robert E. Lee's Army of Northern Virginia in September 1862. Kentucky's population split in its support for North and South, but Union armies controlled much of the state by the end of 1861. In the first months of 1862 a string of military successes expanded the Union influence throughout most of Tennessee. Eastern Tennessee, however, remained under Southern control and became the springboard for the Confederate invasion of Kentucky.

This campaign sought to encourage the commonwealth's secession and to move the Confederacy's border in the west to the Ohio River. The state's populace was expected to provide willing recruits for the invading Southern armies. The battle of Perryville, however, ended these aspirations. After weeks of maneuvering the contending armies finally clashed near this central Kentucky town. On a smaller scale this fight resembled that of Antietam in which a lackluster Union performance on the battlefield nevertheless resulted in a strategic victory. After Perryville the

Confederate invaders withdrew from Kentucky. The state remained firmly in the Union. Moreover, the North regained the initiative in the west after weeks of reacting to Confederate movements. In the wake of both Antietam and Perryville the commanders of the Union armies engaged were both replaced. On the Confederate side the army commander waged a war of words and recriminations with his subordinates over the conduct of the Kentucky invasion. This dissension did not end with the return of the invading forces to Tennessee. Instead, it continued to plague subsequent Confederate operations in the west.

Both sides scrutinized the campaign after its conclusion. Lost in this postmortem analysis was the significance of what the Confederate forces in the west had attempted and achieved. Between June and October 1862 the Army of the Mississippi recovered from its defeat at Shiloh and retreat to Tupelo, Mississippi, regained the initiative, and carried the war deep into Kentucky. The campaign marked a stunning turnaround of Confederate fortunes in the west. Moreover, the invasion of Kentucky proved the only time during the war that the Confederates attempted to coordinate the actions of six different armies drawn from three military departments.[1] The guiding vision behind the campaign lay in mutually supporting operations by forces in Mississippi, Tennessee, and western Virginia. The Confederates also tried to recapture central and western Tennessee, thereby securing their hold on the critical railroad junction at Chattanooga. Thus the invasion of Kentucky must be viewed in the broader context of Confederate goals and operations throughout the theater.

The War in the West, 1861

Between the Mississippi River and the Appalachian Mountains lay a broad expanse that became the principal campaign area for the western theater. While Union forces assembled north of the Ohio River the Confederates worked to raise an army in Tennessee. In between lay Kentucky. Upon the outbreak of war, this state declared its neutrality and its intent to resist incursions from either belligerent. Kentucky's stance effectively protected Tennessee's northern border. Its neutrality shielded Tennessee from both overland invasion and attacks up the Tennessee and Cumberland Rivers. The few Confederate military defenses erected at the war's start focused on the Mississippi River. Kentucky's neutrality permitted the organization of Confederate forces in relative safety. This protective shield was needed since few regiments existed, and those that did lacked weapons, equipment, and training.

Nevertheless, in September 1861 MG Leonidas Polk, temporarily commanding Confederate forces in the west, ordered them to seize Columbus, Kentucky. The town lay on heights overlooking the Mississippi River, and its control could block movement along the river. After its seizure, emplacing heavy cannon transformed Columbus into a Confederate strongpoint. Polk acted to preempt what he believed to be a similar Union effort to capture the town. The Northern commanders, however, had carefully avoided any overt violation of Kentucky's neutrality. Polk's move into the state made such caution unnecessary. Union regiments soon poured into Kentucky, and by year's end much of the state lay under their control.

Polk's tenure as commander ended with the arrival of General Albert Sidney Johnston. When the war commenced Johnston was serving in the US Army in California. He resigned his commission and headed eastward on a lengthy journey. Confederate President Jefferson Davis made him a full general and assigned him to command the Western Military Department. This department stretched from the Appalachian Mountains across Tennessee and the Mississippi River to include Arkansas and the forces operating in Missouri. Johnston had insufficient forces to defend this broad tract, and he possessed little control over operations west of the Mississippi River. He opted for a forward defense of Tennessee, concentrating most of his strength at Bowling Green, Kentucky. Smaller forces led by Polk at Columbus and BG Felix Zollicoffer near the Cumberland Gap protected his flanks. To prevent Union operations up the Tennessee and Cumberland Rivers, construction began on Fort Henry and Fort Donelson.

A steady accretion of Union strength faced these Confederate dispositions. The Department of the Missouri, commanded by MG Henry W. Halleck, included those forces in Missouri and west of the Cumberland River in Kentucky. MG Don Carlos Buell commanded the Department of the Ohio, responsible for the area between the Cumberland River and the Appalachian Mountains. Personal rivalry, however, impeded effective cooperation between these two commanders.

The Union Juggernaut of 1862

The first months of 1862 opened with a string of Union successes against which Johnston seemed powerless to resist. In January political pressure in the North to assist the predominantly pro-Union population of eastern Tennessee resulted in Buell dispatching a 4,000-man column toward the region. Zollicoffer attacked this force near Mill Springs, Kentucky. The resultant battle on 19 January amid mud and rain ended in Zollicoffer's death and the rout of his command. Although poor weather and rugged terrain precluded any further Union advance toward eastern Tennessee the threat of such action remained.

In February BG Ulysses S. Grant received Halleck's permission to attack Fort Henry. The poorly sited and constructed works fell on 6 February. Grant next moved against the better-defended Fort Donelson. Ten days later he captured the fort and 12,000 Confederate soldiers. Johnston could not afford such losses. Indeed he had initially intended to leave only a token force at Fort Donelson but reversed his decision and reinforced the position shortly before Grant attacked. With these Confederate reverses Tennessee lay open to invasion via the Tennessee and Cumberland Rivers.

The fall of Fort Henry and Fort Donelson made the Confederate position at Bowling Green untenable. A strong force remained at Columbus, but Grant's army lay between them and Johnston. Additionally, Buell advanced the Army of the Ohio from Louisville toward Nashville while a newly formed Union army commanded by MG John Pope threatened Columbus. Johnston reacted by retiring to Nashville, but he considered the city indefensible and retreated to Murfreesboro. Left behind were stockpiles of badly needed supplies for the Confederate armies fighting in the west. Within a few days Confederate forces also retreated from Columbus. Only a small force on Island No. 10 remained to contest Union operations down the Mississippi River. By the end of February the areas under Union control included all of Kentucky and much of western and central Tennessee.

West of the Mississippi River Van Dorn assumed control of Confederate forces in Arkansas. He planned an aggressive advance through Missouri to threaten St. Louis and to relieve the pressure on Johnston. His campaign, however, proved short-lived. On 6-8 March the battle of Pea Ridge, fought near the Arkansas-Missouri border, resulted in the defeat of Van Dorn's army. Unable to secure Arkansas from Union invasion, let alone threaten St. Louis, Van Dorn's survivors received orders to march to Corinth, Mississippi. This town became the focus of Union aspirations, following the capture of Nashville.

Through Corinth ran the Confederacy's principal rail link with those states west of the Mississippi River. Railroads also connected Corinth with Columbus, Chattanooga, and Mobile. Corinth's capture would parallel related efforts to secure the Mississippi River and cut the Confederacy in two. Halleck planned the operation to capture the critical town. Following the victories at Fort Henry and Fort Donelson his command responsibilities increased. He now commanded all Union forces west of the Appalachian Mountains, including Buell's and Grant's armies. Halleck intended these forces to concentrate at Pittsburg Landing on the Tennessee River. Grant would move via that river while Buell marched overland to the juncture point. Once combined the entire mass of 75,000 men would move directly on Corinth.

On 15 March elements of Grant's army began arriving at Pittsburg Landing. The next day Buell's force began its 122-mile march from Nashville through rain, mud, and flooded streams. The Confederates understood the significance of these movements and sensed their ultimate objective. Corinth was a logical next step for the Union armies. Therefore Johnston planned to attack Grant before Buell joined him. The Confederate plan owed much to General P.G.T. Beauregard who arrived in the west to serve under Johnston. Beauregard soon became the driving influence for the Confederate counterstrike.

Corinth became the gathering point for the Southern forces. Johnston feigned a retreat from Murfreesboro and arrived on 23 March. MG Braxton Bragg brought troops stripped from defenses along the Gulf of Mexico while Beauregard worked to secure additional soldiers from state governors. Van Dorn, too, received orders to cross the Mississippi River and join the concentration at Corinth, but he arrived too late. Nevertheless some 42,000 soldiers lay poised to attack Pittsburg Landing. Bragg assumed the role of the army's drillmaster and implemented a regimen of harsh discipline and training to improve the army's overall effectiveness.

On 6 April the Army of the Mississippi struck Grant near Shiloh Church. Despite initial success, the Confederates proved unable to rout the Union army or prevent its juncture with Buell. The next day the combined Union forces counterattacked and drove Beauregard's army from the field. Johnston was slain on 6 April, and Beauregard assumed command of a dispirited and defeated army. He retreated to Corinth where Van Dorn's command provided some belated reinforcement. Meanwhile Island No. 10 fell to a combined Union land and naval operation on April 8, opening the Mississippi River as far as Fort Pillow, north of Memphis. At Pittsburg Landing Halleck assumed personal control of Grant's and Buell's combined armies. The arrival of Pope's army soon swelled Union troop strength there to more than 100,000. Halleck, however, first delayed his advance and then crept cautiously toward Corinth.

In the face of the Union juggernaut Beauregard remained at Corinth. However, water scarcity and unsanitary conditions incapacitated many of

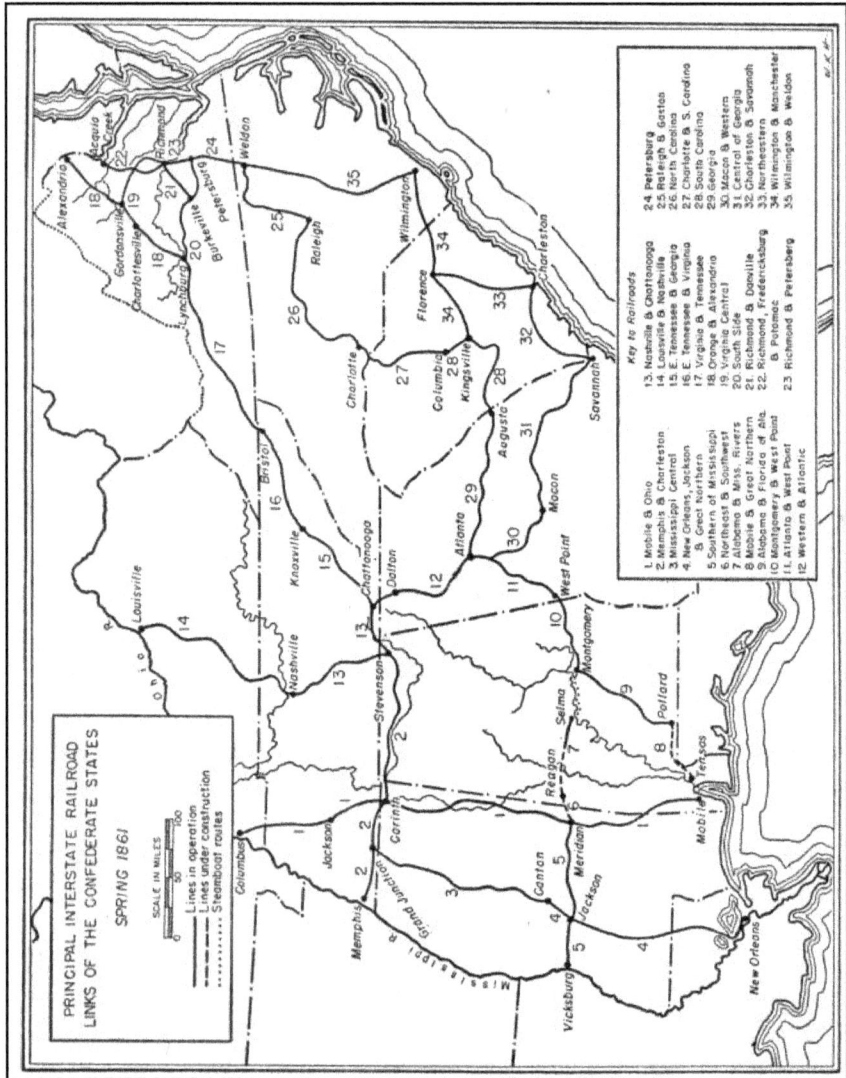

Map 1. Rail net.

Operations of the Army Under Buell From June 10th to October 30, 1862 and the 'Buell Commission'
by James B. Fry and Don Carlos Buell. D. Van Nostrand, 1884.

Map 2. Area of operations.

his soldiers. Beauregard did not believe the army could withstand a siege, despite the town's fortifications. At the end of May the Confederate army abandoned Corinth and withdrew farther south to Tupelo, Mississippi. Halleck did not pursue, but Union raids helped to expand the area under Northern control. Since the battle of Shiloh, 15,000 square miles had been lost to the Confederacy. Beauregard's army shrank through desertions and sickness. Soldier morale plummeted, and public criticism of the army commander for his defeat at Shiloh increased. Beauregard, claiming ill health, left his command to recuperate. Jefferson Davis relieved him for this unauthorized absence. On 15 June Bragg assumed command of the Army of the Mississippi.

Objective Chattanooga

While the Army of the Mississippi languished at Tupelo, Halleck prepared his next move. The principal options open to him were to advance down the Mississippi River valley, secure western Tennessee, or advance into eastern Tennessee. Union numbers, coupled with the Confederates' diminished effectiveness, made each of these actions viable. Political pressure, however, finally resulted in Halleck's army dispersing to secure western Tennessee while Buell led 40,000 men to capture Chattanooga. Since the war's onset Lincoln had urged the Northern commanders in the west to attack into eastern Tennessee and protect the pro-Union population there. When this move was first attempted in January 1862 the victory at Mill Springs resulted. Winter conditions and rugged terrain, however, prevented further operations into eastern Tennessee. With the arrival of spring and a series of Union victories, conditions appeared favorable for resuming this effort. Moreover, seizing Chattanooga would break the primary rail link between the Confederate forces east and west of the Appalachian Mountains. It would threaten Southern small-arms production and arsenals in Georgia. Chattanooga was the gateway to the Deep South, and its fall would deal a major blow to the Confederacy.

The commander of this operation had an impressive military career. Buell graduated from the USMA in 1841 and as a junior officer fought in the Mexican War. He remained in the Army and made it his career, serving in a variety of field and staff appointments while many of his peers left the military. Buell reached the rank of lieutenant colonel by 1861. He demonstrated organizational and administrative abilities that complemented his personal courage and competence. When the Civil War began these qualities ensured his value to the Union Army and his appointment to brigadier general. He assisted in building the Army of the Potomac and in the process forged a lasting personal tie with MG George B. McClellan, who became his friend and mentor. In recognition of his services Buell received command of the Department of the Ohio and was promoted to major general.

Like McClellan, Buell placed great emphasis on discipline and logistics. Both men shared a philosophy of war that focused on maneuver to achieve the most favorable conditions before entering battle. Buell considered war a science governed by principles that must be followed to achieve success. In his view—

> My studies have taught me that battles are only to be fought for some important object; that success must be rendered reasonably certain if possible—the more certain the better; that if the result is reasonably uncertain, battle is only to be sought when very serious disadvantage must result from a failure to fight, or when the advantages of a possible victory far outweigh the consequences of probable defeat. These rules suppose that war has a higher object than that of mere bloodshed; and military history points for study and commendation to campaigns which have been conducted over a large field of operations with important results, and without a single general engagement.[2]

Buell also did not believe that Southern civilians should be exposed to the hardships of war or punished because they supported the Confederacy. Instead he considered it necessary to respect their constitutional rights to ease reconciliation of North and South once hostilities ended. Winning the war meant defeating enemy armies, not waging war on civilians and destroying their property and livelihoods. These views reflected Buell's personal feelings and the US government's policy in 1861. By mid-1862, however, the government began to embrace a more aggressive and ruthless prosecution of the war that did not spare civilians. Buell did not support this trend and continued the soft treatment of noncombatants.

Buell remained aloof to politics, focusing instead on his military responsibilities. In doing so he was out of step with the highly politicized nature of a civil war. Politics and patriotism filled the ranks of his army with citizen soldiers. These Buell trained and molded into a combat force, but he preferred the discipline and efficiency of professional soldiers. He communicated this bias through a cold and uncharismatic demeanor. He did not explain his plans to subordinates, much less to reporters and politicians. He remained a distant figure who concentrated command authority in himself and expected subordinates to obey.

In early June Halleck directed Buell to seize Chattanooga. He was to follow the Memphis and Charleston Railroad east from Corinth, repairing the line as he advanced. This move required the rebuilding of more than 200 miles of railroad through barren country and a hostile populace. Even with repairs complete the railroad's utility remained questionable. It had only limited rolling stock, and no functioning rail links connected it to the Louisville and Nashville Railroad. The latter constituted Buell's primary supply line between his supply source in Louisville and central Tennessee. Nevertheless, despite its null supply benefit, the Memphis and Charleston Railroad would require protection against enemy partisans and cavalry along its length. Thus the army would approach Chattanooga with diminishing strength. Nor could Buell guarantee his army's sustenance even with the railroad properly protected. Therefore he recommended an advance on Chattanooga from central Tennessee where he could better supply his soldiers.

Halleck disagreed and insisted on the original route. Accordingly Buell's forces dispersed along the Memphis and Charleston Railroad to commence repairs, gradually inching their way east. Logistics preparations slowed progress. To facilitate movement across the Tennessee River Buell had a bridge constructed. Louisville, Kentucky, remained the army's primary supply source. From there supplies could be shipped via railroad to Nashville, but the final connection with Buell's army required operating wagon train shuttles to and from the Tennessee capital. Consequently Buell also directed the improvement of the road net between Nashville and towns along the Memphis and Charleston Railroad in northern Mississippi and Alabama. Simultaneously work commenced on the railroads linking Nashville with Decatur and Stevenson in northern Alabama. In the latter town Buell intended to build a forward depot and stockpile supplies to sustain the army once it reached Chattanooga. Upon completion of these actions Buell would possess an efficient, rail-based supply line.

These measures took time. Railroad repairs continued throughout June and July while Buell's army worked closer to Chattanooga. Forward elements reached the town's outskirts by 29 June. There they remained while the rest of the army approached. The Confederates determined to resist Buell but lacked sufficient force to defeat him in battle. Therefore, they resorted to cavalry attacks on the Union supply line. Stretching more than 300 miles from northern Alabama through Tennessee and across Kentucky, Buell's rail link with Louisville now became the Confederate objective. Destroying a single bridge would stop all rail traffic and necessitate time-consuming repairs, further retarding the pace of Buell's advance. In Kentucky COL John Hunt Morgan raided across the state, complementing similar activities by BG Nathan Bedford Forrest in Tennessee and BG Frank Armstrong in Alabama.

To protect his supply line Buell drew on the Department of the Ohio's resources. He sought to provide rear area security while retaining sufficient forward combat power to take Chattanooga. Creating outposts at key points along his supply line improved its protection, but Buell expected the existing forces in Kentucky and parts of Tennessee to fend for themselves. He did not weaken his army by sending detachments far to the rear. Instead he looked to his cavalry to counter the Confederate forays.

Too often, however, the Union cavalry fared poorly in encounters with the raiders. Many units lacked adequate mounts, training, and firearms. Decentralized organization and misuse compounded these problems. Regiments often existed in name only, their components scattered to provide couriers, escorts, and local scouts for a variety of infantry formations. Buell unsuccessfully petitioned the War Department for additional properly equipped cavalry units. He also implemented organizational changes to improve the effectiveness of his mounted force. These efforts included mixed groupings of infantry and cavalry, independent cavalry brigades, and the creation of a cavalry division comprising two brigades. The growing use of entire cavalry regiments and brigades improved their effectiveness, but some mounted organizations continued to be dispersed among infantry formations.

Better organization and use of cavalry, however, did not stop Confederate attacks on the Union supply line. In particular, Morgan's activities in Kentucky resulted in frequent breaks to the Louisville and Nashville Railroad. Buell could not ensure a steady supply flow, and his army in northern Alabama suffered. Ration levels dropped, but foraging parties found little in the barren countryside other than partisan ambushes. In response Buell's soldiers sought to avenge themselves by taking what they needed from the hostile civilian populace and punishing suspected Confederate sympathizers. Buell, however, remained faithful to his own conciliatory views concerning civilian treatment. While placing his army on half rations he prohibited retaliatory measures aimed at noncombatants or their property. His soldiers did not understand this policy, and Buell did not enlighten them. Consequently they began to believe that Buell sympathized with the Confederacy. This view paralleled Washington's criticism of the army commander. Frustration with Buell's seeming inability to take Chattanooga led to allegations of incompetence and disloyalty. A battlefield success might have ended such criticism. Yet as the summer passed Chattanooga remained in Confederate hands, and Buell's offensive ground to a halt short of his objective.

The Confederate Dilemma

The capture of Corinth in May 1862 marked the apex in a string of Union victories that began with the battle at Mill Springs. Conversely Confederate resistance in the West reached its nadir. While Halleck pondered the best means to exploit Corinth's fall, Bragg sought a way to salvage Confederate fortunes. In a few short months the war had shifted from Kentucky to Mississippi. The battle at Pea Ridge effectively ended Confederate aspirations west of the Mississippi River while much of the river itself now lay in Union control. Stripping forces from the Gulf Coast had helped ensure sufficient Confederate strength to attack Grant at Shiloh, but it left the coastal region vulnerable. Within weeks of the battle of Shiloh, New Orleans and Baton Rouge had fallen, and Union naval elements had attacked Vicksburg.

In the wake of Beauregard abandoning his command Bragg became responsible for revitalizing Confederate military operations in the face of these threats. Upon assuming command of the Army of the Mississippi in June 1862 Bragg was one of the Confederacy's senior generals. He had graduated from the USMA in 1837 where he forged lasting ties with classmate Jefferson Davis. As a junior officer Bragg participated in the campaign against the Seminole Indians. During the Mexican War he commanded a battery that became noted for its efficiency and battlefield effectiveness. Subsequently Bragg left the army, resigning as a lieutenant colonel to become a planter.

When the Civil War began Bragg received an appointment as a brigadier general in the Confederate Army and became responsible for defending the Gulf Coast. Promoted to major general in September 1861, he commanded a corps at Shiloh. By June 1862 Bragg was a full general who Davis, Southern politicians, and many of the soldiers in the Army of the Mississippi held in high regard. Although uncharismatic he possessed a flair for organization and administrative work. He also believed in the importance of training and discipline. His emphasis on these qualities in the weeks before Shiloh ensured that Johnston attacked with an effective army.

Bragg set high standards for himself and those under his command. He demanded proficiency from subordinates in executing their duties, and he had little tolerance for those officers who failed to meet his expectations. In the latter category were many officers who lacked formal military training. Like Buell, Bragg preferred the discipline and demeanor of professional soldiers, making him a cold, distant figure to most of his men. His abrasive personality alienated subordinates. Rather than exploit the strengths of his commanders, he openly criticized their weaknesses. He failed to mold his senior commanders into a team and found himself at odds with them. Despite an unrivaled penchant for work, such discord frequently undermined the value of his labor.

Upon assuming command of the Army of the Mississippi, however, Bragg found his abilities as an organizer and administrator in great demand. The army was dispirited and demoralized, and it lacked food. Bragg immediately implemented a regimen of harsh discipline and drill, severely punishing infractions. He intended to ready the army for offensive operations. To do so he also needed capable officers. In many state and volunteer regiments the soldiers elected their own commanders. Unfortunately this democratic process often resulted in the election of popular individuals with no military skills. Bragg therefore established special boards charged with testing newly elected officers' military competence. These boards, in effect, functioned as promotion boards with the power to overturn election results in instances of incompetence or inadequacy. They ensured that all leaders had a modicum of military competence.

Bragg's effort to improve his army's leadership did not stop at the regimental level; he targeted every command echelon. Of his general officers he considered four major generals and four brigadiers incompetent and unfit for command. In his assessment Bragg made no concession to either professional military education or political considerations. Thus, five of these generals had previously graduated from the USMA. Bragg considered Polk useless as a commander, despite Polk's graduation from the academy and his personal friendship with Davis. MG Benjamin F. Cheatham lacked a formal military education, but he proved exceptionally popular among the large Tennessee contingent in the Army of the Mississippi. Bragg, however, saw Cheatham as little more than a ruffian. Efforts to remove these officers, however, foundered upon the Confederate president's opposition. Davis asserted his own authority in appointing and removing generals and denied Bragg's request to have those in his own army dismissed. Unfortunately this attempt to purge senior ranks did not remain a confidential matter, and Bragg's senior subordinates soon learned how their commander perceived them.

Nor did Richmond support Bragg's efforts to develop alternate rail lines to offset the impact of Corinth's loss. He strove to reduce the disruption to

Confederate rail traffic that stemmed from the town's capture. Initially Bragg tried to gain the support of the local railroad companies. When they demurred and proved uncooperative, Bragg commandeered their property and assumed direct responsibility for the work. The affected companies resented such behavior and lodged complaints with the Confederate government. Despite the military value of Bragg's actions, his temporary nationalization of private businesses was not supported in Richmond. Bragg relinquished his control of the railroad companies, and the new rail links he tried to build remained incomplete.

Despite such local failures Bragg continued to study his operational choices. He wanted to assume the offensive but faced a numerically superior army under Halleck. The detachment of Buell toward Chattanooga did not dangerously weaken Halleck's force, but it created another worry for Bragg. The town represented the last direct rail link between the western states and Virginia. It was the gateway into Georgia from whence the supplies for the Army of the Mississippi flowed. Reinforcing Chattanooga might not guarantee that town's security, but it might prompt Halleck to attack Bragg's weakened forces in Mississippi. A Confederate thrust north risked defeat by a superior army. Protecting the Mississippi River Valley left central Mississippi and Alabama vulnerable to invasion.

Faced with an array of poor choices Bragg began to favor moving much of his army to Chattanooga. In addition to the town's importance its location afforded access to central Tennessee, northern Alabama, and the Cumberland Gap. A rapid thrust toward Nashville might recapture the city before Halleck's large but slow-moving army could respond. Alternatively, Kentucky could be invaded. Certainly any such movement lessened the threat to Chattanooga and would likely draw Union forces out of Mississippi and Alabama.

Bragg received continuous attention from displaced Southern politicians and prominent citizens from Tennessee and Kentucky. They lobbied not only for offensive action but also for a powerful Confederate military presence in their respective states. Furthermore, they depicted the local populations as being willing recruits who were simply waiting for Bragg's army to arrive. Reports from Kentucky indicated dissatisfaction with the governor's pro-Union stance. The prospects for Confederate support in both states appeared excellent. Morgan's experiences in Kentucky further encouraged this view. His reports also indicated readily available supplies and a supportive population. Consequently Bragg decided to redeploy much of his army to Chattanooga to prepare for a thrust into both states. In Mississippi he would leave two smaller forces commanded separately by MG Van Dorn and MG Sterling Price.

Buell's advance along the Memphis and Charleston Railroad and the absence of a parallel rail link between Tupelo and Chattanooga forced Bragg's redeployment along a circuitous route. A distance of some 300 miles separated the two towns, but the Confederates would have to travel nearly 800 miles through four states on different railroads and use ferry and steamboat transport across Mobile Bay. Conducting such a move with minimal delay constituted a major logistics undertaking. Bragg supervised and performed much of the required planning himself. Upon completion he dispatched a small division of 3,000 men as a trial run before committing most of his command. On 27 June this formation left Tupelo and arrived in Chattanooga on 3 July. This success led Bragg to prepare his main body to follow suit. The first trains left Tupelo on 23 July. Within four days advance elements began arriving in Chattanooga, but he still had to wait for his supply wagons and artillery to arrive before commencing operations. These elements traveled via a slower overland route. His cavalry support also required time to organize and concentrate at Chattanooga. Nevertheless Bragg had stolen a march on Buell, whose forces remained focused on railroad repairs and security in northern Alabama.

The Department of Eastern Tennessee

Bragg's Chattanooga redeployment moved him into the Department of East Tennessee over which he had no authority. This department encompassed eastern Tennessee, northern Georgia, and western North Carolina. Its creation acknowledged the importance of eastern Tennessee to the Confederacy and the special problems that existed in the region. A separate department ensured that the region's needs would not be lost in the vastness of the Western Military Department. Through eastern Tennessee ran the only direct rail link between the Confederate forces operating in Virginia and those in the western states. The department commander's primary responsibility was protecting the railroad. The Allegheny Mountains provided a natural barrier to the north, but several passes, including the Cumberland Gap, offered Union forces access through the mountains. In eastern Tennessee the pro-Union population's partisan activity posed a less conventional but equally dangerous threat.

MG Edmund Kirby Smith assumed command of this difficult region in February 1862. He graduated from the USMA in 1845 in time to see action during the Mexican War. Cited for gallantry, Smith remained in the US Army, serving on the frontier and returning to West Point as a mathematics professor. In 1861 he resigned as a major to serve in the Confederate Army. The timely arrival of his brigade at First Manassas helped secure a Southern victory, and Smith received the sobriquet of the "Blücher of

Manassas." After recovering from wounds he suffered there Smith was promoted to major general and given command of the newly formed Department of Eastern Tennessee.

Upon assuming command Smith found himself responsible for securing a 180-mile front with 9,000 men. Despite his desire to assume the offensive and strike a decisive blow for the Confederacy, survival soon became his principal endeavor. With a hostile populace to his rear he faced threats on both flanks. Buell's advance endangered Chattanooga while a second Union force commanded by BG George W. Morgan advanced on the Cumberland Gap. Smith used the rail line to shuttle his forces back and forth in response to the most dangerous threat, exhausting his troops in the process. Nor could he stop Union advances. In June Morgan maneuvered Smith out of the Cumberland Gap while Buell's advance elements reached the outskirts of Chattanooga. Although an assault did not materialize, Smith concentrated his forces at the town. He pleaded with Richmond for reinforcements, and he asked Bragg to send additional forces.

Simultaneously Smith sought the means with which to attack. Enthralled by the optimistic reports of COL John H. Morgan Smith wanted to invade Kentucky. He wanted to be freed from the frustrations of protecting his department with minimal forces against multiple threats. In Kentucky, Smith believed an opportunity existed to realize his ambition of conducting an offensive for the Confederacy that might lead to the war's end. His plans and aspirations, however, languished until Bragg arrived.

Planning the Invasion of Kentucky

Bragg established his headquarters in Chattanooga and there met with Smith on 31 July. The two commanders pledged their mutual cooperation and developed a notional plan of operations. First Smith would concentrate his forces and regain the Cumberland Gap. Bragg would remain at Chattanooga until joined by his artillery and wagon train. He would then strike central Tennessee, threatening Nashville. Should the latter's defenses prove too strong he would march north into Kentucky. In either event Smith would support Bragg. Both armies would seek an early juncture, and Bragg would assume command of the combined force.

Subsequent planning efforts expanded the operation's scope. Smith secured the support of BG Humphrey Marshall, commanding 3,000 soldiers in western Virginia. Once Smith secured the Cumberland Gap Marshall would advance into Kentucky and block the escape of George W. Morgan's Union force. Bragg also involved his principal subordinate commanders, Van Dorn and Price. Still in Mississippi their separate forces would undertake operations into western Tennessee to prevent the dispatch of reinforcements to Buell whose Army of the Ohio posed the principal military obstacle to an invasion of Kentucky. Recovering western Tennessee if possible Price and Van Dorn might also enter the commonwealth if conditions permitted. Finally Bragg enlisted the support of MG John C. Breckinridge, a prominent Kentuckian with a division command. He would follow in the wake of Bragg's main body. Ideally these separate operations would result in a concentration of Confederate forces in Kentucky under Bragg's unified command. The planned invasion of Kentucky thus resembled three prongs: Van Dorn and Price on the left, Marshall and Smith on the right, and Bragg's main effort supplemented by Breckinridge in the center.

Specific guidance from the Confederate government that was responsible for coordinating the military departments' actions proved scarce. The military departments constituted a collection of independent commands given broad authority within their geographically defined regions. The Confederate president or his Secretary of War coordinated the department commanders' actions. While planning for the Kentucky invasion continued, guidance from these offices was noticeably absent, despite the planned involvement of three different military departments. Davis cautioned Bragg against any action that risked destroying his army and indicated the importance of installing a Confederate governor in Kentucky. However, he provided no instructions regarding how the campaign should be executed or what objectives should be sought. Nor did Davis make any deliberate effort to coordinate planning for the invasions of Kentucky and Maryland beyond providing a sample proclamation to Generals Lee, Smith, and Bragg. This proclamation would be issued to people in Maryland and Kentucky once Southern forces entered those states.

Unlike Buell's Chattanooga offensive none of the Confederate operations relied on railroads. Intended advance routes were determined independent of the rail net, much of which already lay in Union hands. Nor would the pace of the advance be tied to the rate at which rail lines could be repaired. Instead the Confederates would carry their own limited supplies with them via wagon train. Once in Kentucky they would sustain themselves from the countryside, relying on the accuracy of John Morgan's reports of abundant food and forage. Invulnerable to the type of raiding tactics employed against Buell the Confederate armies would have considerable freedom of maneuver.

The planned Confederate offensive possessed considerable merit. It marked a unique effort to articulate a theaterwide strategy for the west that transcended a single department commander's more localized views. Success would change the entire tenor of the war in the west, recovering Tennessee and potentially adding Kentucky to the Confederacy. Moreover, it accorded with the more general Southern goal in 1862 of achieving a major military victory to trigger European intervention. Confederate forces arriving along the Ohio River would also provide added impetus to those Northern politicians seeking a negotiated settlement to the war.

Success depended on the Confederate components' ability to act in a coordinated fashion. Given the distance separating the various armies and the limitations of mid-19th-century communications, a critical need existed for each commander to understand his purpose, objectives, and relation to the broader campaign plan before operations commenced. No such directive was ever issued. Each army commander received only a general statement of intent. Moreover the overall campaign purpose never matured beyond a desire to install a Confederate governor in Kentucky and arm the anticipated masses of new recruits. The political goal remained unconnected to specific military or geographic objectives. A viable pro-Confederate state government could not be installed without either defeating Buell's army or capturing Kentucky's principal cities. Yet specific guidance regarding how either event would be engineered did not exist.

The absence of a unified command discouraged the articulation of a clear and executable plan. Bragg's redeployment to Chattanooga removed him from his own department's boundaries and placed him within the Department of Eastern Tennessee's jurisdiction. Bragg never considered subordinating himself to Smith, nor could he command the latter. Having left his own department, Bragg retained only limited ability to influence the actions of Price and Van Dorn. Marshall lay within yet another department. Bragg recognized the need for a single commander with authority over all forces participating in the campaign. He petitioned Richmond to be allowed to assume this role, but his request was denied. Instead Bragg relied on informal agreements to secure necessary cooperation among the various armies. He did not force the issue with Davis, and although willing to think "outside of the box" represented by his own department, Bragg remained uncertain of his authority.

Unfortunately he failed to exercise the authority he possessed. Van Dorn, Price, and Breckinridge received no specific orders outlining their roles in the upcoming offensive. Having indicated his intent to invade Kentucky via central Tennessee, Bragg expected his subordinates to support his endeavor. Expectation did not equate with clear guidance. Moreover, Bragg's notion of a theaterwide campaign in which all Confederate forces

78

provided mutual support did not align with Van Dorn and Smith's separate ambitions. Smith sought to single-handedly strike a blow for the Confederacy. Bragg's arrival in Chattanooga relieved Smith from its defense. With troops borrowed from Bragg he prepared for an independent invasion of Kentucky. Van Dorn sought a decisive victory that would satisfy his personal desire for glory and remove the tarnish of defeat he incurred at Pea Ridge. While providing tacit support to Bragg's Kentucky invasion, in fact, Van Dorn pursued his own objectives. He worked to gain control over all Confederate forces in the Western Military Department. Instead of preparing Breckinridge to advance in Kentucky Van Dorn launched him in an unsuccessful attack on Baton Rouge, Louisiana, on 5 August. Without informing Bragg, Van Dorn successfully lobbied Richmond for authority over Price's command.

In effect Van Dorn established a unity of command in Mississippi and western Tennessee. By subordinating Price's command to his own, Van Dorn established a more effective command structure in contrast to the uncertain relationship between Bragg and Smith. Moreover, Price had served under Van Dorn previously in operations west of the Mississippi River. Both generals believed in the importance of joining their armies, but they disagreed on how the forces should be employed. Price wanted to follow Bragg's instructions and move into central Tennessee. Van Dorn favored an attack on Corinth, followed by an advance into western Tennessee. His view ultimately prevailed, and the left prong of the planned Kentucky invasion never materialized.

Opening Moves

During the early days of August Bragg remained at Chattanooga awaiting his artillery and wagons. Smith, however, desired a rapid start of operations. The two commanders agreed that Smith should move against the Cumberland Gap. Bragg detached some of his troops to reinforce Smith's operation, leaving 27,000 men at Chattanooga and swelling Smith's force to 19,000. Bragg intended Smith to seize the strategic gap and prepare to support his own pending move into central Tennessee. Some discussion ensued regarding Smith's possible move on Lexington, Kentucky, but Bragg considered the main emphasis of the campaign to lie with his army.

Smith prepared his forces by concentrating them at Knoxville. On 13 August he began his move against the Cumberland Gap. The Union force there had a strong defensive position and ample supplies. Smith, however, had no intention of attacking the gap. Instead he intended to invest it with a blocking force and march around it. While his infantry and artillery crossed the Cumberland Mountains via several smaller passes, one division

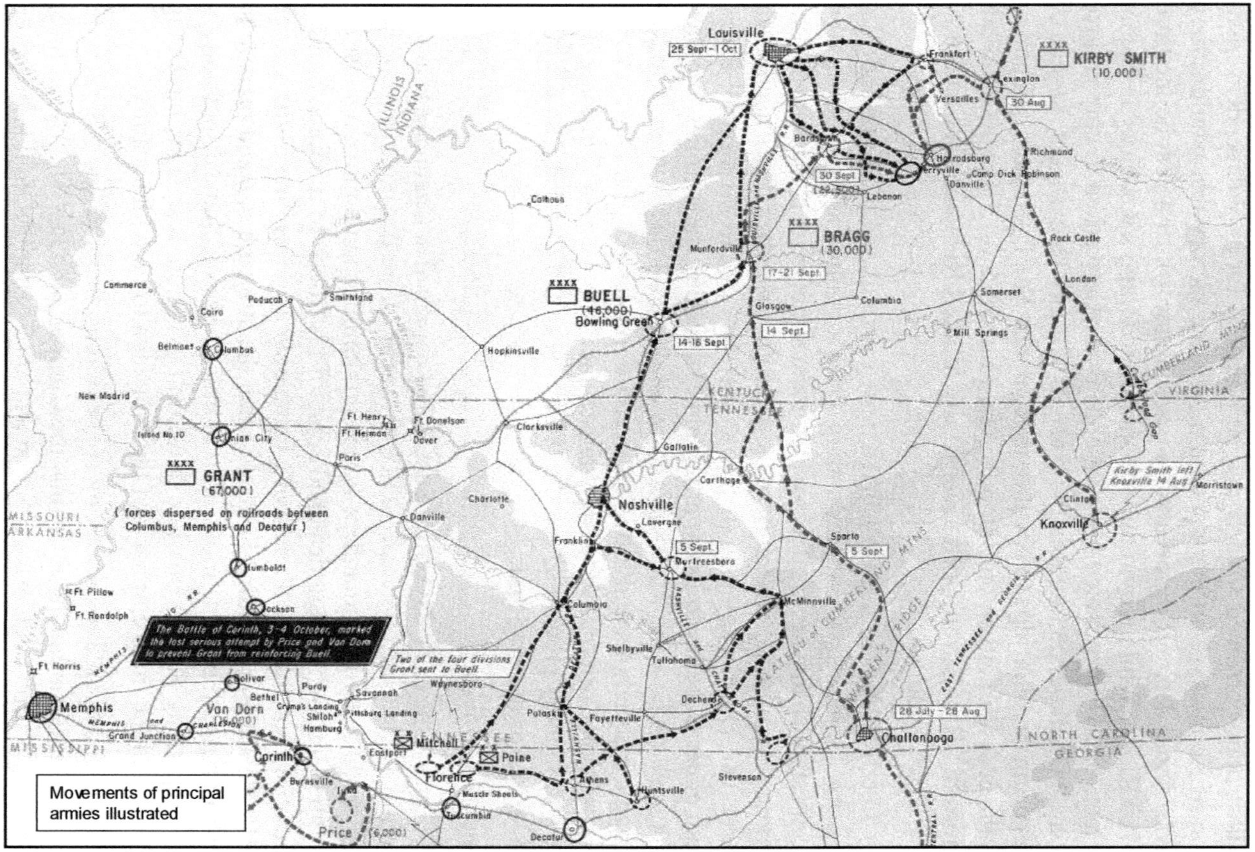

Map 3. The march to Perryville.

blocked the Cumberland Gap. Smith's cavalry ranged ahead to screen the advancing columns and cut the Union supply line at London, Kentucky. COL John Morgan also embarked on a raid into central Tennessee to draw Union attention there.

The march through the Cumberland Mountains' rugged terrain proved difficult and exhausting. However, the morale of Smith's men remained high. The campaign came as a welcome relief from months of reacting to Union threats. Filled with confidence and an expectation of success undiminished by the natural obstructions in their path the Confederates crossed the mountains without mishap. The first elements arrived at Barboursville on 18 August astride the principal road between Lexington and BG George Morgan's Union force at the Cumberland Gap. The Northern commander did not abandon the strategic location. Smith now lay between Union forces gathering in northern Kentucky and those still at the Cumberland Gap. Rather than retreat he opted to advance on Lexington.

Smith notified Bragg of his intent but did not await a response before moving. Bragg had little choice but to concur, even though Smith's independent action precluded him supporting Bragg's pending advance into central Tennessee. Smith's sudden eruption into Kentucky, however, benefited from surprise. Unopposed he moved quickly toward Lexington. A hastily formed Union formation tried to block his advance at Richmond. On 30 August Smith attacked and destroyed this force in a series of well-fought engagements. Confederate cavalry pursued the retreating survivors, and many were captured.

For the time being the battle effectively ended further resistance to Smith's advance. By 3 September he had captured Lexington and the state capital of Frankfort. Having seized the Bluegrass region Smith was determined to hold it. Having insufficient force to assault either Louisville or Cincinnati the Confederates dispersed to ensure control over a broad tract of Kentucky. Supplies proved ample and the populace sympathetic, although few indicated a desire to fight for the South. In a lightning operation Smith had achieved considerable success. Unfortunately he considered his work complete, contenting himself with securing his gains. He made little further effort to undertake offensive operations and left Bragg to cope with Buell's Army of the Ohio alone.

Bragg Enters Kentucky

While Smith invaded Kentucky, Bragg remained at Chattanooga awaiting the rest of his army. He continued to prepare for the coming offensive. He reorganized his army into two wings, each comprising two divisions and a cavalry brigade. MG William J. Hardee and Polk received command of the left and right wings, respectively. Bragg's opinion of Polk remained unchanged, but Polk's seniority, personal friendship with Davis, and rank left little alternative to a senior command. Of the four division commanders only Cheatham had not graduated from West Point, and MG Jones M. Withers suffered from poor health. Promotion boards continued to sit, and Bragg continued to try to remove those officers he considered unfit. He also sent his chief of staff and inspector general to oversee prisoner exchanges and prepare for returned Confederates to rejoin fighting regiments.

Bragg encountered less success in his efforts to reorganize his headquarters. His chief of staff was unwilling to continue in that capacity during the coming campaign because of age and the physical strain that sustained field operations required. Bragg unsuccessfully petitioned the Confederate War Department for an experienced replacement. Instead the officer assigned to this important position lacked command and staff experience. Bragg therefore largely performed the roles of army commander and chief of staff himself. Such a dual role risked major command decisions becoming overshadowed by the army's daily affairs. Bragg, however, had few options. Most of his other staff officers lacked experience in their duties. Bragg's efforts to secure more seasoned personnel met with the same failure as his effort to obtain a new chief of staff. Nor would the army benefit from a chief of cavalry to oversee the mounted force's administrative needs and coordinate its actions. Bragg wanted to appoint COL Joseph Wheeler to this position, but he could not do so, given Forrest's seniority. Rather than use Forrest as chief of cavalry Bragg left the position vacant.

The arrival of the Army of the Mississippi's artillery and trains permitted it to begin operations. On 28 August it left Chattanooga and began crossing the Cumberland Plateau. Cavalry screened its movement and spread misinformation about the size and route of Bragg's army. While the main Confederate force moved through the mountains Forrest returned from a raid into central Tennessee to strike the Union positions from behind. Forrest suffered defeat, but his presence helped create additional confusion. These cavalry actions prevented early detection of Bragg's march route and ensured that the Confederate advance through the mountainous terrain went unmolested. Bragg first crossed the Cumberland Plateau into the Sequatchie River valley before turning north toward Sparta. From there he could either move west against Nashville or north toward Kentucky.

Bragg's move to Sparta ended Buell's efforts to capture Chattanooga. Since June he had labored to build a logistics support system to sustain the army after the town's capture. He selected Stevenson, Alabama, as the site of a forward depot. The town marked the juncture of the Nashville and Chattanooga and Memphis and Charleston Railroads. By 12 July the rail link with Nashville was open, permitting the direct flow of supplies into the depot via train from Buell's base in Louisville. However, Confederate cavalry operations in Tennessee and Kentucky ensured that there was no speedy accumulation of supplies. Buell responded by increasing security along the rail line in Tennessee. Guard posts, additional soldiers, and the use of small, mobile forces kept the railroad to Nashville reasonably functional, but the link between Nashville and Louisville remained vulnerable and subject to repeated attacks. Nor was a sustained effort made to effect repairs in the wake of Confederate raids.

With his army reduced to half rations Buell dispatched MG William Nelson to Louisville. He was to collect the newly available troops there and organize Kentucky's defenses. In addition, Buell directed him to repair and secure the railroad link between Louisville and Nashville, thereby restoring his line of supply. Buell also sent additional officers and two artillery batteries to support Nelson. The former included BG Charles Cruft, BG Mahlon D. Manson, BG James S. Jackson, and Captain Charles C. Gilbert. Nelson arrived in Louisville on 23 August to discover that Buell no longer had any authority over military activities in Kentucky. The Department of the Ohio had been reorganized to include Ohio, Indiana, Illinois, Michigan, Wisconsin, and eastern Kentucky, including the Cumberland Gap. It also had a new commander, MG H.G. Wright. Buell's army became an independent command directly responsible to the general in chief. His supply base at Louisville now lay outside his jurisdiction. Moreover, the primary focus of the new command structure in Kentucky lay in relieving George W. Morgan at the Cumberland Gap rather than Buell's supply line.

On 24 August Nelson arrived in Lexington to assume command of the newly raised Army of Kentucky. It comprised several newly raised infantry and cavalry regiments. The infantry regiments were formed into a division of two brigades, and the cavalry regiments were formed into a single brigade that BG Jackson commanded. Nelson deployed his forces to block a Confederate move west toward the Louisville and Nashville Railroad or north toward the Kentucky River. The latter represented a natural defense that would bolster his green infantry's effectiveness. However, through a series of miscommunications, Nelson's infantry division advanced south of the Kentucky River. On 30 August Smith attacked and effectively destroyed the entire force during the ensuing battle of Richmond, Kentucky.

Nelson was absent for much of the battle. He arrived on the field too late to prevent defeat, but he was wounded. He escaped to recover in Louisville where he assumed command of the city's defenses.

Outside Chattanooga Buell received reports of Bragg's arrival in the town and the buildup of Confederate strength there. With a force estimated to be at least 60,000 men, a Southern offensive into central Tennessee appeared likely. Buell deployed most of his army across the most direct routes to Nashville. To cover the multiple passes through the mountainous region necessitated a dispersion of force. However, special instructions were issued to all commanders to guide their movements in the event of a Confederate advance. Preselected coordination points were established, and rockets and signal equipment were issued to provide timely warning of the enemy's appearance. These measures would permit a speedy concentration of force once Bragg's intentions became clear. In the days before the Confederate departure from Chattanooga, conflicting rumors of enemy activity deluged Buell's command. The effective Confederate cavalry screen made confirmation difficult. Unable to discern the enemy's intent or location, Buell directed his army to concentrate at Murfreesboro by 5 September. From there he could safeguard Nashville against a sudden thrust by Bragg.

Meanwhile Bragg marched to Sparta, bypassing Buell's original defenses, and there lay ready to strike toward the Tennessee capital or into Kentucky. Arriving on 4 September Bragg's army remained at Sparta for several days resting amid a supportive populace. Before leaving Chattanooga Bragg had sent instructions to Van Dorn and Price to move into central Tennessee as soon as possible. At Sparta he reiterated these instructions, requesting that Price move toward Nashville. When Forrest reported the erection of Union fortifications there Bragg resolved to advance into Kentucky. Turning north, the army reached Carthage on 9 September.

Another report from Forrest helped to spur Bragg's movement. Buell appeared to be leaving Nashville and moving his entire force north. The city, however, was not being left unguarded. These developments surprised Bragg, who feared Buell's army might move toward Louisville and threaten Smith while the main Confederate army remained to the south. Bragg therefore ordered Polk's wing to advance to Glasgow, Kentucky, with orders to cut the Louisville and Nashville Railroad and await the rest of the army. Glasgow provided access to a good road net that would support movement into north central Kentucky. Bragg also hoped to find food and forage for his soldiers. Operating without a fixed supply line the Confederates relied on those supplies carried and what could be found in the countryside. Much of the supplies they carried had already been consumed during the march to Carthage.

On 14 September both wings of Bragg's army reunited at Glasgow. There Bragg issued a proclamation to the populace announcing the arrival of a Confederate army to liberate the state from the "tyranny of a despotic ruler." It called on citizens to join Bragg's ranks and demonstrate their support for the Confederacy through force of arms. In preparation for the expected flood of recruits, Bragg's wagons carried 15,000 extra muskets. These weapons symbolized the political goal of the campaign: to mobilize a friendly population awaiting the appropriate opportunity to join the Confederate cause.

Less visible to observers were the military problems facing Bragg. Glasgow and surrounding Barren County lacked sufficient food to sustain an army. Foragers had long since scoured the area. Bragg also received news that General Grant, who had replaced Halleck as commander of Union forces in western Tennessee and northern Mississippi, had dispatched forces to secure Nashville. Van Dorn and Price had failed to prevent reinforcements being sent to Buell. Moreover, Buell was reported to be marching with a superior force toward Bowling Green. Believing himself to be outnumbered Bragg favored a speedy juncture with Smith. He also contemplated a combined strike against Louisville, but he did not make clear his intent or issue any instructions for such an action. The absence of a clear plan for the army once it entered Kentucky now began to make itself felt. While Bragg considered his next move, events overtook him.

Upon Polk's arrival in Glasgow, BG James R. Chalmers received orders to advance his brigade to Cave City and cut the Louisville and Nashville Railroad there. Chalmers accomplished his mission and dispatched a scouting party toward Munfordville. En route it found a mill with a supply of wheat, and this discovery soon resulted in the infantry arriving to operate the mill and provide food for the brigade. While thus engaged Chalmers made contact with COL John C. Scott's cavalry brigade. This force belonged to Smith's army and had been sent toward Munfordville to establish a link with Bragg and raid the Louisville and Nashville Railroad. The railroad crossed the Green River via an 1,800-foot span at Munfordville. The bridge beckoned raiders since its destruction would stop rail traffic for months.

On their own initiative Chalmers and Scott resolved to attack the Union garrison in Munfordville on 14 September. The defenders provided determined resistance from behind fortifications. The Confederate attack collapsed amid confusion and casualties. Apprised of the attack and its failure Bragg felt obligated to capture the town and its garrison. He moved his entire army to Munfordville, and after prolonged negotiations, this demonstration of force led the garrison to surrender on 17 September. The same day Lee's invasion of Maryland ended at the battle of Antietam. Bragg's Kentucky campaign was now the only principal Confederate operation that might yet achieve success.

The victory at Munfordville earned Bragg's army a day of thanksgiving and rest. It lay along a river line astride Buell's supply line. However several factors weakened this seemingly strong position. Bragg's army had sufficient rations for only a few days and could not depend on the barren country for sustenance. Buell's army, initially thought to be at Bowling Green, was found to be only 10 miles away at Cave City. The close proximity surprised Bragg. He had expected Buell to move slowly. He also had relied on his cavalry to give him timely notice of Buell's movements. During the march to Glasgow, Forrest and Wheeler successfully screened the army, provided steady information regarding Buell's status, and conducted delaying actions. From Glasgow, however, Forrest's brigade became responsible for screening the army's advance while Wheeler continued to operate against Buell. The Army of the Ohio's sustained, rapid movement caught the Confederates off guard. Moreover, Buell's use of better-organized and aggressive cavalry to screen his own march forced Wheeler to fight rearguard engagements at the expense of reconnaissance.

What news of the Union army Bragg did possess suggested he was outnumbered. Despite the defensive strength of the Munfordville position, it was not the only crossing point on the Green River. Indeed Buell was rumored to be crossing farther west and moving to outflank the Confederate army. Additional Union forces were believed to be forming in Louisville, and Smith remained at least several days' march away. Bragg feared being caught between enemy forces. Further undermining his resolution was Davis' personal instructions not to risk the defeat of his army. Now facing an enemy of uncertain strength in close proximity Bragg hesitated to act. He vacillated between affecting a juncture with Smith at Bardstown and remaining on the Green River line. Movement orders were issued only to be cancelled and then reinstated. This uncertainty did not remain invisible to the soldiers in the ranks. Cheatham's division started on the road to Bardstown and reversed itself before once again departing Munfordville.

Bragg finally resolved to move to Bardstown. He requested Smith to march to the same place and assemble supplies there since Bragg's men had only three days' rations remaining. Bragg also asked Smith to maintain his watch on BG George Morgan at the Cumberland Gap. This force was not to be allowed to escape. On 20 September the Army of the Mississippi left Munfordville, arriving at Bardstown two days later. In doing so, Bragg left his position astride Buell's supply line, permitting Buell direct access to Louisville. The Confederates had not seriously entertained an attack on that city, but Bragg's stop at Munfordville delayed his intended union with Smith. Smith, however, had not marched to Bardstown as instructed.

The Unfinished Business of the Cumberland Gap

When Smith invaded Kentucky he did not secure the Cumberland Gap. Considering the Union position there to be too strong, Smith instead left a division to guard the pass. He also relied on Marshall's army from western Virginia to intercept any attempt by this force to escape north. Relying on these dispositions, Smith dispersed his forces to occupy the region around Lexington and Frankfort. His presence caused consternation for the North, whose commanders remained unclear as to his strength and objective. Reinforcements were hastily sent to Louisville and Cincinnati to protect those cities. In reality, however, Smith posed little threat to either city. He lacked sufficient strength to take either one and proved content to let Bragg cope with Buell's army and Louisville.

BG Morgan interrupted this complacency by making a sudden dash for the Ohio River. Following his capture of the Cumberland Gap in June, Morgan had fortified his position and begun to construct a depot to support further operations into eastern Tennessee. Smith's invasion of Kentucky and the Confederate victory at Richmond, however, cut his supply route and left him isolated. By mid-September Morgan's command began to run short of food and faced starvation. The Union commander resolved to escape via the rugged terrain of eastern Kentucky and reach the Ohio River and safety. The route selected had little food, forage, or water, and it was considered barely passable for wagons and artillery.

On the night of 17 September the Union force began its trek. Destroying the nearly complete depot at Cumberland Gap, BG Morgan led his force north to Manchester for a short rest. To deceive the Confederates he dispatched a commissary officer along a different route to purchase supplies as though preparing for the Union division to arrive. However, Confederate cavalry assigned to watch the Cumberland Gap soon pursued the retreating column. COL John H. Morgan also interfered with its movement, creating barriers and removing potential sources of food along its path. These measures delayed but did not stop the Union force. It continued through Hazel Green, West Liberty, Greyson, and finally crossed the

Ohio River after a 200-mile march through rugged terrain bereft of supplies. The soldiers had repeatedly cleared defiles of rock barriers and on occasion built their own road through wooded areas. The entire operation resulted in 80 casualties, but not a single cannon or wagon was lost.

Confederate efforts to intercept the Union force suffered from a lack of coordination and aggressiveness. When Smith entered Kentucky, Marshall was to enter the state from western Virginia. However, the Confederate War Department had not been apprised of this action, and the Department of Western Virginia's commander flatly opposed the move. Consequently Marshall remained in western Virginia until the issue could be resolved. When finally released to enter Kentucky, Marshall moved slowly and made little serious effort to prevent BG Morgan's escape. Smith raced much of his command toward Mount Sterling, but he also failed to intercept the Union column.

Bardstown

Bragg's army arrived in Bardstown on 22 September. Supplies that Smith had gathered awaited it, but Smith had marched away into eastern Kentucky. Bragg's army was exhausted and required rest. While it camped at Bardstown its commander considered his next move. Of the various forces outlined for the Kentucky invasion, only Bragg's, Smith's, and Marshall's had actually entered the state. Bragg knew that Van Dorn and Price had not prevented Buell from receiving reinforcements from western Tennessee. Nor had these Confederate commanders moved toward Nashville as directed. Price initially tried to move into central Tennessee and had advanced to Iuka on 14 September. There he remained for several days while Grant dispatched forces to attack him. While the Union columns moved into position, Price attacked on 19 September. Poor coordination ensured that only a portion of the Union forces available actually participated in the fight. While the Northern columns prepared to renew the battle the next day, Price withdrew and marched toward a juncture with Van Dorn. Van Dorn began to prepare for an attack on Corinth rather than to move into central Tennessee as Bragg desired.

Commanding the forces in the Western Military Department in Bragg's absence Van Dorn also blocked the northward movement of Breckinridge's division. Breckinridge intended to follow in Bragg's wake, joining the main army in Kentucky. However, Van Dorn had no orders to release the Confederate division and sought to include it in his own operations. The absence of clear guidance from Bragg coupled with Van Dorn's separate campaign plans created command confusion and delayed Breckinridge's effective employment. Finally released by Van Dorn, Breckinridge arrived in Chattanooga on 2 October out of place to influence either the attack on Corinth that occurred on 3-4 October or the deciding battle of the Kentucky campaign at Perryville on 8 October.

At Bardstown Bragg faced Buell's Army of the Ohio, another Union army forming in Louisville, and a third enemy force massing in Cincinnati. Bragg was sufficiently concerned about the campaign's outcome to order the creation of a chain of supply depots to support the army should it be forced to retreat from Kentucky. He did not believe he could successfully attack Louisville without Smith's direct assistance, especially with Buell closing on the city. After returning from eastern Kentucky, however, Smith preferred to remain in the vicinity of Lexington and Frankfort to safeguard gathered supplies and attempt to recruit new soldiers.

Kentucky's populace hardly flocked to the Confederate colors. With Buell's army the entering the state and new units arriving at Cincinnati and Louisville the success of Confederate arms seemed less than certain. Little incentive existed to join Southern regiments until a clear military victor appeared in the state. In the event of a Confederate defeat, a potential recruit risked property confiscation for supporting the rebellion. This cautious attitude undermined Confederate aspirations. The invasion had been planned in part on the assumption that the presence of a Southern army would automatically draw volunteers. Faced with the irresolution of the population, Bragg focused on the only clear objective of the campaign—installing a Confederate governor in Kentucky. On 28 September Bragg left Polk in command at Bardstown and traveled to Frankfort to prepare the inauguration. Once established, the new Confederate governor could implement a conscription act. Kentuckians would be forced to fight for the South, but the compulsory nature of the law would theoretically protect their property from being confiscated while they were in Confederate service.

With the commander and his attention at Frankfort, Bragg's army remained in the vicinity Bardstown. It dispersed to maximize the geographic area under Confederate control, relying on cavalry patrols to report on Union activity. These dispositions, however, assumed Buell would remain in Louisville for several weeks. Both Smith's and Bragg's forces now lay idle, dispersed, and separated from one another. Polk received no specific guidance concerning his actions should Buell actually attack.

The Confederate cavalry's ability to provide sufficient warning in such an eventuality also remained uncertain. Since the start of the campaign it had been continuously employed. Responsible for screening the advance into Kentucky, delaying Buell's movements, protecting the army's wagon train, securing information on enemy activities, and raiding the Union supply line, the cavalry suffered from overuse. The nature of these missions ensured frequent engagements with Buell's cavalry that further sapped the Confederate cavalry's strength.

The army Bragg led into Kentucky included 10 cavalry regiments and battalions plus additional detachments. Events in late September, however, resulted in the effective loss of three regiments. The 6th Confederate Regiment had become combat ineffective because of the expiration of one-year enlistment terms and the ongoing election of new officers. Following the resignation of its commander, the 2d Georgia became a regiment of detachments performing escort and administrative duties for the army. On 29 September Union cavalry attacked the 3d Georgia at New Haven and nearly destroyed the regiment. In each instance an experienced cavalry colonel was lost to the service either through his failure to be reelected by his soldiers, resignation, or capture.

This leadership loss increased with Forrest's relief. On 25 September Bragg sent him back to Tennessee to raise a new mounted force and conduct operations against Nashville. In effect Bragg sought to compensate for Price and Van Dorn's failure by threatening Nashville with those resources under his immediate command. Forrest's demonstrated success in building effective cavalry units and leading independent commands made him ideal for this mission. Yet Bragg's army at Bardstown also lost its most senior and experienced cavalry officer while the enemy's intentions remained unclear.

Despite its ragged state Bragg's cavalry received no respite. While the army rested near Bardstown the cavalry assumed responsibility for protecting the town. Wheeler covered the roads from the west, while Forrest's much smaller brigade, now commanded by COL John A. Wharton, defended the critical routes from Louisville. The Confederate cavalry formed a line stretching across north central Kentucky with active patrols toward Elizabethtown and Louisville. Neither brigade, however, had the strength to sufficiently cover its assigned area. Moreover, the defeat suffered at New Haven demonstrated their vulnerability to defeat in detail by increasingly aggressive and capable Union cavalry brigades. A chief of cavalry might have permitted better coordination of cavalry, but this position lay vacant on Bragg's staff.

Nor did the presence of Wheeler's and Wharton's brigades ensure a steady and timely flow of information to the army commander. At the campaign's start the brigade commanders reported directly to Bragg, but Bragg subsequently placed each cavalry brigade under a wing commander. Although the cavalry represented the eyes and ears of the army, no mechanism existed to directly transmit critical information to the army commander. Reports on enemy activities flowed first to the brigade commander, then to the wing commander, and finally to the army commander. Timeliness depended on the information's ability to reach the brigade commander and receive his immediate attention, an unlikely occurrence given the broad fronts over which the cavalry screen at Bardstown operated. By the time Bragg received a report it was often outdated. Without direct access to forward cavalry elements he depended on the second-hand assessments his wing commanders provided him.

The Savior of Louisville

When Bragg marched from Chattanooga Buell withdrew his forces in northern Alabama and eastern Tennessee toward Nashville. Uncertain whether the Confederates would march on the city or invade Kentucky he remained in position until the enemy's intent became clear. On 7 September Buell received word that Bragg had crossed the Cumberland River at Carthage, heading north into Kentucky. Including the reinforcements sent by Grant, Buell had eight divisions. One division he immediately dispatched to secure Bowling Green along his supply line where a small garrison and supply cache lay. With five divisions under his immediate command Buell followed shortly afterward. MG George H. Thomas remained in Nashville with three divisions. Bragg's continued northern movement, however, reduced the threat to that city, and Thomas joined Buell with one division. By 15 September the Union army at Bowling Green numbered 35,000 men organized into six divisions. A faster concentration could not be accomplished because all formations had to use the single major road connecting Bowling Green and Nashville.

Bragg arrived in Glasgow the day before. Thirty miles east of Bowling Green the town marked the juncture of several excellent roads that provided access into north and central Kentucky. Buell did not know whether the Confederate commander intended to attack his supply base at Louisville or link up with Smith's army. He nevertheless moved to attack Bragg at Glasgow on 16 September. Unknown to Buell the Confederate Army had already marched to Munfordville, but its wagon train with Bragg's remaining supplies was still in Glasgow. However, the determined rearguard efforts of Wheeler's cavalry permitted the wagons to escape. The next day Buell learned that Bragg had captured Munfordville and its garrison. The move surprised Buell. While Munfordville lay astride his supply line, it was also farther from Smith and lacked access to good roads. Bragg's army was believed to be short of supplies, and Smith had plenty. A rapid concentration of the two Confederate armies seemed the most likely course of action. Instead Bragg continued to threaten Louisville and moved away from those roads whose condition and direction made them ideal for a rapid march toward Smith.

Buell felt obligated to attack the Confederate position at Munfordville. Bragg's presence posed a threat to Louisville that the collection of raw troops there might not withstand. Bragg lay between the only veteran Union army in Kentucky and the state's principal city. When the Confederates withdrew, Buell pursued them closely. Simultaneously he prepared for the city's garrison to collect provisions for his army and prepare an alternate crossing site on the Salt River. Should the need arise he planned to bypass the Confederate army to reach Louisville. Bragg's move to Bardstown, however, made these preparations unnecessary. Buell's army began arriving in Louisville on 26 September.

The Union commander believed he had accomplished a significant achievement. In the face of the Confederate buildup at Chattanooga, Buell conducted a well-planned retreat toward Nashville. He secured the city against capture and followed Bragg into Kentucky. He had pushed his soldiers hard during the march to Louisville despite a scarcity of rations. In doing so he had sustained a pace of operations that surprised Bragg and restricted Bragg's operational freedom. Buell had moved his army intact to Kentucky to contest control of the state and secure his own supply base. He considered his actions a success and a logical response to the enemy's movements.

In Washington few agreed. There, Buell's failure to take Chattanooga after a frustratingly slow campaign contrasted unfavorably with his rapid dash rearward out of northern Alabama, across Tennessee, and on to the Ohio River. Criticism of Buell's actions rose amid allegations of treasonous behavior and incompetence. Lincoln also expressed his dissatisfaction with Buell. Nor did the soldiers in the Army of the Ohio consider their march to Louisville to be a positive and significant accomplishment. They, too, saw the rapid withdrawal as further evidence of their commander's Confederate sympathies. Buell appeared unwilling to pursue an aggressive campaign against the South and too eager to retreat. Some officers lobbied actively for his dismissal. Buell, however, remained indifferent to politicians' criticism and ignored the dissension in his own ranks.

His army's arrival in Louisville helped to allay the panic in the region that the Confederate invasion of Kentucky triggered. After Smith captured Lexington and Frankfort martial law was declared in Cincinnati. Businesses closed and able-bodied men with weapons were urged to rally to the city's defense. However dubious their military abilities, these "squirrel hunters" gave a sense of protection to a city that was afraid of imminent attack. Ohio's governor sought to concentrate newly raised regiments in Cincinnati but found himself competing with his counterparts in Kentucky and Indiana. The latter believed that Louisville, Kentucky's largest city, had a more pressing need for soldiers. Its loss would effectively ensure Confederate control of the state and permit further incursions across the Ohio River. To prevent this eventuality Louisville became home to a host of new regiments. Entrenchments arose around the city, but the soldiers that would man them lacked training and experience. In those parts of the state still subject to Northern authority a string of arrests occurred as the state government attempted to suppress support for the Confederacy. These measures generally backfired and encouraged pro-Southern sympathies.

In Louisville Buell assumed command of all the Union forces there. He immediately applied his organizational and administrative talents toward reorganizing his army. Within each brigade he integrated the green regiments in the city with his own veteran units. In accordance with the War Department's July authorization of a corps structure he formed three corps each of three divisions. To each corps he assigned a cavalry brigade, while smaller cavalry detachments remained available to the division commanders. Appointing corps commanders, however, posed a problem. The Union armies in the west had never previously employed corps, although armies in the east had employed a corps structure since March 1862. Within Buell's army there was no cadre of leaders who were familiar with the operation of such a formation. Buell therefore intended to appoint his most senior subordinates as corps commanders, and Thomas became his second in command. MG Alexander M. McCook and MG Thomas L. Crittenden, both prior division commanders, would command I and II Corps, respectively. Nelson, who had organized Louisville's defenses before Buell's arrival, would command III Corps.

Simultaneously with reorganizing his army Buell planned his next move. With his arrival in Louisville he considered a Confederate attack much less likely, despite reports of enemy cavalry within miles of the city. He also benefited from Smith's preoccupation with BG George Morgan. Smith and Marshall had moved their forces into northeastern Kentucky in a vain attempt to intercept the Union force as it sought the Ohio River's safety. This sideshow had further separated the Confederate armies in Kentucky. Buell planned to launch a feint toward Frankfort while marching most of his army toward Bragg's army at Bardstown. Buell intended to either engage Bragg separately or cause him to withdraw toward Smith's army. In the latter event Buell planned to herd the Confederates into northern Kentucky and block their retreat out of the state. He envisioned a final battle in which the concentrated Union strength would attack and destroy the isolated Southern invaders.

As Buell prepared to march on Bardstown two events disrupted his plans. On 29 September BG Jefferson C. Davis murdered Nelson. Davis had arrived in Louisville only recently with reinforcements from Grant's army, but a series of bitter altercations between the two generals finally resulted in this deadly encounter. Nelson's death left a corps command vacancy, and Buell appointed MG Charles C. Gilbert to replace him. Gilbert graduated from the USMA in 1846, and he had seen service in the Mexican War and on the frontier. However, he had been only a captain in August. His meteoric promotion to major general reflected the desperate need for military leaders to organize Kentucky's defenses in the wake of Smith's invasion. With no senior command experience Gilbert now assumed command of a 22,000-man formation. The same day Nelson died Buell received orders relieving him of command and replacing him with Thomas. Thomas, however, refused. With no other senior army commander available the relief order was suspended but not rescinded. The War Department's message was clear: Buell must become more aggressive and defeat the enemy if he wished to retain his command.

The Road to Perryville

The events of 29 September forced Buell to delay his planned departure by one day. On 1 October his army filed out of the city. His three corps moved along parallel roads that converged on Bardstown. Simultaneously BG Joshua W. Sill led a smaller force of infantry and cavalry that marched directly toward Frankfort. Comprising two infantry divisions with supporting cavalry, Sill's column aimed at convincing the Confederates that the state capital constituted Buell's objective. A powerful cavalry screen moved several miles ahead of each column to cloak Union movements and drive away Confederate cavalry.

Buell's total strength numbered nearly 80,000 men, with 19,000 under Sill's command; 13,000 in I Corps; and 22,000 in each of the II and III Corps. I Corps' smaller size reflected the detachment of an infantry division to Sill's column. Despite these numbers many of Buell's regiments remained green and untested, having only recently formed. Total Confederate forces in Kentucky numbered about 50,000 men, many of them veterans. However, they were strewn across the state in a rough arc stretching from Bardstown across the Kentucky River to Mount Sterling. Nor did they have a unified command or plan of action. Polk was left to his own devices at Bardstown while Bragg addressed political affairs in Frankfort and Smith remained focused on northeastern Kentucky.

The Union advance benefited from good roads and Confederate surprise. The columns moved rapidly. By 2 October Sill had reached Shelbyville, halfway between Louisville and Frankfort. The same day I Corps neared Taylorsville, II Corps moved to Mount Washington, and III Corps approached Shepherdsville. Confederate cavalry patrols were driven back without being able to secure accurate information regarding Union dispositions. Against the avalanche of Union forces advancing on Bardstown from the north Wharton's small brigade struggled for survival. To the west Wheeler's larger force fared better, but it, too, failed to slow the Union advance. On the road to Frankfort Scott's cavalry brigade retired in the face of Sill's column.

News of Buell's advance surprised Bragg. He had expected no action from his counterpart for several weeks. Instead he now faced a powerful Union thrust against his scattered forces. Nor did Bragg have any clear sense of the enemy's intentions. Apprised of the advance of Union infantry and cavalry to Shelbyville Bragg believed this force constituted Buell's main effort with Frankfort as its objective. On 2 October Bragg assumed command of Smith's army and ordered a concentration of the army's force at Frankfort. He also directed Polk to march toward the state capital where the combined Confederate forces would attack the advancing Union column from front and flank.

These movements required time. Polk's army lay more than 50 miles from Frankfort, and Smith's forces remained scattered east of the Kentucky River. Buell, however, continued his aggressive advance. On 3 October Union movements threatened to drive a wedge between Polk at Bardstown and Bragg at Frankfort. While II Corps arrived at High Grove, I Corps' cavalry entered Bloomfield farther east. Had Polk followed his orders he would have moved across both Union corps' fronts. Instead, aware that enemy forces of unknown strength were moving between himself and Bragg, Polk decided to ignore his commander's orders. He resolved to abandon Bardstown and retire toward Danville. He informed Bragg of his actions, but he only hinted at the factors influencing his decision.

While Polk retreated Bragg and Smith attended the Confederate governor's 4 October inauguration ceremony. Enemy action eroded much of the event's political value. Union cavalry advanced to within 10 miles of Frankfort and engaged the Confederate rearguard. The sound of artillery hastened the conclusion of the inauguration. Bragg and his entourage of Southern officers and politicians soon departed. Believing that a major assault was imminent while his own forces remained dispersed, Bragg abandoned Frankfort and ordered a concentration of Smith and Polk at Harrodsburg. Accordingly Smith's still-dispersed forces began moving toward Versailles before crossing the Kentucky River. Bragg, meanwhile, established his headquarters in Harrodsburg on 5 October.

Polk, too, moved his command toward this town. He divided his force into two columns; one he led and the other Hardee led. Polk's column marched toward Harrodsburg over a good road that led through Springfield. Hardee followed a more direct route leading through Mackville, but poor road conditions slowed his progress. Therefore he redirected his column onto the same route as Polk. Changing the line of march delayed Hardee further while Buell's army drew nearer. III Corps soon closed on the Confederate column, and cavalry skirmishing ensued. Wharton and Wheeler conducted rearguard actions to delay Buell's advance, but the Union cavalry's aggressiveness nearly destroyed Wharton's brigade. The Confederate cavalry was thrust onto the defensive and forced to fight for its survival as it screened the retreating infantry columns. In doing so it lost its ability to obtain accurate information about Buell's army.

Polk further reduced his reconnaissance capability when he dispatched Wharton's brigade to Lebanon. With Union columns of undetermined strength advancing upon him from the west and north, Wharton now guarded the Confederate Army's unthreatened southern flank. Wheeler assumed sole responsibility for covering the retreat to Harrodsburg, but the execution of this mission again occurred at the expense of gathering information. None of the senior Confederate commanders possessed accurate information regarding Buell's intent and dispositions. They relied on the cavalry to provide this input, but reconnaissance was not the current priority for the mounted force. In effect key command decisions were being made on the basis of guesswork. Bragg depended on assessments his wing commanders and Smith provided; they, in turn, relied on their respective cavalry brigades to gather information. The brigades' failure to do so directly impaired the army's decision-making process.

Nevertheless, for the first time in the campaign the scattered Confederate forces moved toward a concentration. On 6 October Bragg met with

Smith in Harrodsburg. Rumors continued to give an imprecise picture of the enemy's activity. Buell's intentions remained a mystery, and reports of Union forces' locations and strengths continuously changed. Amid this uncertainty Smith recommended keeping his troops east of the Kentucky River. There he could retain Confederate control over the Bluegrass region and its valuable supplies. He believed he could quickly reinforce Polk at Harrodsburg if it became necessary. Bragg agreed. The Union column outside Frankfort for the moment remained inert. The army commander was also unaware of the threat Polk faced. While Buell's army bore down on a portion of Bragg's army the Confederate forces remained separated.

Plans again changed on 7 October. In the morning Smith reported 20,000 Union soldiers crossing the Kentucky River into Frankfort, indicating an imminent advance east or south from the capital. Subsequent reports reduced the Union presence to only a small cavalry force. Hardee, however, requested reinforcement. His column had finally reached Perryville, but the close pursuit of III Corps made further movement toward Harrodsburg impractical. The Confederate force risked being attacked while en route, and its vulnerability triggered Hardee's request for assistance. He did not, however, describe these circumstances to Bragg, who could only speculate at his wing commander's situation.

While the threat of a Union advance from Frankfort remained minimal Bragg decided to attack at Perryville. He believed Hardee faced only a small enemy force that could be destroyed. Then he would join Smith and march on Frankfort. Bragg ordered Polk and Wharton to join Hardee at Perryville. The cavalry quickly complied, but the two infantry divisions under Polk's command were then approaching Harrodsburg. They dutifully turned around and retraced their steps toward Perryville, but this movement required time. By the morning of 8 October only Cheatham's division had joined Hardee. The second division, commanded by MG Jones Withers, remained en route. Three Confederate divisions and two cavalry brigades with a combined strength of nearly 17,000 men had gathered at Perryville. Moving toward them were 58,000 Union troops.

Buell's feint toward Frankfort confused the Confederates. He had successfully concentrated most of his army against a portion of Bragg's forces. Moreover, since his determination to retire on his supply base at Louisville, Buell's rapid pace exerted constant pressure on Bragg. As the campaign progressed Confederate actions lost all semblance of coherency. The notional plan of a three-pronged thrust into Kentucky disintegrated through the absence of a unified command, nebulous objectives, and the growing pressure of Union activity.

Conversely, Buell had a clear operational concept and the will to implement it. From the moment his army departed Louisville, Buell dictated the pace of events. Bragg responded with a series of snap decisions based on inadequate information. His principal objectives lay in installing a Confederate governor and combining his army with Smith's. The latter, however, required time and Smith's cooperation. Buell's rapid advance denied the Confederates time, and Smith's determination to retain an independent command east of the Kentucky River precluded a juncture of Southern forces.

The success of Buell's maneuvers, however, did not occur without mishap. The confusion among the Confederate commanders remained invisible to him. The march toward Bardstown and Perryville proved difficult. Severe drought conditions afflicted much of northern Kentucky. Water scarcity increased the hardship the many green soldiers in the Union army experienced. Unaccustomed to the rigors of campaigning, they suffered from thirst and fatigue. Buell's popularity remained low. While the army marched toward the enemy several of his officers drafted a letter to the president requesting his dismissal. In charge of III Corps, Gilbert proved ineffective. He quickly gained a reputation as a martinet and earned the enmity of his own men.

On 7 October Gilbert's corps remained in close pursuit of Hardee as the latter retired into Perryville. Union cavalry clashed with Wheeler's rearguard throughout the day. Accompanying III Corps, Buell learned that the Confederates had halted at Perryville and were deploying their infantry. He therefore planned an attack. The enemy force was his principal objective, but the availability of water also made control of the town and surrounding area desirable. Buell issued orders for all corps to move at 0300 the next day and deploy abreast before attacking at 1000. However, late transmission and receipt of these orders delayed I and II Corps' movements. Both formations had deviated several miles from their line of march in search of water. They marched toward Perryville but too late to meet the commander's timeline. Apprised of these delays Buell opted to delay his attack one day to complete his corps' deployment. Thus the Union attack would occur early on 9 October with all three corps and an entire day for the battle. Each corps commander received orders not to trigger a general engagement on 8 October. As his army marched toward Perryville Buell was unable to oversee their deployment. Thrown from his horse, he suffered injuries that prevented him from riding.

The Confederates remained oblivious to these developments. Polk arrived at Perryville and assumed command of the forces concentrated there. Ordered to attack he demurred, preferring to await Union action before responding. Bragg intervened, and on 8 October the Confederates attacked. In a hard-fought contest that continued past sunset Bragg's forces nearly destroyed the Union I Corps. Having detached one division to support the feint against Frankfort this formation was the smallest in Buell's army, and it had the greatest number of green troops. Moreover I Corps fought the battle largely unsupported. Buell's absence from the battlefield and his orders to his corps commanders not to trigger a general engagement undermined effective cooperation among his three corps. The Confederates were able to concentrate their outnumbered forces on one portion of the Union line and defeat it. Buell remained at his headquarters throughout the day where atmospheric conditions effectively shielded him from the sounds of heavy fighting. He remained unaware of I Corps' plight until a courier arrived late in the day.

During the night after the battle Bragg learned the extent of the Union's presence. He had defeated one corps but at considerable human cost. His soldiers were exhausted, and he had no reserves. Smith lay too far away to provide effective support. Buell still had two full corps that were rested and had only been slightly engaged. Bragg opted to retreat over the objections of some of his soldiers who believed they had won a partial victory and should remain to complete it. Leaving their dead and many of their wounded behind the Confederates marched toward Harrodsburg. Unknown to the Confederate commander, additional Union troops were en route to Perryville. One division was marching toward the town from Frankfort. Smith tried to intercept this force using his own troops and Withers' division. However, despite some skirmishing and a small engagement also fought on 8 October, the Union formation escaped.

Closing Maneuvers

On 9 October Buell prepared to renew the fight at Perryville only to find the Confederates gone. Despite the absence of opposition the Union army spent much of the day moving into the town and securing the battlefield. Buell pondered his next move. He wanted to advance on Danville and Bryantsville to threaten the Confederate retreat path to Tennessee. However Bragg's retreat toward Harrodsburg implied his effort to join Smith's army. Buell hesitated to move aggressively on Danville with the combined Southern armies poised to strike his own flank and line of communication. He resolved the issue by sending forces toward both Danville and Harrodsburg. Until the Confederates' intentions became clear, Buell was determined to act with caution.

Bragg's focus was on his supply situation and his ability to retire into Tennessee via the Cumberland Gap. He previously directed the creation of supply depots at Bryantsville and Camp Dick Robinson to support such a move. Buell's advance toward Danville now threatened these depots. Only Wheeler's cavalry protected this town while Bragg concentrated the rest of his army at Harrodsburg. There he expected to join Smith and fight Buell on more even terms. Smith agreed, but Buell's arrival at Danville forced a change in plans. Concerned over the growing threat to his supplies and his path to Tennessee, Bragg directed both armies to retire upon Camp Dick Robinson via Bryantsville.

On 12 October the Confederate leaders decided to quit Kentucky. Several factors spurred this decision, although Smith preferred to fight Buell before committing to a retreat. Bragg considered a defensive battle along Dick's River with the finally combined Confederate armies. Logistics considerations, however, forced him to reject this notion. Instead of a stockpile of supplies at the Bryantsville and Camp Dick Robinson depots Bragg found only a few days' rations. The food and forage Smith's army collected lay abandoned in the Bluegrass region. Their removal to the depots had been overlooked amid the confusion following Buell's rapid advance from Louisville. Now the combined armies of Smith and Bragg lacked sufficient supplies whether they fought or retreated. The route to the Cumberland Gap, however, led through rugged and barren terrain. Postponing the retreat would increase the passage's difficulty, especially with the approach of more inclement fall weather.

Bragg's headquarters also received news of Van Dorn and Price's fate. Van Dorn led their combined armies to Corinth. On 3-4 October the 22,000-man force launched a series of unsuccessful assaults on Union fortifications there. The Confederates suffered heavy casualties and retreated in the face of a powerful Union counterattack. The battle symbolized Price and Van Dorn's failure to render effective support to the Kentucky invasion. They did not prevent Grant from dispatching reinforcements to Buell, failed to advance into Tennessee, and finally met defeat while still in Mississippi.

With limited supplies and no prospect of additional support Bragg retreated. Marshall retired into western Virginia, and Smith and Bragg led the rest of the army toward the Cumberland Gap. Several hundred captured Union supply wagons accompanied them, but they carried weapons and munitions rather than food. Cavalry again screened the marching columns and maintained a rearguard presence to delay pursuit. To coordinate his mounted units Bragg belatedly appointed Wheeler as his chief of cavalry. The retreat commenced on 13 October, and the entire force passed through the Cumberland Gap nine days later. The journey proved grueling. The rugged terrain complicated wagon and artillery movement and quickly fatigued the infantry. The limited food supplies were quickly consumed, and hunger added to the misery of the retreat. When the columns finally arrived in Tennessee they comprised exhausted and dispirited men. A sense of failure and frustration pervaded the army. Many soldiers felt that Kentucky had been nearly won only to be abandoned. However, the army had not been defeated, and it remained a powerful force.

Buell's army did not interfere with Bragg's retreat. In the days following the battle at Perryville the Union commander remained uncertain of Confederate dispositions and intent. He moved cautiously rather than risk a surprise move against a portion of his army or his line of communications. Wheeler's aggressive delaying tactics further encouraged the deliberate pace. Buell's forces reached Crab Orchard on Dick's River on 15 October. By then Bragg's intention to retire toward the Cumberland Gap had become clear. Buell decided to break off his pursuit. Familiar with the rugged terrain the Confederates planned to traverse, he did not believe he could keep a pursuing army properly supplied. Moreover the rocky defiles along the route favored the type of delay and ambush tactics the Southern cavalry practiced. Rather than risk his army on an uncertain venture through inhospitable terrain after an elusive foe Buell assigned II Corps to monitor the Confederate retreat. The rest of the army marched away toward Nashville. Once in central Tennessee it would be poised to resume operations against Chattanooga.

Unmolested, Bragg's army reached Knoxville and a much-needed rest. The army commander traveled to Richmond to confer with Davis. There Bragg outlined the course of the recent campaign and the rationale behind his decisions. Polk and Smith also met separately with the Confederate president. Polk spoke on behalf of Hardee and most of the division commanders. He dubbed the Kentucky campaign a failure, blaming Bragg's vacillating leadership. Smith similarly criticized Bragg's leadership and refused to serve with him in any capacity. Both generals recommended that Bragg be replaced. Davis, however, refused to remove Bragg. Indeed, with the campaign over he now gave Bragg command authority over the combined Confederate armies in Tennessee.

The meetings with Davis did not end the command dissension among the members of the Army of the Mississippi. Aware of their efforts to remove him Bragg blamed his subordinate commanders for the campaign's outcome. He considered those officers who disagreed with his interpretation of events to be disloyal. Hardee, Polk, and several of the division commanders lost their confidence in Bragg. They continued to lobby for his removal and questioned his actions. In turn, Bragg questioned their competence. Effective command and control withered in this atmosphere of acrimony and mistrust, although several officers supported Bragg. The command climate did not improve until General Joseph E. Johnston replaced Bragg following the November 1863 defeat at Missionary Ridge.

Once the Confederate commanders returned from Richmond, Bragg's army moved to Murfreesboro. There the Southern presence posed a threat to Nashville and provided forward protection to Chattanooga and eastern Tennessee. The farmlands outside Murfreesboro also provided ample food for the soldiers. With the previously independent commands of Breckinridge, Smith, and Bragg now concentrated under a single commander the army remained in place awaiting the next Northern move.

Buell, however, would conduct no further operations. On 24 October Lincoln relieved him of command and replaced him with MG William S. Rosecrans. Buell's failure to pursue the Confederates directly into eastern Tennessee triggered the change in command. However, the action marked the president's and the War Department's general dissatisfaction with Buell since his abortive campaign against Chattanooga. He was perceived as being too cautious and either unwilling or unable to satisfy the government's desire to more aggressively prosecute the war. Consequently Buell was not only relieved but his leadership throughout the Kentucky campaign also was subjected to a War Department investigation. A special commission convened to determine whether he had permitted the invasion of Kentucky and the capture of the Munfordville garrison. It also focused on his leadership at the battle of Perryville and his subsequent failure to intercept the retreating Confederate armies.

The commission rendered its verdict in April 1863. It found that Buell could have preempted the invasion of Kentucky by attacking Bragg's army as it marched north through Tennessee. The commission also censured Buell for using his signal facilities at Perryville poorly, and it found that his pursuit of the Confederates after that battle lacked initiative and drive. However, in investigating Buell's operations against Chattanooga and subsequent actions in Tennessee and Kentucky, the commission ruled in Buell's favor. No formal charges or punishment resulted from the inquiry. He was released for reassignment, but the War Department found no further use for him. Buell resigned from the Army in June 1864.

At Nashville Rosecrans inherited the mission of seizing Chattanooga and liberating eastern Tennessee. He spent all November and most of December 1862 preparing his command and its logistics support for the campaign. Like Buell he ignored pressure from the War Department and the president to advance until he felt ready to do so. On 31 December he engaged Bragg's army at Murfreesboro in a bloody three-day contest. Bragg withdrew, and Rosecrans prepared eventually to march on Chattanooga. Ironically he opted for an advance along the same axis that Buell recommended the previous June. Rosecrans maneuvered Bragg out of Tennessee and captured Chattanooga in September 1863.

Notes

1. The forces used in this campaign included armies commanded by General Braxton Bragg, MG Edmund Kirby Smith, MG Earl Van Dorn, MG Sterling Price, BG Humphrey Marshall, and MG John C. Breckinridge. These armies were drawn from the Departments of the West, Eastern Tennessee, and Western Virginia.

2. MG Don Carlos Buell, "Statement of Major General Buell in Review of the Evidence Before the Military Commission," 5 May 1863, 38. This document may be found at the US Army Military History Institute Library, Carlisle Barracks, Pennsylvania.

Chapter 3. Suggested Route and Vignettes

Introduction

On 8 October 1862 more than 70,000 Union and Confederate soldiers gathered near Perryville. In the early morning hours elements of the Union III Corps attacked Peter's Hill just west of the town. This skirmish did not trigger a full-scale battle. It ended after III Corps secured the hill mass. South of Perryville Confederate cavalry demonstrated against the Union II Corps for much of the day. North of the town most of the Confederate force deployed and attacked the Union I Corps in an attempt to envelop the Army of the Ohio's left flank. This action and the bitter combat that followed comprise the essence of the battle of Perryville. Much of this fight occurred within or in the immediate vicinity of the Perryville Battlefield State Historic Site boundaries.

This chapter is a detailed guide to the principal events associated with the Confederate attack. It constitutes the core of the handbook's instructional orientation. In particular it links key actions as they occurred on the battlefield. To the extent possible, details concerning key personalities, command decisions, unit backgrounds, and weaponry have been included. Situational awareness, the human experience of combat, command and control, and troop leadership constitute the most important themes addressed. However, the overall thrust lies in understanding the battle and the complex set of variables that influenced its course and outcome. From such comprehension stem insights that can be applied to current military actions.

Consequently this section identifies a series of locations on park property from which you can analyze specific combat events. It also includes a recommended route that connects these points in a manner that best illustrates the battle's flow sequentially and chronologically. This route exploits the park management's interpretation efforts, including the readily identifiable informational markers and maintained walking paths. Although it is possible to walk over much of the battlefield in any direction, using the existing paths and the recommended route will simplify your movement from one location to another and help you understand the battle's flow. The paths are laid out logically and are easy to follow.

The following pages provide specific information for each point, or stand, along the route. The precise location of each stand is identified, including an eight-digit grid coordinate. (See Chapter 4 for specific information regarding the nature and use of these coordinates.) A vignette will describe each tactical situation. The vignettes comprise a participant's account or report of events. In some instances special information follows that provides additional insights into units, commanders, or weaponry. Recommended teaching points identify key topics for discussion and instruction. Directions to the next stand are also included. The stands are numbered in the sequence in which they should be visited. Nearly every stand is located near an existing park sign or readily identifiable landmark. Note that the stand numbers do not correspond to the numbers the park has assigned to informational markers. However, the location description provided for each stand indicates both the stand number and the corresponding park sign number. Most of the informational markers include a diagram showing unit positions and movements.

The maps provided in this chapter are intended to support planning and navigation. The first map shows the path net and location of each park informational number. The second one shows the stands superimposed on a topographic map. Together with the directional guidance provided for each stand these maps offer a clear sense of the staff ride route. The other maps illustrate different phases of the battle and include unit locations.

The park museum offers a collection of exhibits and wall displays. For groups that are unable to prepare before arriving on the battlefield the museum should be the first stop. There, maps are available to overview the campaign and battle. Exhibits depicting weaponry, equipment, flags, and uniforms also introduce you to the nature of the Civil War battlefield. The museum building also includes a gift shop. Both are open 0900-1700 daily from 1 April through 31 October.

The recommended staff ride route begins with a discussion of the army commanders, their intent, command climate, and leadership style. This background provides a context for understanding subsequent events. Stands 1 through 9 trace the initial Confederate dispositions and the attack of MG Benjamin F. Cheatham's division. This formation constituted most of the Confederate right wing at Perryville. Incorporated into these stands are the status of the defending Union brigades and the details of the tactical movements and combat that follow. Stands 10 through 16 also trace a loop, but they focus on the actions of the Confederate left wing. Its two infantry divisions attacked shortly after Cheatham, but little coordination occurred between the left and right wings. Each fought its own separate battle at the same time. The recommended route, therefore, completes analysis of developments in Cheatham's sector before moving to the Confederate left wing. Stand 17 marks the scene of the final engagements before the battle's end. Discussion of the battle's significance and the integration phase follow.

None of the positions highlighted in this chapter require special authorization to access. Nor do they require the use of a vehicle on the battlefield. All points can be reached by walking and using the paths provided. For planning purposes, groups should allow six hours to cover all of the stands provided. Prior coordination with the park staff will provide advance notice of the ground conditions and any special events that may interfere with the staff ride. Typically the paths are muddy from late fall through early spring. In the summer waist-high grass covers much of the park. Appropriate clothing should include long pants with boots or hiking shoes regardless of the season. Particularly in the summer months the combination of high heat, humidity, and tall grass ensures the presence of a variety of bugs and insects. It is essential to bring water to the park. There are no water fountains along the park paths, and water is only available near the museum and visitor center. The principal restroom facilities are located near the museum.

The staff ride route outlined in this chapter focuses on those events within or near the park's boundaries. Much of the emphasis lies on the battle's preparation and execution rather than on the operational setting. The latter can be addressed through preparatory study and analysis of the 1862 Kentucky campaign. However, it is possible to expand the staff ride to include additional sites. For assistance in doing so, see the points of contact indicated in chapter 4 of this handbook.

Maps 6, 7, 8, 9, 10, and 11 that appear in this chapter are reprinted with permission from *Perryville: This Grand Havoc of Battle* by Kenneth W. Noe, University Press of Kentucky, 2001.

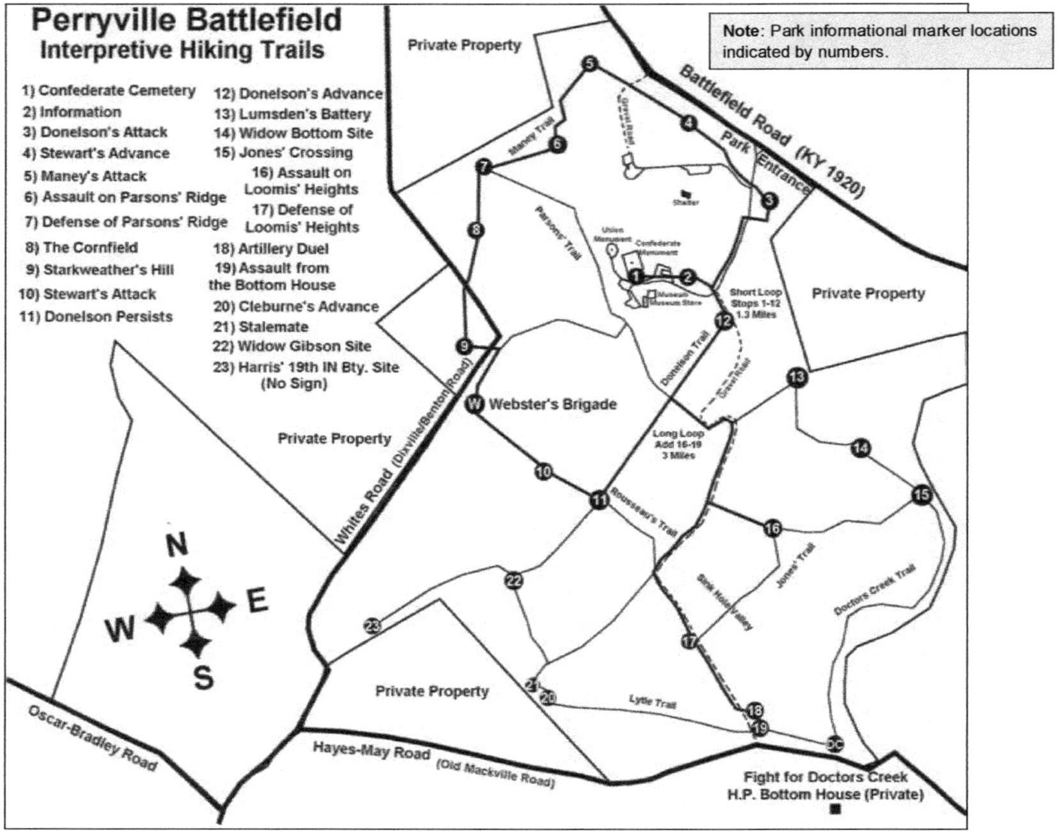

Perryville Battlefield
Interpretive Hiking Trails
1) Confederate Cemetery
2) Information
3) Donelson's Attack
4) Stewart's Advance
5) Maney's Attack
6) Assault on Parsons' Ridge
7) Defense of Parsons' Ridge
8) The Cornfield
9) Starkweather's Hill
10) Stewart's Attack
11) Donelson Persists
12) Donelson's Advance
13) Lumsden's Battery
14) Widow Bottom Site
15) Jones' Crossing
16) Assault on Loomis' Heights
17) Defense of Loomis' Heights
18) Artillery Duel
19) Assault from the Bottom House
20) Cleburne's Advance
21) Stalemate
22) Widow Gibson Site
23) Harris' 19th IN Bty. Site (No Sign)
Note: Park informational marker locations indicated by numbers.
Private Property
Battlefield Road (KY 1920)
Park Entrance
Maney Trail
Parsons' Trail
Donelson Trail
Short Loop Stops 1-12 1.3 Miles
Webster's Brigade
Whites Road (Dixville/Benton Road)
Long Loop Add 16-19 3 Miles
Rousseau's Trail
Sink Hole Valley
Jones' Trail
Doctors Creek Trail
Lytle Trail
Hayes-May Road (Old Mackville Road)
Oscar-Bradley Road
Fight for Doctors Creek
H.P. Bottom House (Private)
N
E
W
S

Map 4. Perryville battlefield paths.

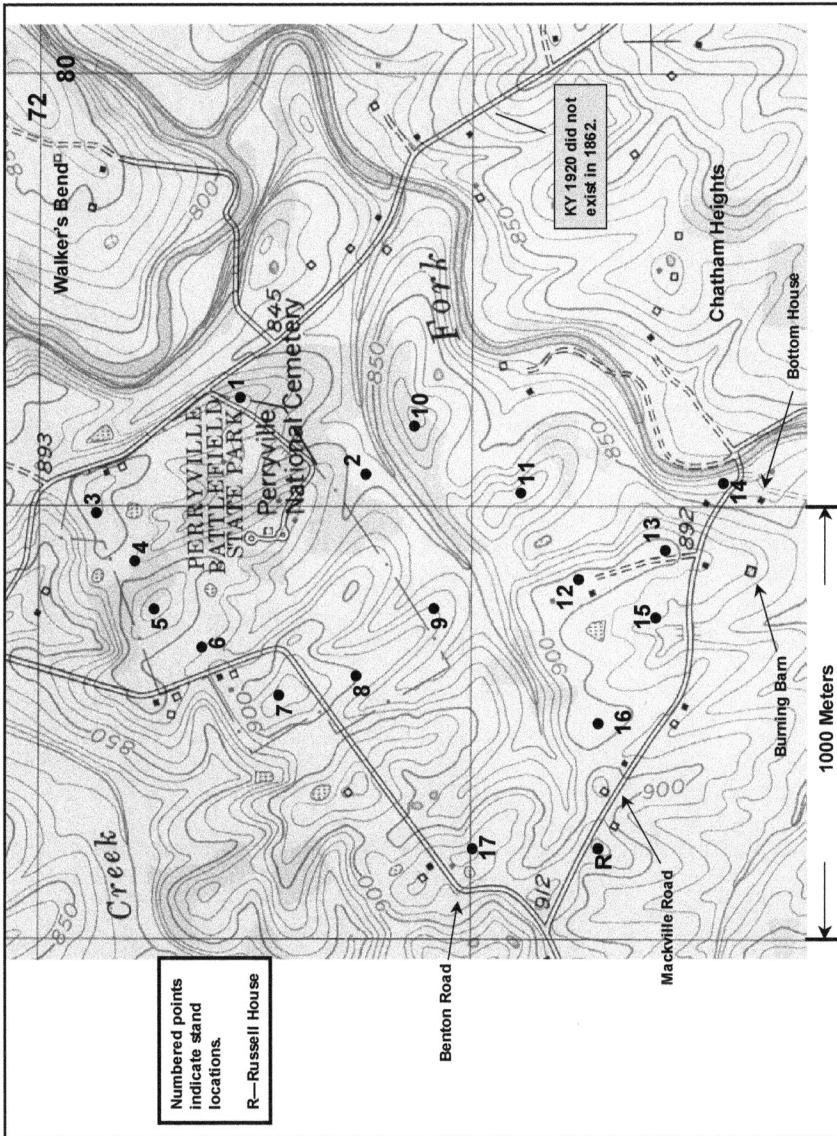

Map 5. Location of battlefield stands.

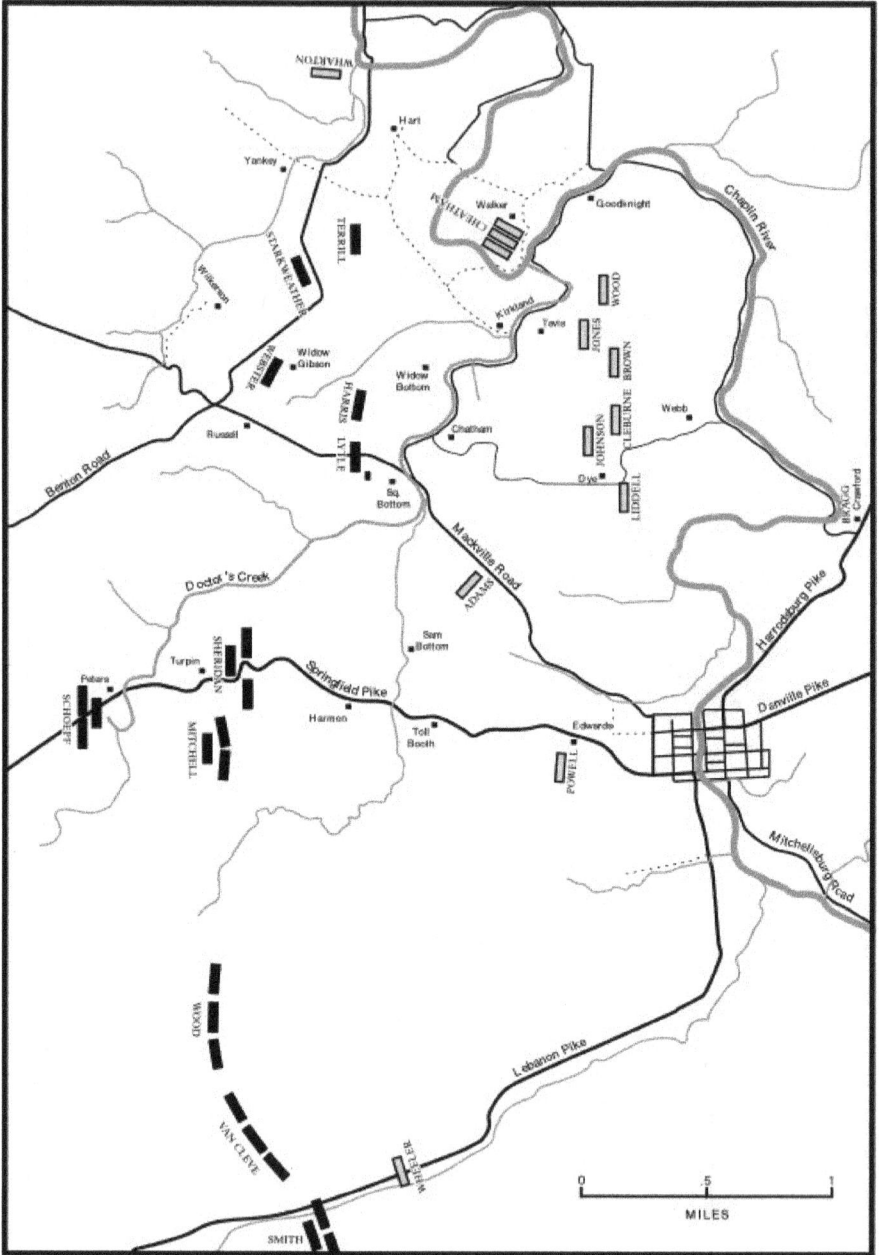

Map 6. Battlefield deployment, 1400.

Battle Orientation (Army of the Ohio)
MG Don Carlos Buell

Location: Pavilion (near museum building—UTM grid 7895 7147).

Note: The location given is recommended for simplicity. Buell's head-quarters actually lay at the Dorsey House. This structure no longer exists, but it stood about 2.5 miles southwest of the museum near the intersection of Route 150 and Coconaugher Drive. At the time of this publication there is no sign to identify the site. Nor is there a pulloff or parking area suitable for a large bus or multiple vans. Hence for ease of access and safety the pavilion is recommended for this portion of the staff ride.

Situation: Throughout 7 October III Corps advanced along the Springfield Pike (now Route 150) in the wake of elements of the Confederate Army of the Mississippi, retiring toward Harrodsburg. On Peter's Hill to the south of this position astride the Springfield Pike, Confederate infantry deployed to contest the Union advance. Additional infantry and cavalry were reported in and near Perryville, suggesting that General Bragg's Army of the Mississippi intended to stand and fight near the town. In preparation MG Buell established his headquarters on the Springfield Pike behind his most forward corps and 2.5 miles from where much of the fighting would occur.

Commander's intent: On the evening of 7 October Buell issued orders directing I and II Corps to advance early the next day and deploy on the left and right, respectively, of III Corps. He intended to concentrate his entire army, develop the Confederate position, and attack. I and II Corps, however, strayed from their intended march routes, searching for water amid the then prevailing drought conditions. By the time the corps commanders received their orders they could no longer meet Buell's timetable. Instead of arriving abreast the III Corps early on 8 October as directed I and II Corps did not arrive until nearly noon.

With less than 6 hours of daylight left to mount an attack by his entire army Buell opted to delay his attack one day, using the intervening time to deploy his corps and prepare. Buell communicated his revised intent to corps commanders as they reported to him. He also directed that no action be taken that would trigger a general engagement before 9 October when his army would be concentrated, deployed, and rested. Buell knew that Smith's and Bragg's two Confederate armies remained separate. At Perryville Buell intended to defeat Bragg's army before it could be reinforced. Then he would herd the remaining Confederate forces into northern

Kentucky and away from their line of supply and communications. Buell expected to fight and win; he did not expect to be attacked.

Vignette: "On discovering that the enemy was concentrating for battle at Perryville I sent orders on the night of the 7th to General McCook and General Crittenden to march at 3 o'clock the following morning, so as to take position respectively as early as possible on the right and left of the center corps, the commanders themselves to report in person for orders on their arrival, my intention being to make the attack that day if possible. The orders did not reach General McCook until 2.30 o'clock, and he marched at 5.

"The Second Corps, failing to find water at the place where it was expected to encamp the night of the 7th, had to move off the road for that purpose, and consequently was some 6 miles or more farther off than it would otherwise have been. The orders did not reach it in time, and these two causes delayed its arrival several hours. Still it was far enough advanced to have been pressed into the action on the 8th if the necessity for it had been known early enough.

"Between 10 and 11 o'clock the left corps [I Corps] arrived on the Mackville road. General McCook was instructed to get it promptly into position on the left of the center corps and to make a reconnaissance to his front and left. The reconnaissance had been continued by Captain Gay toward his front and right, and sharp firing with artillery was then going on. I had somewhat expected an attack early in the morning on Gilbert's corps while it was isolated; but, as it did not take place, no formidable attack was apprehended after the arrival of the left corps.

"The disposition of the troops was made mainly with a view to a combined attack on the enemy's position at daylight the following morning, as the time required to get all the troops into position after the unexpected delay would probably make it too late to attack that day." (US War Department, *The War of the Rebellion: A Compilation of the Official Records of the Union and Confederate Armies*; series I, vol. XVI, *Part I: Reports*, Washington, DC: US Government Printing Office, 1886, 1025, hereafter referred to as *OR*.)

Command climate: Buell's leadership skills were shaped by his career in the military. In the years before the Civil War he remained in the Army when many of his peers left to pursue civilian careers. As a junior officer he led troops in battle and acquitted himself well during the Mexican War. He shared the risks of his soldiers in combat, and he developed an organizational and administrative expertise that complemented his emphasis on training and strict discipline. As a commander Buell centralized authority in himself. He had the energy to make major policy decisions and supervise the execution of routine affairs. These qualities enabled him to build the Army of the Ohio from a motley collection of volunteers into an efficient fighting force. Yet he disdained the unsoldierly conduct of many of those same volunteers, preferring the professionalism of regulars. Moreover his personal aloofness and centralization of authority discouraged his subordinate commanders from exercising personal initiative.

Buell's view of warfare did not include a role for political influences, despite the political nature of the Civil War. As an army commander Buell ignored congressmen and state governors' views on organizing and employing his soldiers. In so doing he alienated the same people who were responsible for mobilizing volunteers for the war effort and sustaining President Lincoln's administration. Buell further antagonized them by diligently respecting Southern property and rights in occupied areas long after the government abandoned the policy. During the abortive effort to take Chattanooga, Buell's soft policies fostered resentment among his officers and soldiers. Subject to partisan raids and reduced rations his soldiers did not understand why they could not live off the land or punish suspected raiders. Buell did not explain his views to his command. When he retired first to Nashville and then to Louisville in response to the Confederate invasion of Kentucky his loyalty soon came into question, and he was accused of being a Southern sympathizer.

Buell's command style emphasized careful planning and deliberate movements that would outmaneuver rather than outfight the enemy: "My studies have taught me that battles are only to be fought for some important object; that success must be rendered reasonably certain if possible—the more certain the better; that if the result is reasonably uncertain, battle is only to be sought when very serious disadvantage must result from a failure to fight, or when the advantages of a possible victory far outweigh the consequences of probable defeat. These rules suppose that war has a higher object than that of mere bloodshed; and military history points for study and commendation to campaigns which have been conducted over a large field of operations with important results, and without a single general engagement. In my judgment the commander merits condemnation who, from ambition or ignorance, or a weak submission to the dictation of popular clamor, and without necessity or profit, has squandered the lives of his soldiers." (Major General Don Carlos Buell, Army of the Ohio, in *OR*, series I, vol. XVI, *Part I*, 51.)

Such a methodical approach to warfare was not in accord with the desire of the president, congress, and the state governors to more vigorously prosecute the war. Instead it made Buell appear overly cautious and lacking initiative. Following the Confederate invasion of Kentucky this perception led to his relief from command on 29 September. He soon resumed command, when his intended replacement refused to relieve him. Such support was not widespread among Buell's subordinate commanders. As the army marched to Perryville, a group of officers, including at least one division commander, conspired against him. They drafted a letter to the president requesting Buell's removal from command of the Army of the Ohio. On the eve of the battle of Perryville he was thrown from his horse following an altercation with a soldier. The injuries sustained prevented him from riding for several days.

Buell did not lack ability as a commander. However, his unwillingness to explain his views and intentions, his centralization of responsibility in himself, and his unresponsiveness to the political climate of the Civil War undermined his credibility. At Perryville Buell successfully concentrated his army against a portion of the Confederate forces. Simultaneously he fostered a climate of personal resentment among his command and dampened personal initiative. When the Confederates unexpectedly attacked, three Union corps followed their instructions to the letter and failed to provide mutual support. Buell remained immobilized at his headquarters unaware of the battle.

Acoustic shadow: Despite the close proximity of this headquarters to the battlefield Buell remained unaware that an engagement was under way. The sound of artillery and musket fire, synonymous with a major battle, did not reach his headquarters. A combination of wind, hilly terrain, and temperature tended to distort and mute the sound of battle. Known as acoustic shadow, this phenomenon was not unique to the battle of Perryville.

Vignette: Major J. Montgomery Wright, Buell's assistant adjutant general, gave the following depiction of acoustic shadow. Wright was at Buell's headquarters when dispatched to MG Charles C. Gilbert, commander, III Corps, to send two brigades to reinforce I Corps. Delivering his message Wright was directed to head to I Corps and determine where the two brigades would deploy. In the process of doing so Wright encountered the sights and sounds of battle without warning.

"Directed by the officers in charge of the ambulances I made another detour, and pushing on a greater speed I suddenly turned into a road, and there before me, within a few hundred yards, the battle of Perryville burst into view, and the roar of the artillery and continuous rattle of the musketry first broke upon my ear. It was the finest spectacle I ever saw. It was wholly unexpected, and it fixed me with astonishment. It was like tearing away a curtain from the front of a great picture, or the sudden bursting of a thunder-cloud when the sky in front seems serene and clear. I had seen an unlooked-for storm at sea, with hardly a moment's notice, hurl itself out of the clouds and lash the ocean into a foam of wild rage. But here there was not the warning of an instant. At one bound my horse carried me from stillness into the uproar of battle. One turn from a lonely bridle-path through the woods brought me face to face with the bloody struggle of thousands of men." (J. Montgomery Wright, Major, Assistant Adjutant General, USV, "Notes of a Staff Officer at Perryville," extracted from public domain documents at <http://www.battleofperryville.com> accessed 6 March 2003.)

Communications: At Perryville communication among division, corps, and army headquarters occurred through staff officers and personal interface. Each command echelon had several aides de camp and orderlies who carried messages between headquarters. Before the Confederate attack Buell required each corps commander to report in person to him. The I and III Corps commanders complied and in turn received instructions directly from Buell. The Army of the Ohio also included a Signal Corps element that operated semaphore stations at each corps headquarters and the Dorsey House. When the Confederates attacked I Corps, however, none of these means was used to apprise the army commander in a timely fashion. Buell only learned of the battle late in the day when a staff officer finally arrived at his headquarters. No clear explanation ever emerged as to why the signal stations were not used to relay this critical information earlier. The failure to inform the army commander immediately that his forces were under attack resulted in I Corps fighting its own private battle with little support and at considerable cost in lives.

Teaching points: Command, leadership, situational awareness, political awareness, communications.

Route to next stop: Follow the road leading back to the park entrance a short distance to Park Informational Marker 2 on your left. Proceed to the sign.

Battle Orientation (Army of the Mississippi)
General Braxton Bragg

Location: Park Information Marker 2 (map stand near Civil War Hall—UTM grid 7907 7140).

Note: Bragg's actual headquarters on 8 October was at the Crawford House. This structure lies on Route 68 just east of the town of Perryville. It has been purchased for restoration and public visitation. At the time of this publication the house remains closed and its restoration incomplete.

Situation: General Bragg commanded the Army of the Mississippi during the invasion of Kentucky. When Buell advanced from Louisville, Bragg's army was at Bardstown under MG Leonidas Polk's temporary command. Bragg had traveled to Frankfort to oversee preparations for the inauguration of the Confederate governor. The Union Army's sudden movement surprised him. Frankfort was abandoned while Bragg sought to concentrate his army with MG Edmund Kirby Smith's at Harrodsburg.

The Confederate forces remained dispersed as they moved over multiple routes toward a juncture. Smith's army remained scattered east of the Kentucky River. Polk retired from Bardstown in two columns, one led by him and the other by MG William J. Hardee. Each column followed a separate route. Polk's column moved rapidly toward Harrodsburg. Hardee, however, made little progress over poor roads and altered his march route onto the better roads Polk had taken. These movements delayed Hardee and permitted the Union III Corps to close on the Confederate force as it neared Perryville. Hardee found himself the target of an aggressive Union pursuit. On 7 October he requested reinforcements to deal with this threat.

Commander's intent: Bragg received Hardee's request simultaneously with a series of conflicting reports of Buell's location and objective. With the Union presence near Frankfort seemingly inactive Bragg determined to attack. He intended to defeat what he believed was a small Union force at Perryville, combine his army with Smith's, and advance on Frankfort. Accordingly, Bragg directed Polk's column to support Hardee at Perryville and attack early on 8 October. When Polk joined Hardee, however, he opted to remain in a defensive posture until Union intentions and dispositions became clear.

In Harrodsburg Bragg failed to hear the sounds of battle in the early morning hours of 8 October. He rode toward Perryville and established his headquarters at the Crawford House on the Harrodsburg Pike (now Route

68). Learning of Polk's decision, Bragg conducted a personal reconnaissance of the terrain. He then renewed his orders to attack and directed the necessary deployments himself. Most of the Union strength lay across the Springfield Pike (now Route 150) with a smaller force astride the Mackville Road (now the Hayes May Road). Bragg intended to roll up the Union left, first crushing the force on the Mackville Road before turning into the larger concentration on the Springfield Pike. The entire operation resembled a giant left wheel with the three Confederate divisions available attacking in echelon from right to left. MG Benjamin Franklin Cheatham's division would conduct the initial assault following an artillery bombardment. Cavalry would screen both flanks.

The artillery bombardment began at 1230 as scheduled, but it was not followed by Cheatham's advance. While Confederate attack preparations proceeded, the Union left flank extended farther to the north. In response Bragg moved Cheatham's division farther to its right into Walker's Bend to ensure that its advance would strike an open Union flank. Reshuffling the Confederate forces delayed the initial attack until after 1400. Less than four hours of daylight remained for the pending attack.

Vignette: "Finding the enemy pressing heavily in his rear near Perryville, Major General Hardee, of Polk's command, was obliged to halt and check him at that point. Having arrived at Harrodsburg from Frankfort I determined to give him battle there and accordingly concentrated three divisions of my old command (the Army of the Mississippi, now under Major General Polk)—[MG] Cheatham's, [MG Simon B.] Buckner's, and [BG James P.] Anderson's—and directed General Polk to take the command on the 7th and attack the enemy next morning. [BG Jones M.] Withers' division had gone the day before to support [MG] Smith.

"Having on the night of the 7th learned that the force in front of Smith had rapidly retreated, I moved early next morning to be present at the operations of Polk's forces. The two armies were formed confronting each other on opposite sides of the town of Perryville. After consulting with the general and reconnoitering the ground and examining his dispositions I declined to assume the command, but suggested some changes and modifications of his arrangements, which he promptly adopted.

"The action opened at 12.30 p.m. between the skirmishers and artillery on both sides. Finding the enemy indisposed to advance upon us, and knowing he was receiving heavy re-enforcements, I deemed it best to assail him vigorously and so directed." [General Braxton Bragg, Army of the Mississippi, in *OR*, series I, vol. XVI, *Part I*, 1087.]

Command climate: General Bragg assumed command of the Army of the Mississippi on 15 June 1862. He did so under trying circumstances. His predecessor in effect abandoned his command, while the defeat at Shiloh and subsequent abandonment of Corinth demoralized the army. Bragg reorganized his command and restored discipline. His immense personal capacity for work, administrative ability, organizational talent, and strict adherence to discipline transformed the Army of the Mississippi from a motley collection of dispirited individuals into a combat-effective force.

Bragg's vision of operations in the western theater transcended the geographical limits of his own command. He understood the Confederacy's need to regain the initiative. Moreover the overwhelming strength of Union forces in western Tennessee did not dampen his determination to mount an offensive. He refused to be pinned along the Mississippi River or keep his army in an idle defensive posture at Tupelo. Instead he resolved to regain freedom of maneuver by redeploying much of his force to Chattanooga. There he could secure that key railroad junction and mount an operation into central Tennessee and Kentucky. He applied considerable administrative and logistics talent in rapidly moving 30,000 soldiers over a circuitous rail route spanning nearly 800 miles.

However, during the invasion of Kentucky a rift began to emerge between the army commander and his senior subordinates. Before Bragg left Chattanooga he sought to remove several of his generals, whom he considered inept. The Confederate government disapproved his efforts, but Bragg's views became common knowledge. An anomalous situation emerged in which Polk became second in command due to his seniority despite Bragg's perception that he was ineffective. Cheatham similarly retained command of a division although Bragg considered him a ruffian lacking military ability. Cheatham, however, proved popular among the large contingent of Tennessee troops serving in the Army of the Mississippi. Bragg's efforts to remove him only alienated Bragg from the Tennesseans, whose primary loyalty lay with Cheatham.

Bragg proved more successful at improving unit commanders' efficiency. Many regiments followed the traditional practice of electing their officers, resulting in popular leaders who did not necessarily possess the skills necessary for an effective commander. Bragg established promotion boards comprising proven battlefield commanders. Newly elected officers had to demonstrate their military competency before these boards before they could assume their new responsibilities. These boards helped to ensure a basic skill level for commanders. However, by interfering with a practice soldiers saw as their right, the boards did little to raise Bragg's popularity within his command.

Nor did an experienced staff serve the Army of the Mississippi. It comprised several officers who were unfamiliar with their duties. There was no chief of cavalry to coordinate cavalry and information-gathering activities. Moreover, the senior and most experienced cavalry commander, BG Nathan B. Forrest, was relieved at the height of the campaign to return to Tennessee and raise a new mounted force. In the days before the battle of Perryville the lack of central coordination became manifest in the absence of solid intelligence regarding Union movements. Bragg also failed to secure an experienced officer to serve as chief of staff so he assumed this role himself. Despite his immense personal energy this dual role prevented Bragg from focusing his attention on key command decisions. Instead he remained partially mired in the routine details of his army's operations.

Bragg's wing and division commanders questioned how their commander handled the campaign. Following an auspicious beginning in which the Confederates advanced from Chattanooga, sidestepped Buell's army, and invaded Kentucky, Bragg vacillated regarding his proper course of action. He did not make Louisville his principal objective, despite his subordinates' urgings. Instead of making the Union forces' defeat a goal, he refused battle on several occasions. When Bragg marched from Munfordville to Bardstown, many of his subordinates believed he had lost an opportunity to either defeat Buell or seize Louisville. The army commander seemed to hesitate at critical moments instead of making decisions. Bragg, however, bore personal instructions from President Jefferson Davis not to risk his army. In the days before the battle of Perryville he had little information regarding the disposition of Buell's forces. Instead of intelligence Bragg's commanders sent him requests for reinforcements without explanation and offered advice on how to run an army. At Perryville Polk ignored Bragg's instructions to attack without informing Bragg of his rationale for doing so. Bragg responded by intervening and assuming personal control of the attack preparations. In the aftermath of the battle of Perryville Bragg would begin to view his commanders as disloyal while his commanders would seek his removal.

Vignette: On 7 October Bragg desperately sought firm information regarding the dispositions and intent of Buell's army. Instead he received no clear information from his subordinate commanders at Versailles, Perryville, or en route to Harrodsburg. Desperate for news of the enemy, instead Bragg received the following missive from Hardee who was commanding the left wing at Perryville:

"Permit me, from the friendly relations so long existing between us to write you plainly. Do not scatter your forces. There is one rule in our profession which should never be forgotten; it is to throw the masses of your troops on the fractions of the enemy. The movement last proposed will divide your army and each may be defeated, whereas, by keeping them united success is certain. If it be your policy to strike the enemy at Versailles take your whole force with you and make your blow effective; if, on the contrary, you should decide to strike the army in front of me first let that be done with a force that will make success certain." (*OR*, series I, vol. XVI, *Part I*, 1099.)

Teaching points: Situational awareness and understanding, political awareness, command and staff organization, impact of personality, role of subordinate commanders.

Route to Stand 1: Return to the road leading toward the park entrance. Before reaching the entrance turn right and proceed to Park Informational Marker 3.

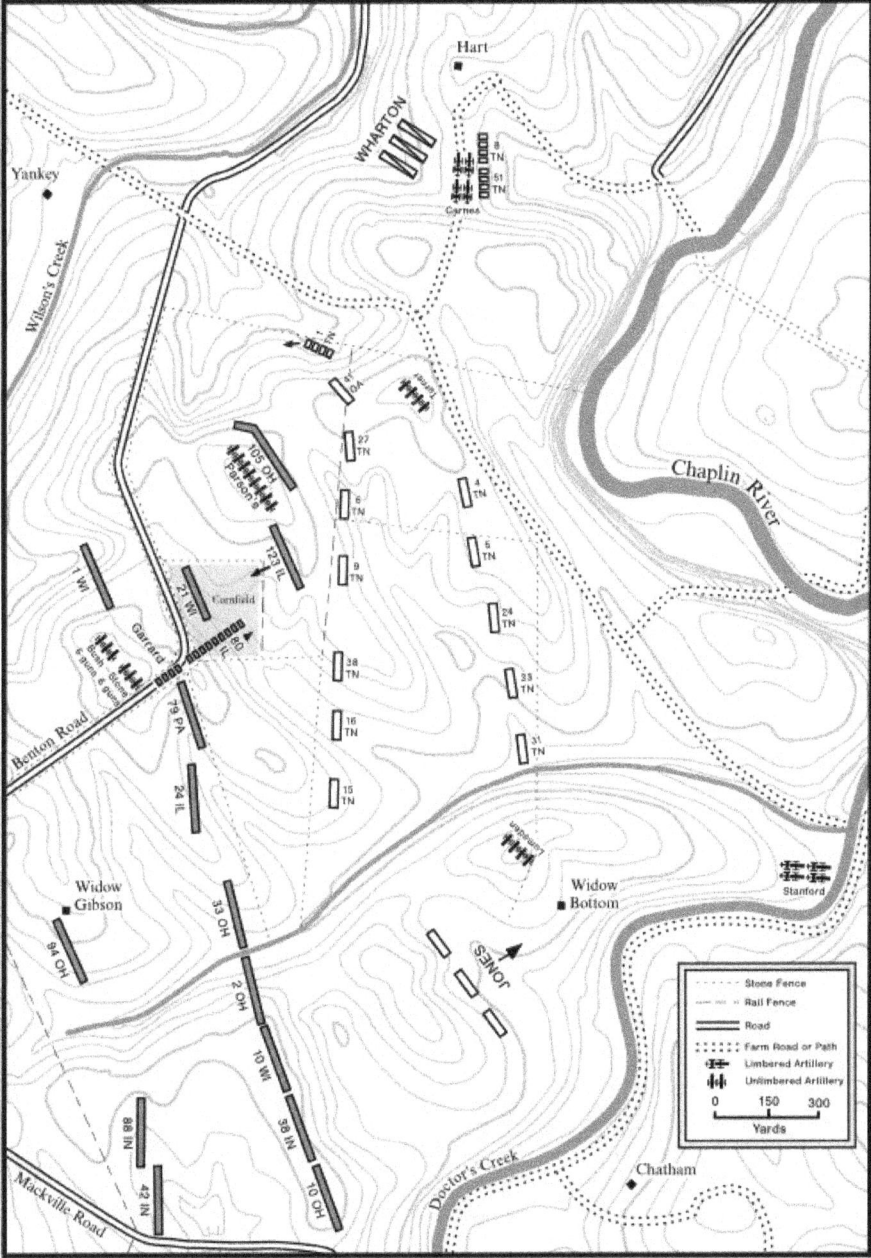

Map 7. Cheatham's attack, 1500.

Hart

WHARTON

Yankey

8 TN

51 TN

Cornea

Wilson's Creek

Chaplin River

2

4 OA

27 TN

105 OH
Parsons

6 TN

4 TN

6 TN

1 WI

123 IL

9 TN

21 WI

Cornfield

24 TN

Garrard

80 IL

Bush's Battery
6 guns & guns

38 TN

33 TN

79 PA

16 TN

31 TN

Benton Road

24 IL

15 TN

Widow
Gibson

33 OH

Widow
Bottom

Stanford

84 OH

2 OH

JONES

Stone Fence
Rail Fence
Road
Farm Road or Path
Limbered Artillery
Unlimbered Artillery

0   150   300
Yards

10 WI

38 IN

88 IN

42 IN

10 OH

Mackville Road

Doctor's Creek

Chatham

University Press of Kentucky

121

Cheatham's Attack

Stand 1

Donelson's Brigade

Location: Park Informational Marker 3 (park entrance—UTM grid 7926 7153).

Situation: In 1862 a wood line ran along this hill. To the east across the Chaplin River lies Walker's Bend where Cheatham's division deployed before its attack. The three brigades formed one behind the other with BG Daniel S. Donelson's brigade in front. At 1330 Confederate cavalry commanded by COL John A. Wharton swept along this hill from the north, clearing it of Union skirmishers in preparation for Cheatham's advance. Having accomplished his mission and receiving Union artillery fire from COL John C. Starkweather's batteries (Stand 7), Wharton withdrew to the north to screen Cheatham's flank.

MG Alexander McDowell McCook's I Corps remained unaware of the pending Confederate attack. Instructed by Buell to conduct a reconnaissance toward the Chaplin River, McCook oversaw the deployment of BG William R. Terrill's brigade on an open hill (Stand 5). This move extended the Union left flank still farther, but the Confederates did not observe this development. By the time Terrill's brigade began to move onto the hill Wharton's cavalry had withdrawn.

Cheatham began his attack shortly after 1400 by ordering Donelson's brigade to advance. While the unit crossed the Chaplin River and formed in the open area to the east of this position Donelson and his regimental commanders moved onto this hill to survey the terrain over which the brigade would attack. Their objective was Captain Samuel J. Harris' battery to their front (Stand 17). Its position had been engaged during the artillery bombardment, and it was mistakenly believed to mark the Union left. Expecting a lightly held flank instead Donelson and his commanders observed several Union regiments formed for battle. To reach Harris' battery they would need to cross open ground subject to enemy infantry and artillery fire. Moreover the Confederates would do so at reduced strength and without fire support.

Donelson's brigade included Captain William W. Carnes' Tennessee battery of four smoothbore six pounders. During Cheatham's movement to the army's right flank, one of Carnes' cannon became entangled on a fence gate. Donelson's infantry tore down the fence and continued moving, separating the brigade and its artillery. Carnes finally extracted his cannon only to be diverted to support BG Sterling A.M. Wood's brigade.

123

While moving into position between Cheatham on the right and Brown's and Jones' brigades on his left (see map 6), Wood identified COL William H. Lytle's infantry and artillery as a potential threat (Stand 13). With his own artillery still moving forward Wood requested artillery support from Polk. In response Carnes moved onto a prominence behind Wood's infantry from which he could observe and engage Lytle. During the subsequent artillery duel Carnes' battery suffered damage and withdrew to make repairs. Upon completion Carnes found himself without orders and separated from his parent brigade. Detailed to provide battery support, the 8th and 51st Tennessee Infantry Regiments also remained idle with Carnes. Consequently Donelson opened the Confederate attack with only a portion of his combat power.

Donelson moved his three remaining regiments onto this hill in a single line. Here they became visible to the Union forces and offered the first evidence of a Confederate attack. Amid Union artillery fire from front and left, Donelson advanced. The 16th Tennessee quickly raced ahead of the brigade line, aiming for the depression in front of this position (Stand 2).

Vignette: "I remember we went into the battle close to a small creek. We had just got to the top of a small hill when we saw the enemy rise to their feet and then business began, and things were hot for a time. There was a battery on our left that was giving us grape and canister and the bullets were singing around us. A man was standing just in front of me while I was loading my gun and I happened to have my eyes on him just as a canister struck him in the breast and I saw the white flesh before it bled. He was a dead man." ("Civil War Memories of Robert C. Carden, Company B, 16th Tennessee Infantry," chapter II, transcription of scrapbook contents, including newspaper clippings, *The Independent*, Boone, Iowa, 12 April 1912.)

Command climate: The 16th Tennessee's sudden dash away from the rest of Donelson's brigade demonstrates the battlefield influence of personality. COL John H. Savage commanded the regiment. He considered Donelson a drunkard with limited military ability. Before Perryville Savage had repeatedly ignored orders from his brigade commander. Donelson responded by having him arrested and court-martialed. The latter action, however, proved unsuccessful, and relations between the two men remained strained. When Donelson issued orders for his brigade to attack toward Harris' battery, Savage believed he was being deliberately sent to his death. In this mindset, he raced his regiment toward the enemy battery, quickly outdistancing the rest of the brigade. Instead of an entire brigade's coordinated movement on a single battery Donelson's advance disintegrated into a collection of disjointed regimental actions.

Teaching points: Intelligence preparation of the battlefield, situational awareness, command climate.

Route to Stand 2: Head west along the path to Park Informational Marker 12. This route traces the initial attack of Donelson's brigade.

Stand 2
Donelson's Brigade

Location: Forward of Park Informational Marker 12 (depression—UTM grid 7909 7124).

Situation: Amid artillery fire from its left and front Donelson's brigade advanced off the hill (Stand 1) and onto the lower ground here with the 16th Tennessee well forward. COL Savage sought to use the low ground to shield his regiment from the Union artillery fire that was taking a toll of his regiment. Instead he now received fire from Lieutenant Charles C. Parsons' battery of Terrill's brigade on the right (Stand 5). Surprised and suffering considerable loss the 16th Tennessee turned to face the new threat while Donelson brought his other regiments forward for a concerted attack on Parsons' battery. Before these movements could be completed Cheatham intervened, ordering Donelson to continue his attack toward his initial objective. To silence Parsons' battery he dispatched BG George E. Maney's brigade. Donelson's regiments again faced in the direction of Harris' battery and advanced with Savage leading the 15th and 16th Tennessee in front of the 38th Tennessee. As it did so it entered a crossfire that Union artillery and infantry created to its left, front, and right.

Vignette: "The boys were falling dead and wounded all around me and I thought all would be killed. Some of my schoolmates and playmates, neighbors and friends lost their lives there. . . . If you wish to know how a soldier feels in such a battle as that, you must ask someone else. I cannot explain, but I had no hope of getting out alive." (Carroll Henderson Clark Memoirs, quoted in Kenneth W. Noe, *Perryville: This Grand Havoc of Battle*, Lexington, KY: University Press of Kentucky, 2001, 199.)

Unit profile: The 16th Tennessee Infantry Regiment comprised 10 companies formed between May and June 1861 and assembled at Camp Harris. It followed the traditions of other state units organized on both sides by electing its officers. Sent to Virginia, it became part of Donelson's brigade in August. After participating in some minor skirmishing the brigade relocated to South Carolina in December. In April 1862 the brigade went back into the western theater via railroad, arriving in Corinth, Mississippi to join the Army of the Mississippi after the latter's retreat from Shiloh. Donelson's brigade accompanied the army during its retreat to Tupelo. Redeployed to Chattanooga, the 16th Tennessee remained with Bragg's main force as it invaded Kentucky. The regiment participated in the battle of Munfordville. At Perryville the regiment entered the battle with a strength of 370 men and lost 219. These catastrophic losses were repeated at Murfreesboro when the regiment again suffered 50-percent casualties. Savage resigned his command after that battle.

Teaching points: Intelligence preparation of the battlefield, use of terrain, situational awareness, battlefield command and control, effect of mass casualties.

Route to Stand 3: Retrace your steps to Park Informational Marker 3 near the park entrance. Head in a northerly direction along the path along the ridge to Park Informational Marker 5.

Stand 3
Maney's Brigade

Location: Park Informational Marker 5 (hill—UTM grid 7899 7186).

Situation 1: The presence of a Union battery on the open hill to your front (Stand 5) surprised the Confederates. Instead of attacking the Union left flank Donelson's brigade advanced into the center of I Corps. In response to this unexpected development Cheatham ordered BG Maney forward from Walker's Bend with instructions to take Parsons' battery on the open hill. The division commander also instructed BG Alexander P. Stewart to advance to support Donelson.

Maney's brigade comprised five regiments and one battery. Initially this force constituted the division reserve, charged with sustaining the momentum of the division's advance. Now Maney found himself committed to battle within minutes of its commencement. He moved his brigade by the right flank out of Walker's Bend and across the Chaplin River. Once across the Confederate infantry still had to move through Wharton's cavalry, which had retired behind this position after its initial brush with Union skirmishers.

In the open ground east of this location Maney formed his first line of three regiments. From left to right it comprised the 9th Tennessee, 6th Tennessee, and 41st Georgia. The tree line on this hill mass concealed them from the Union troops on the open hill (Stand 5). While his regiments formed Maney rode forward to personally view his objective and the terrain over which he would advance. To ease the pressure on Donelson he led his first line forward without waiting for his remaining two regiments or the brigade's artillery to deploy. The terrain and trees permitted him to advance to within 200 meters of his objective before being spotted.

Vignette: "The opposite bank of this creek directly in front of our approach was a precipitous bluff from twenty to forty feet high, the ground beyond it woodland, not more than ordinarily undulating and extending forward to open fields. To ascend the bluff directly in front in anything like order would have been impossible, and in approaching it I was instructed by staff officers of both Major-Generals Polk and Cheatham to move my command by the right flank past the creek by a crossing at the lower point of the bluff and take possession of the woods in the highlands beyond. This crossing was perfectly practicable for a movement by the flank, but the general ruggedness and irregularity of the ground on either side rendered the passage impracticable to any extended front of line, and in a strong degree imparted to it the character of a defile. About the same time I commenced my movement by the flank a gallant dash was made by COL Wharton's cavalry command through the woods to which I had been directed, and while this was going on I received orders ordered from Major-General Cheatham in substance as follows: 'To advance as rapidly as practicable through the woods toward the enemy; attack, drive, and press him.' There had been considerable firing, but the movement of our cavalry appeared a success in clearing the woods, and deeming it important to appropriate the advantage of any confusion which might exist with the enemy, in consequence, I pressed on with all rapidity practicable, turning to the left after crossing the creek bed and following the sound of the action. In passing through the wood, I encountered much of our cavalry, which had been engaged in the dash just made, and knowing that when deployed my command was to constitute the extreme right of our infantry line, and being unable at the moment to find the commanding officer, I instructed the cavalry whether in squads or companies to pass rapidly to the right, so as not to enfilade my infantry movement, and to take position for the protection of my right flank. Meeting COL Wharton a few moments afterwards, I mentioned my action and wishes with respect to his cavalry and requested his personal efforts in carrying them out, which was promptly given. During my movement by the flank, to avoid delay so far as possible, my staff were kept almost constantly passing to the rear to deliver necessary orders and keep the command closed up. My own time was occupied in directing the cavalry to my right and examining the ground forward with the view of advantageous engagement.

"After proceeding several hundred yards through the woods in the course I had first taken, I was informed General Donelson had become hotly engaged and was in great need of reinforcements. The action seemed but a short distance to my front and appeared to be fiercely waged, both with infantry and artillery.

"A depression in the ground, protected in front by a slight ridge and extending some distance to my right, afforded shelter for and favored the convenient formation of line of battle by filing to the right, halting and fronting when proper space was attained. My line was here and by this movement commenced, and in a few moments I ascertained by a personal reconnaissance the position of the enemy. Facing my approach and slightly to the right of General Donelson's command was a strong battery placed on a hilltop in an open field and less than 120 yards from the nearest edge of the woods, in which I was. The battery was actively engaged, partly on General Donelson's command at short range and partly in firing into the woods through which I was approaching. General Stewart's Brigade, which was to form between General Donelson's and mine, had not yet arrived, but my instructions as well as the immediate assistance needed by General Donelson's command committed me to engagement without delay and my preparations to attack the battery were made forthwith.

"Colonels [Charles A.] McDaniel's, [George C.] Porter's and [John W.] Buford's Regiments were fronted into line for the immediate attacking force (these constituting as much front as could be brought to bear advantageously against the battery) and a staff officer sent back to direct Colonels [William] Frierson and [Hume R.] Feild, so as to form in rear of and as a supporting line to the three first regiments. These arrangements being made without waiting for the supporting line to get into position, I commenced the advance of the attacking line, directing it so as to reach the open field at the nearest point to the battery. From the nature of the ground the right of my line first emerged from the shelter of the ridge under which it had been formed, and immediately the enemy's fire was opened upon it. Steadily and rapidly, however, the advance was continued to the fence dividing the woodland from the field, about an average of 120 yards from the battery." (BG George Maney in *Supplement to the Official Records of the Union and Confederate Armies*, Janet B. Hewett, ed., serial no. 94, vol. 2, *Part III: Correspondence*, Wilmington, NC: Broadfoot Publishing Company, 1999, 668-70.)

Situation 2: Maney's battery, commanded by Lieutenant William B. Turner, moved into this position from the gravel road visible across KY 1920. The rough terrain around Walker's Bend delayed this movement, preventing the availability of Maney's fire support until after the entire brigade had been committed and pinned along the fence to your front (Stand 4). Turner was still moving forward from Walker's Bend when Maney's first line attacked.

Vignette: "I had not reached the top of the hill, when orders were brought to me from General Cheatham, by Capt. [Melanchon] Smith, chief of artillery, to advance rapidly, and was conducted by the latter to a position on the hill to the extreme right, and overlooking the enemy, who was then in a fighting attitude before our forces. I immediately opened an enfilading fire on them, at the distance of 250 or 300 yards, with canister, and continued it with shell and spherical case as the enemy retired. This continued until our forces had so far advanced as to be between our battery and the enemy's infantry, when we commenced replying to a battery of the enemy, which had annoyed us considerably, opening upon us with guns of heavier caliber than ours as soon as we commenced our firing. I continued this until I received orders from General Cheatham to cease firing, and our infantry advanced and took the battery opposing us." (First Lieutenant William B. Turner, Smith's Mississippi Battery, in *OR*, series I, vol. XVI, *Part I*, 1156-57.)

Teaching points: Intelligence preparation of the battlefield, use of terrain, movement to contact, surprise, fire support, use of reserves.

Route to Stand 4: Proceed down the hill along the path to the fence line at Park Informational Marker 6.

Stand 4
Maney's Brigade/Terrill's Brigade

Location: Park Informational Marker 6 (tree and fence line—UTM grid 7889 7177).

Situation: Maney's first line continued its advance toward this point. In 1862 the fence followed the course of the existing tree line and private fencing in a north-south direction. The two groves of trees on the eastern slope of the hill did not exist at the time of the battle. Instead the ground was clear between the fence and the hillcrest. As they approached the fence the Confederate regiments received fire from the Union artillery and infantry on the open hill. The large size of the 123d Illinois supporting Lieutenant Charles C. Parsons' battery led the Confederates to believe they faced an entire brigade.

The sudden and close appearance of Maney's brigade, however, surprised Terrill. He responded by ordering the green 123d Illinois to attack toward the fence. With minimal training and in battle for the first time this regiment quickly became disordered. As its novice soldiers approached the fence Maney's veteran regiments would have appeared to them to be in perfect formation and order. In the brief firefight that ensued Confederate musketry shattered the 123d Illinois, and it fled back up the hill. Total casualties for this regiment numbered 189 of 772 that entered combat. Most of this loss occurred during the unit's initial clash with Maney's brigade.

Maney's regiments reached the fence line, but they promptly became pinned by canister and musket fire from Terrill's brigade on the open hill. Maney tried to maintain the momentum of his attack by bringing his remaining two regiments forward, but the brigade remained stalled at the fence line. Regiments became intermingled, and casualties mounted. The brigade faced heavy losses whether it retreated, advanced, or remained in place, notwithstanding the effective fire support Turner's battery offered once it deployed. At this critical juncture the 1st Tennessee began moving to the right to outflank Terrill. The personal example and exhortation of the brigade and regimental commanders, however, finally drove the brigade over the fence and up the hill. The assault carried the hill and overran Parsons' battery.

Obstacle definition: In 1862 the fence astride Maney's advance stood at least chest high and comprised interlocking wooden rails. This fence line proved among the longest of the many fences and stone walls present on the battlefield. It ran across the entire frontage of Cheatham's division, but it changed from a wooden fence to a stone wall south of Maney's position. Each of Cheatham's brigades had to negotiate this barrier before facing the enemy. A partial reconstruction of the wooden portion of the fence can be seen to the left of this position. It posed a physical and psychological obstacle to formed bodies of soldiers. Conversely it offered little protection from either artillery or rifled muskets. To cross such a fence regiments often relied on skirmishers to break down the fence or employed company columns to hit the fence and break gaps in it. The unit moved through and reformed before continuing its advance. Alternately an entire line of soldiers would try to open the fence and/or climb over it. Maney's brigade did the latter.

Vignette 1: "They had gone but a short distance when one of the most deadly and destructive fires that can possibly be imagined was poured in their whole line by the enemy, who occupied a strong and well chosen position on an eminence in an open field about 300 yards to the front. Here had a battery of eight guns, strongly supported by infantry. This command still pressing steadily forward, all the time having the contents of this battery, consisting of grape, canister, and shell, together with the small arms of the strong supporting force, it came to a high fence at the edge of the wood, at which time it seemed impossible for humanity to go farther, such was the havoc and destruction that had taken place in their ranks. A temporary halt was the inevitable result. Here, at this critical juncture, General Maney passed along the line from the right of the Georgia regiment to the left of the Ninth Tennessee, ordering and encouraging us to still press forward, as it was our last and only chance of safety and success. His presence and manner having imparted fresh vigor and courage among the troops the fence was crossed, the ascent gained, the battery taken, and the infantry, with terrible slaughter, driven from the field. It was here at the fence and between the fence and the point where this battery was in position that this regiment sustained its greatest loss. Here was the hottest part of the engagement. It was near the fence on entering the field that Capt. Thomas B. Rains, Company C, and First Lieut. Ed. Seabrook were killed, while acting nobly at the head of their respective companies. No truer and braver men fell that day. The color-bearer, John Andrews, was here too badly wounded to proceed farther and had to be carried to the rear. They were then seized by John Ayeres, one of the color guard, who carried them gallantly for a short distance and was killed. A.M. Pegues then carried them to the summit where the first battery was placed, where he was badly wounded, being shot in three places. They were then seized by Ed. Quin, private, Company H, who bore them in advance of the regiment across the field into the wood, where he was killed." (COL George C. Porter, 6th

133

Tennessee Infantry, *OR*, series I, vol. XVI, *Part I*, 1115.)

Vignette 2: "Ninety yards east of the battery's position began a heavy wooded slope. No skirmishers were thrown forward, nor was any examination made of this wood. Just beyond the crest, at that very moment, lay one of the most noted brigades of the Confederate army. They had only to climb the slope on the other side; deploy into line under cover of the wood and advance to the edge of the wood, along which ran a high rail-fence, to make the battery's position wholly untenable. No sooner did they open fire and the peril of the battery become apparent to General Terrill, than he ordered the One Hundred and Twenty-third Illinois, which had just been rushed into position at the double, rear rank in front, to charge the enemy's line. Such an order was justifiable only to gain time to withdraw the battery or for the arrival of expected succor. As an attempt to carry the enemy's position, or repel their attack, it was simple madness. The front already developed by their fire was more than double that of the assailing force. They were under cover in a thick wood with a high rail-fence along its edge. The perfectness of their cover may be judged from the fact that one of the Thousand [105th Ohio] said to the writer: 'I can see nothing to shoot at but the smoke of their guns. Shall I aim at that?' Against such a position, held by more than double their number, the One Hundred and Twenty-third was thrown across an open field. That they should be repulsed was inevitable; that there should be confusion was natural." (Albion W. Tourgee, *The Story of a Thousand; Being a History of the Service of the 105th Ohio Volunteer Infantry, in the War for the Union from August 21, 1862 to June 6, 1865*, Buffalo: S. McGerald and Son, 1896, 132-33.)

Unit profile: The 123d Illinois Infantry Regiment experienced its first battle at Perryville with minimal training. It formed in August 1862, and officer elections occurred on the 17th. The elections largely confirmed prior appointments, including the Illinois Adjutant General's selection of James Monroe as the regiment's commander. Monroe proved a doctrinaire officer, and he had accumulated considerable military leadership experience since the war's start. He led troops in battle at Belmont, Fort Henry, Fort Donelson, and Shiloh. Indeed, for his actions at Fort Donelson he received a brevet promotion to major. During this service he established a reputation for excellence in drill and discipline. The rest of the regiment's leadership, however, lacked military experience.

The regiment began its soldierization process at Camp Terry, near Mattoon, Illinois. The three weeks spent at this encampment constituted the only formal training the unit received. The rush to send new units forward to meet the Confederate offensive in Kentucky left the rookie soldiers with insufficient time to master the basic drills necessary for a Civil War regiment to function properly. Few company drills and no battalion drills occurred. On 6 September the 123d Illinois Infantry mustered into federal service with 10 companies. The regiment traveled by railroad to Louisville, Kentucky, where its soldiers dug defensive works for the city's defense. Few opportunities existed for unit training. On 1 October the regiment marched from Louisville as part of BG James S. Jackson's 10th Division in I Corps. (Sam M. Blackwell, Jr., "The History of the 123rd Illinois Infantry in the Civil War," student paper prepared at Northern Illinois University, 7 July 1976, US Army Military History Institute.)

Teaching points: Situational awareness, combat leadership, unit behavior under fire, unit training, unit cohesion, battlefield mobility.

Route to Stand 5: Advance up the hill to Park Informational Marker 7. This path traces the assault of Maney's brigade on the open hill.

Stand 5
Terrill's Brigade

Location: Park Informational Marker 7 (open hill—UTM grid 7879 7172).

Situation: I Corps' first elements began arriving on the battlefield in the vicinity of the Russell House (see map 5, point R) at about 1100. General McCook directed their initial deployment near that point before reporting in person to Buell at his headquarters. There the army commander indicated his intent to delay his attack by one day, allowing both I and II Corps to arrive and deploy. McCook was further instructed to move one brigade forward to this location as a reconnaissance brigade. Here it would have access to the Chaplin River, thereby easing the water shortage throughout I Corps. However, McCook was also cautioned not to take any action that would trigger a general engagement.

When McCook returned to the battlefield he sent Terrill's brigade forward to this hill. Parsons' battery arrived first, followed by the 123d Illinois in support. The rest of the brigade was still in the process of deploying when the Confederate attack began. The division commander, BG Jackson, accompanied Terrill's brigade onto this hill and remained to oversee the developing tactical situation. This hill offered a commanding view, but the open terrain to its north made it vulnerable to a flanking attack while trees to the east limited visibility to the vicinity of the fence line. Neither Jackson nor Terrill were aware of the nearness of Cheatham's division.

When Donelson attacked Parsons engaged him with at least part of his battery (Stand 2). However, the sudden appearance of Maney's brigade near the fence line surprised Terrill. Concerned for the safety of Parsons' battery he ordered the cannon turned to bear on this new threat and ordered the 123d Illinois to attack. Confederate muskets shattered the regiment as it neared the fence line (Stand 4) and killed Jackson. The 123d Illinois Regiment fled back up this hill while the rest of Terrill's brigade continued to deploy. The 105th Ohio moved onto the crest of the hill to the left of Parsons' battery while the 80th Illinois and COL Theophilius T. Garrard's detachment formed to its right. The combined firepower of these forces pinned Maney's regiments at the fence line. However, Confederate support arrived with the deployment of Turner's battery (Stand 3). Maney finally got his brigade over the fence and moving up the hill.

The Union line faltered in the face of Maney's advance. Parsons' battery lost many of its horses to Confederate fire. Withdrawal became nearly impossible when the gun crews fled. In their place Terrill employed soldiers from the 105th Ohio to man the battery. He also ordered the same regiment to charge down the hill. His efforts failed, and Maney overran the position, capturing all but one cannon. Terrill formed a second line along the hill's reverse slope. The Confederates, however, pressed their attack. Upon reaching the hilltop they did not pause to re-form. Instead they immediately assaulted Terrill's newly formed line. After a short exchange of fire the Union infantry fled. It suffered considerable loss to Confederate muskets that continued to shoot the soldiers as they ran.

Command and soldier welfare: BG Jackson commanded an infantry division in combat for the first and last time at Perryville. A native Kentuckian born in 1823, he studied and practiced law. He volunteered for service in the Mexican War, joining the 1st Kentucky Cavalry as a first lieutenant. However he soon resigned from the Army to avoid court-martial proceedings stemming from a duel he fought with another officer in the same regiment. He then pursued a political career and was serving as a Kentucky congressman when the Civil War began. Authorized by President Lincoln to raise a regiment, he recruited, organized, and commanded the 3d Kentucky Cavalry. During the winter Jackson's unit operated in western Kentucky against Confederate raids. In spring 1862 he accompanied Buell's army south to Nashville. Although present at the battle of Shiloh the 3d Kentucky played little role in it. Afterward the regiment participated in the siege of Corinth and the preparatory movements of Buell's advance on Chattanooga. In August Jackson was promoted to brigadier general shortly before being dispatched with several other officers to help organize Kentucky's defenses in response to Smith's Confederate invasion. Jackson assumed command of the cavalry in the newly formed Army of Kentucky. After the defeat at Richmond Jackson's cavalry retreated to Louisville where new regiments were concentrating.

Jackson assumed command of the 10th Division, which comprised entirely green units. He soon earned a reputation as a tyrant. Inattentive to his soldiers' care and needs, he had few admirers after parading his division in full kit around the city in high heat and stifling humidity. The new soldiers lacked training and conditioning. At least four soldiers died from heatstroke, and many more suffered from heat exhaustion.

The march toward Perryville marked the first field march for the soldiers in Jackson's division. They suffered not only from the simple rigors of campaigning but also from lack of water because of the prevalent drought conditions. In the early morning hours of 8 October they stumbled into Mackville seeking rest. When Jackson learned of Buell's order to advance to Perryville he quickly readied his division to move. Many of the soldiers lacked sleep, food, and water, but they remained in march formation waiting for Rousseau's division to lead the corps movement. When Jackson's men finally arrived on the battlefield Terrill's brigade was immediately moved forward to an exposed position on the army's extreme left flank. The soldiers had no time to rest or eat before they found themselves the target of a very aggressive assault by Maney's Confederate veterans. Their state of exhaustion and the apparent callousness of their division commander eroded their morale and undermined their effectiveness even before the battle began. Poor command decisions at the brigade level then accelerated the disintegration of Terrill's regiments.

Vignette 1: "On a little knoll to our right front, the battery was firing with frenzied rapidity. The shells from the enemy's battery flew over our heads and cut the limbs of the trees by which we stood, sending down a shower of acorns. Bullets pattered about us. We could see the artillerymen dashing back and forth as the smoke lifted from the guns. Men were coming back from the hell which the crest hid from our view, some wounded, some stragglers. Somebody suggested that the guns were empty, and the order to load was given in some of the companies. Our division and brigade generals were standing, unmounted, just in the rear of the battery. Both had accompanied it to the position assigned and remained to watch its action; General Terrill leaving the duty of posting his brigade to his staff officers. He was by training, almost by instinct, an artilleryman, and his battery's action eclipsed in interest the maneuvering of his brigade. When Maney's brigade appeared in line of battle in the woods upon its right, as it stood facing northward, advancing with a steady fire until they reached the fence a hundred yards away, its peril absorbed his whole attention. Ordering Colonel Monroe of the One Hundred and Twenty-third Illinois, to charge the enemy's line, he remained beside the battery, directing and encouraging the men in its operation.

"When the Thousand came up, the right of the brigade had fallen back, and the enemy, checked by the hot fire which greeted them, had halted in the edge of the wood along the fence below. The battery stood alone upon the crest of the hill, half its guns silenced, its men and horses being cut down by the fire of the enemy. It was said the order to withdraw the battery had been given. Even then it was too late. A mounted aide pointed out our position and rode beside our adjutant at the head of the column as we advanced. A caisson, the horses of which had become unmanageable, dashed through our line to the rear." (Albion W. Tourgee, *The Story of a Thousand; Being a History of the Service of the 105th Ohio Volunteer*

Infantry, in the War for the Union from August 21, 1862 to June 6, 1865,
Buffalo: S. McGerald and Son, 1896, 119-20.)

Unit profile (Parsons' battery): In September 1862 BG Terrill directed the creation of an artillery battery to support his command, the newly
formed 33d Brigade of General Jackson's 10th Division. Before assuming
brigade command Terrill served with distinction as a battery commander.
As a result of his service at Shiloh he was promoted to brigadier general.
His artillerist's background inspired Terrill to acquire a battery for his
brigade. He secured two 12-pound howitzers, five 12-pound Napoleons,
and one 10-pound Parrott rifle. To man this battery Terrill employed volunteers from his infantry regiments. The new battery became a focal point
of his interest. He appointed another artillery officer, Lieutenant Charles
C. Parsons, to command the battery. Together Terrill and Parsons trained
and molded the motley collection of cannon and soldiers into an effective
battery. Their efforts were only partially complete when Buell's army left
Louisville on 1 October. Parsons' battery was the largest artillery unit of
either side at Perryville, but it had no combat experience and lacked the
cohesion of more veteran organizations. (Albion W. Tourgee, *The Story of
a Thousand; Being a History of the Service of the 105th Ohio Volunteer
Infantry, in the War for the Union from August 21, 1862 to June 6, 1865,*
Buffalo: S. McGerald and Son, 1896, 132, 137-39; James H. Hillard, "
'You Are Strangely Deluded': General William Terrill," *Civil War Times
Illustrated*, February 1975, 15; "Artillery Breakdown at the Battle of Per-
ryville," chart prepared by the Perryville Battlefield State Park staff, 21
October 1999.)

Vignette 2: "Here Captain Parsons was located soon after, and by 2
p.m. opened with round shot and shell. The One hundred and twenty-third
Illinois had been previously brought on the field forming our extreme left
and angling toward the rear of the battery. Soon after the battery was in
position the One hundred and fifth Ohio, Colonel Hall, came up and took
position to the left and rear of the battery, and the Eightieth Illinois, Colonel Allen, through misdirection of the guide, came up later and formed in
the valley near the edge of the woods, as will be seen by the report of Capt.
William P. Anderson, assistant adjutant general, herewith submitted.

"The battery had fired but a few shots when we heard rifle shots below
in the woods, when the enemy soon advanced and came in sight in the
edge of the woods fronting our troops. No sooner was this seen by General
Terrill and Lieutenant Parsons, then directing the fire of the guns, than they
changed the direction of the fire, and opened at short range (about 90 yards)
on the flank of the enemy with grape with deadly accuracy. It checked the

advance of the enemy, and after a few more rounds they changed front and faced the battery, which then flanked our left. General Terrill, seeing this, ordered the advance of the One hundred and twenty-third Illinois, Colonel Monroe, and to charge bayonets. It advanced bravely, but unfortunately the enemy had not then left the woods, and there was a rail fence on its edge, which prevented their advancing promptly. The regiment fired a volley and fell back, when almost immediately afterward General Jackson, who was standing on the left of the battery, was killed, two bullets entering his right breast." (Captain Percival P. Oldershaw, Assistant Adjutant General, 10th Division, *OR*, series I, vol. XVI, *Part I*, 1060.)

Teaching points: Command responsibility in battle, leadership, psychological effects of combat, fire support.

Visibility note: Looking east toward Starkweather Ridge (Stand 7) it is possible to see several buildings that appear close together on the same ridgeline. In fact a series of ridges separate these structures. When Wharton's cavalry made its earlier sweep against the 33d Ohio skirmishers, it was fired on by Starkweather's batteries. Because of the optical illusion, however, Wharton misidentified the source of the fire and mistakenly confirmed Harris' battery as the Union left flank.

Route to Stand 6: Move down the path toward the cornfield and Park Informational Marker 8.

Stand 6
21st Wisconsin

Location: Park Informational Marker 8 (cornfield—UTM grid 7868 7162).

Situation: On the morning of 8 October BG Lovell Harrison Rousseau directed the deployment of his 3d Division. Starkweather's 28th Brigade occupied the hill behind this location (Stand 7) and constituted the division's left flank. The 21st Wisconsin Infantry initially deployed on the same hill. Rousseau, however, directed the regiment to assume an advanced position in this cornfield. Subsequently Terrill's brigade moved on to the hill to your front (Stand 5). When Maney's brigade attacked the men of the 21st Wisconsin heard but could not see the fighting to their front. On the hill to their rear (Stand 7) the two batteries supporting Starkweather fired over their heads, resulting in stray rounds and the wooden sabots from the artillery ammunition falling into the 21st Wisconsin's ranks. This unit received its first glimpse of the battle when terrified soldiers from Terrill's brigade fled through and around their ranks.

While the 21st Wisconsin re-formed its temporarily disordered ranks Maney's brigade attacked them. Alone and unsupported the regiment held its position against Confederate infantry firing into their front and flanks. The effect of this fire and gradual awareness of the regiment's exposed position finally triggered the unit's retreat. To reach relative safety behind Starkweather's position the soldiers had to turn away from the Confederates and scramble up the hill under continuous fire. The Confederates pursued closely, using the retreating 21st Wisconsin to cover their advance on Starkweather's position (Stand 7). The regiment rallied in the depression behind Starkweather and rejoined the fight. For a short time the 21st Wisconsin had served as a breakwater in the path of Maney's victorious regiments. It entered the battle with a strength of 663 and suffered 41 killed, 101 wounded, and 36 missing, nearly 27-percent casualties.

Cornfield: In October 1862 the corn stalks stood several feet high, partially obstructing visibility. The corn did not conceal the regiment, but the high stalks and weeds hindered the deployment and movement of linear formations.

Unit profile: The 21st Wisconsin Infantry Regiment exemplifies the experience of several Union regiments in I Corps seeing combat at Perryville for the first time with minimal training. The 21st Wisconsin formed in late summer 1862 under the command of COL Benjamin Sweet. After its formation in its home state the unit moved to Covington, Kentucky.

There it joined a mass of soldiers and "squirrel hunters" hurriedly assembled to protect the approaches to Cincinnati. In September the regiment moved to Louisville where it built defensive works. On the eve of its departure the unit received its first tents only to be instructed to leave them in Louisville. The unit comprised part of the 28th Brigade commanded by COL Starkweather. An indication of the regiment's combat readiness is documented in one veteran's account: "In consequence of the numerous changes of camp, the drawing of full equipage, constant fatigue duty in digging trenches, it had been impossible to hold battalion drill down to this date [1 October], but three times. The men were absolutely without any experience, and could not obey commands from not knowing what they imported. To add to the trials of the new situation the weather was hot in the day and cold at night. No rain had fallen for days and the country passed over was singularly destitute of water for either man or beast. Like all new troops, they endeavored to carry too much and consequently many gave out, and all, after the first day's march, either threw away or otherwise disposed of surplus clothing, blankets, etc." (Michael H. Fitch, *Echoes of the Civil War As I Hear Them*, New York: R.F. Fenno and Co., 1905, 54-55.)

Vignette: "Very soon the broken and bleeding troops of Jackson's division overpowered, exhausted by heat and marching, many of them wounded, and the rest demoralized (for they were mostly new troops), came pouring back upon the line of the twenty-first in crowds, and several hundred of them halted just in front of the twenty-first, but without any formation. At this point, General William R. Terrill, who commanded a brigade in Jackson's division, dismounted, and apparently almost overcome with vexation and exhaustion, passed to the rear by the right of the twenty-first. He said to the adjutant as he passed, that the rebels were advancing in terrible force, and that the only way in which the twenty-first could avoid being crushed was to wait until they came near enough, and then charge bayonets upon them. This information the adjutant hurried to carry to the colonel, who was opposite the centre of the line, but found him wounded. In the meantime, the firing had become terrific, and it seemed at that time strange, that all the firing from the Federal troops, came from the rear of the twenty-first. Reports came from the captains along the line that the men of the twenty-first were being killed by shots from a battery in the rear, and that there were no supports on our flanks, but then it was too late to change position by the slow movement of military tactics, for in less time than it takes to write this, a frightful rush of the disorganized troops who had gathered in the front of the twenty-first, was made to the rear

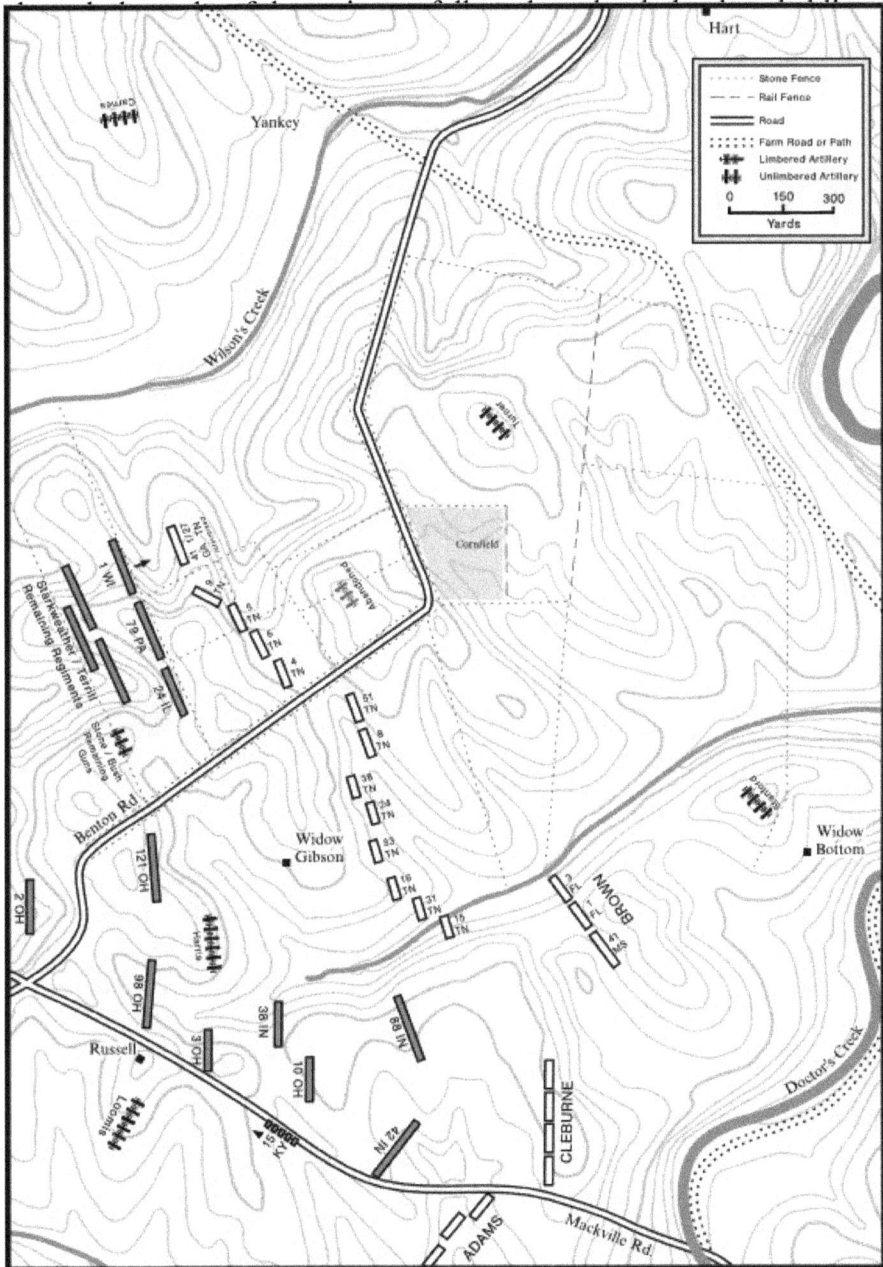

Map 8. Cheatham's attack continued, 1615.

University Press of Kentucky

143

Stand 7
Starkweather's Brigade

Location: Park Informational Marker 9 (hill—UTM grid 7857 7143).

Situation: In the evening of 7 October Buell issued orders to his corps commanders to attack the Confederate positions at Perryville the next morning. He directed I Corps to advance from Mackville at 0300, assume its position on III Corps' left, and prepare to attack at 1000. However, although written in a timely manner, the delivery of these instructions was inexplicably delayed. Thus MG Alexander M. McCook, commander, I Corps, did not receive his orders until 0230, shortly after his command had entered bivouac for the night. Not until 0500 did elements of the corps begin preparations to advance. Rousseau's division led the movement with only the brigades of COL William H. Lytle and COL Leonard A. Harris. Assigned to the corps' rear area to protect the formation's trains, Starkweather's brigade required additional time to move forward and rejoin its parent division. As it did so it also stopped to draw supplies.

McCook intended for Jackson's green division to follow Rousseau. Jackson, however, was determined to move rapidly on Perryville despite his soldiers' exhausted state. When the corps finally received its orders to advance, Jackson immediately roused his command and readied his men to march. Many of the soldiers had not been fed and lacked water, but they remained in formation while Lytle's and Harris' brigades cleared Mackville. Impatient to move Jackson finally opted to advance without allowing Starkweather to first rejoin Rousseau's division. At about 0800 Jackson began marching along the Mackville Pike (now the Hayes May Road). This action effectively split Rousseau's division and left Starkweather once more in the rear of I Corps. The absence of an alternative route to Perryville channeled I Corps down a single, narrow, twisting roadway. Bottlenecks ensued, but Starkweather remained at the rear of the column unable to bypass Jackson. As the three Union brigades neared the Russell House they could hear the fighting for Peters Hill and subsequent exchanges of artillery fire. Jackson's brigades deployed skirmishers on their flanks and continued their approach more cautiously. Starkweather, however, increased his pace and moved rapidly toward the sound of guns. He also moved his brigade cross-country to get around Jackson and assume a position on I Corps' left flank. Nevertheless Starkweather's brigade was the last one in I Corps to arrive on the battlefield.

Starkweather ultimately deployed his brigade along this ridge on the morning of 8 October in accordance with his division commander's instructions. The brigade benefited from the presence of two batteries, one commanded by Captain Asahel K. Bush and the other by Captain David C. Stone. Together these two batteries included 12 cannon, a uniquely high level of organic artillery support for any brigade on the battlefield. Starkweather's command also included four infantry regiments. Except for the 21st Wisconsin all deployed on this high ground, facing generally toward Terrill's position (Stand 5). From left to right Starkweather's line comprised the 1st Wisconsin, 79th Pennsylvania, and 24th Illinois. The position dominated the terrain behind Terrill's open hill, and it marked the extreme Union left flank.

The collapse of Terrill's brigade placed Starkweather's position on the front line. By 1545 it had become the focal point for Cheatham's efforts to turn the Union left flank. Starkweather faced Maney on his left, Stewart to his front, and Donelson's renewed attack on his right. When the 21st Wisconsin retreated Maney's Confederates pursued closely, using the broken regiment to shield their own advance from Starkweather's guns and infantry waiting on this hill. Fear of hitting their own men, however, did not prevent Bush's and Stone's batteries, or their supporting regiments, from firing into the onrushing mass. Although elements of Stewart's brigade attacked simultaneously on their left, Maney's attack disintegrated with heavy losses.

However, the 1st Tennessee maneuvered onto the left (north end) of this hill. Despite close-range fire from Bush's battery, the Confederate infantry reached a point just under the hill's crest from which the cannon could not be depressed sufficiently to engage them. The 1st Wisconsin therefore advanced and fired into their midst. The Tennessee regiment continued forward, and a melee ensued in which Bush's battery was overrun. This seeming victory was negated when the disorganized Confederates failed to consolidate their position and soon retired. The 1st Tennessee incurred particularly high losses, including Lieutenant Colonel John Patterson. He had led the charge in lieu of the regiment commander who had helped orchestrate the advance of Maney's brigade.

Maney prepared for a second assault. While he re-formed his infantry, Captain William Carnes' battery deployed in an enfilade position that Wharton's cavalry previously identified. The location of the battery lies outside the park's boundaries, but it can be readily identified by the white barn with partially rusted roof visible north of Starkweather's position. Carnes' battery belonged to Donelson's brigade, and two regiments of the parent organization still accompanied him. Turner's battery also

146

displaced forward to the open hill that Terrill abandoned. Starkweather found himself in a crossfire. Behind his line Terrill rallied elements of his own brigade. He advanced them to support Starkweather only to be killed by an artillery round. The artillery fire, the signs of another Confederate attack, and continued pressure on his right led Starkweather at about 1630 to order his cannon withdrawn to the hill west of this location. His infantry covered their withdrawal in a continuous exchange of musket fire with Maney's and Stewart's regiments. Losses in horses and gun crews resulted in the abandonment of some of the cannon. The rest displaced rearward and recommenced firing. The Union infantry then began a stubborn retrograde movement and formed a new line near the cannon.

Carnes' deployment: After Carnes completed repairs to his battery he tried to reenter the fight. His parent brigade had already begun its efforts to seize Harris' battery, leaving Carnes and the two supporting infantry regiments on their own. Carnes vainly sought orders from his brigade and division commanders. He finally encountered COL John A. Wharton whose cavalry brigade secured the Confederate right flank. Wharton's cavalry had discovered an optimal firing position but had no cannon. With Donelson's approval Carnes led his battery to the designated location and commenced an enfilade fire on Starkweather. Although equipped with 6-pound smoothbore cannon firing at close to their maximum range, Carnes' actions contributed to Starkweather's decision to retire.

The Confederates moved onto Starkweather's original position, but they could not sustain the momentum of their attack. They advanced into a setting sun amid a storm of musketry and canister. Having taken two hill positions defended by artillery and infantry they now confronted a third. The intensity of the fighting continued to escalate in tandem with the defenders' stubbornness. The 1st Tennessee again attempted a flanking move. It moved into a depression on Starkweather's left, but exceptionally intense fire decimated its ranks. A charge by the 1st Wisconsin captured the Tennessee regiment's colors and completed its repulse. Physical and psychological exhaustion contributed to the Confederates' inability to drive home another assault. Starkweather's second position held, and Maney's spent regiments—even with Stewart's support on their left—could not convert their initial successes into a more complete victory.

Visibility note: The ridge immediately west of this position marks Starkweather's second line. The ground slopes downward to the north. At the base of the tree line along this slope a stone wall is clearly visible, particularly in the late fall through early spring months. The wall marks the engagement area between the 1st Wisconsin and 1st Tennessee.

Vignette 1: "This disposition of my forces was hardly complete before General Maney's brigade attacked me in front, assisted by a battery, and General Donelson's [Stewart's] brigade again attacked on the extreme right, the enemy at the same time placing a battery on my extreme left, upon a well-chosen position to flank me. The flank movement on the left was prevented by Stone's battery shelling the position chosen, and Donelson's brigade was again forced to retire by the well-directed and continuous fire of the Twenty-fourth Illinois and Seventy-ninth Pennsylvania. I then ordered the Twenty-first Wisconsin to fire and charge the front, but, being a new regiment, their colonel being severely wounded and their major killed at about the time such order was given, no field officer was left to carry the command into execution, although several companies, hearing the order, attempted to obey it, but being sorely pressed by the brigade and battery in front, it retired in some disorder and confusion. I immediately advanced the First Wisconsin to the front, supported by an oblique fire from the Seventy-ninth and with canister from my artillery, and held such position until many of the artillery horses were killed and the balance became unmanageable, creating such confusion that proper discharges could not be continued. Other regiments on my right at his time were retiring, and being unable to obtain any support from them, I ordered the Seventy-ninth, Twenty-fourth, and First to hold their positions, while Stone's battery, of four guns, and Bush's battery, of two (all that was manageable), were retired to a new and safer position. The retirement was made in good order, and the fire from the artillery again opened." (COL John C. Starkweather, 28th Brigade, *OR*, series I, vol. XVI, *Part I*, 1155-56.)

Vignette 2: "We did not recoil, but our line was fairly hurled back by the leaden hail that was poured into our very faces. Eight color-bearers were killed at one discharge of their cannon. We were right up among the very wheels of their Napoleon guns. It was death to retreat now to either side. Our Lieutenant Colonel Patterson halloed to charge and take their guns, and we were soon in a hand-to-hand fight—every man for himself—using the butts of our guns and bayonets. One side would waver and fall back a few yards and would rally, when the other side would fall back, leaving the four Napoleon guns; and yet the battle raged. Such obstinate fighting I never had seen before or since. The guns were discharging so rapidly that it seemed the earth itself was in a volcanic uproar. The iron storm passed through our ranks, mangling and tearing men to pieces. The very air seemed full stifling smoke and fire which seemed the very pit of hell, peopled by contending demons." (Sam R. Watkins, *"Co. Aytch": A Side Show of the Big Show*, New York: Collier Books, 1962, 53.)

Starkweather's artillery: The previous excerpts are confusing in terms of the number of cannon the batteries assigned to Starkweather's brigade possessed. To clarify, Stone's battery included two 6 pounders, two Parrott rifles, and two 3.8" rifled guns. Bush's battery comprised two 6 pounders, two 12 pounders, and two 3.8" rifled guns. With 12 cannon total Starkweather had the greatest organic support of any brigade on the battlefield. However this number diminished through losses. When Starkweather withdrew from his first position (Stand 7) the loss of gunners and horses complicated the artillery's retreat. Infantry and the surviving gunners dragged as many caissons, limbers, and cannon rearward as possible, but several cannon were abandoned. Stone left four cannon, while Bush appears to have lost two. The remaining six pieces were then reemployed as three sections supporting Starkweather's second line, whose left held the stone wall.

Teaching points: Terrain use, fire support, combat leadership, withdrawal under fire, situational awareness, psychological experience of combat, actions on the objective

Route to Stand 8: Follow the path in a southerly direction along the ridgeline to Whites Road. Cross the road and pass through the gate (cross the fence if the gate is locked). Continue south on the park path to Park Informational Marker 10. Face east.

Stand 8
Stewart's Brigade

Location: Park Informational Marker 10 (hill—UTM grid 7862 7126).

Situation: Initially Stewart's brigade deployed with the rest of Cheatham's division into Walker's Bend. When Donelson attacked and became caught in a crossfire, Cheatham intended Maney to attack Parsons' battery and Stewart to advance in support of Donelson. However, once Maney attacked, Cheatham became absorbed in the fight for the open hill and issued no further orders to Stewart, who refused to act without instructions. Thus Donelson's initial attack occurred without support from Stewart. As Donelson prepared to renew his attack at about 1515, he requested Stewart's assistance. In response, the five regiments of Stewart's brigade finally advanced.

Stewart crossed the Chaplin River and formed his five regiments—from left to right, the 31st, 33d, 24th, 5th, and 4th Tennessee—into a single line. This line advanced over the hill between Stands 1 and 3. As it moved forward it filled the gap between Donelson and Maney's brigades. Although it did not directly participate in the fight for the open hill (Stand 5), the presence of Stewart's regiments helped Maney to rally his brigade and overrun Parsons' battery. The left of Stewart's brigade line also finally linked with Donelson's regiments after their second failed attack toward Harris' battery. However Stewart, too, advanced without his brigade's battery. It had been detached to reply to long-range Union artillery fire during the prebattle artillery duel.

As Maney's brigade attacked first the cornfield (Stand 6) and then Starkweather's left (Stand 7), the 4th and 5th Tennessee of Stewart's brigade attacked toward this location. In 1862, the tree line immediately east of this position did not exist, and the Tennessee regiments were in plain view as they advanced. They angled toward Stone's battery to the right and become intermingled with Maney's 6th Tennessee. Amid canister fire from the battery and musket fire from the supporting 79th Pennsylvania the Confederates reached the hillcrest and fired into the battery's crew. The latter fled, but a small group of Union infantry remanned the guns and drove the Confederates back with close-range canister fire.

By 1615, although forced to retreat, Donelson's, Stewart's, and Maney's combined efforts placed pressure all along Starkweather's line and nearly broke it. Indeed while Stewart and Maney prepared to renew their assault with artillery support from Carnes and Turner, Starkweather withdrew to the ridgeline to his rear. Stewart's brigade participated in the final but unsuccessful attacks by Cheatham's division on this new line.

Vignette: "By four o'clock, when the battle was thickest, the odds were fearful. "There they come again!" and filing out of the edge of the woods was the long even line of the enemy once more. All that afternoon's slaughter seemed only to have augmented their numbers. One, two, three lines of battle, fresh men every time, with the precision of a parade they came; in their front rank rode a general on a white horse, conspicuous for his gallantry; around him were clustered a numerous staff; the rebel ensign floated haughtily above. Our columns shattered, our ammunition almost gone, our companions bleeding about us; but the thinned and wasted ranks closed up yet once more, and with bated breath waited the word of command. In the awful silence of that moment you could hear the cannoneers, away on our left, drive their canister home. A moment the oppressive stillness lasted. Then the fires of death were lighted, the earth trembled with the shock of artillery and the volleyed thunders of the musketry as they poured their leaden hail into that 'valley of the shadow of death.' 'Pale horse' and rider and flag went down together; yet their column, with firm step, and leveled pieces, surged on. Our cartridge boxes were empty, so we borrowed from the dead; our rifles heated with the incessant firing that we could not clutch the barrel with our hands; shrouded by smoke, deafened by the rattle of musketry, our throats parched and husky." (Private E.K. Martin, 79th Pennsylvania, quoted in Geoffrey L. Blankenmeyer, "The Seventy-ninth Pennsylvania at Perryville," in essays on Perryville at <http://www.battleofperryville.com/> accessed 6 March 2003.)

Teaching points: Command responsibility, battle command, situational awareness, fire support, psychological effect of combat.

Route to Stand 9: Continue along the path in a southerly direction to Park Informational Marker 11.

Stand 9

Rousseau's Division

Location: Park Informational Marker 11 (hill—UTM grid 7876 7108).

Situation: This position lies close to the center of the Union I Corps when it initially deployed. The corps began arriving on the field before 1100. While the corps commander reported in person to Buell at army headquarters senior division commander BG Lovell H. Rousseau oversaw the corps' deployment. He subsequently began moving forces into the line of battle in response to the 1230 Confederate artillery bombardment. Except for Terrill's movement onto the open hill (Stand 5), Rousseau was directly responsible for the basic Union dispositions immediately before the Confederate attack. Note the positioning of infantry and artillery on key heights. This deployment contributed to Bragg's intended envelopment devolving into a collection of brigade fights for select hills and ridgelines.

The 33d Ohio deployed forward of this point with skirmishers along the hill line near the park entrance (Stand 1). These soldiers fell back when Wharton's cavalry swept along the hill from the north. The 33d Ohio belonged to COL Leonard A. Harris' brigade of Rousseau's 3d Division deployed on the hill south of this location and readily identifiable by the twin utility poles and power lines. Starkweather deployed his units on the left, concentrated near Bush's and Stone's batteries (Stand 7). COL George Webster's brigade formed to the rear on high ground overlooking the Widow Gibson Site with Captain Samuel J. Harris' battery forward (Stand 17). Its field of fire encompassed some of the ground to the front of this location.

No Union soldiers initially occupied this position, despite the close proximity of three brigades. Harris' and Starkweather's two brigades did not have enough troops to man a continuous line between their positions. Donelson's first attack aimed directly into this gap. The low ground and creek flowing from the direction of the park entrance provided an avenue of approach that the Confederates exploited in their drive toward Harris' battery. However neither Donelson nor his brigade commanders realized they had struck along a unit boundary and threatened to split I Corps at its center.

When the 16th Tennessee emerged from the low ground where Parsons' battery enfiladed him (Stand 2) the Confederates encountered the 33d Ohio formed behind a fence. After a brief melee the Union regiment retreated, leaving behind considerable casualties, including its commander,

152

Lieutenant Colonel Oscar F. Moore. MG McCook, commanding I Corps and observing this action from the Widow Gibson Site, reacted by trying to close the gap between Harris' and Starkweather's brigades. On his right he personally ordered the 2d Ohio forward to support the retreating 33d Ohio and extend the left flank of Harris' brigade. On his own initiative Harris also reinforced his center. McCook also directed Rousseau to move a regiment of Starkweather's brigade toward Harris. Rousseau led the 24th Illinois toward this location with skirmishers advanced.

Commander profile: Lovell H. Rousseau was born in 1818 in Lincoln County, Kentucky. At age 15 he lost his father to cholera. He abandoned his formal education and worked for a period as a common laborer building roads in Kentucky. Later he settled in Lexington and studied law. He moved to Indiana where he opened his own practice and entered politics. He was elected to the state legislature in 1844. During the Mexican War he commanded a company with distinction, particularly at Buena Vista. In 1849 he moved his law practice to Kentucky where he soon became a prominent figure in both the General Assembly and the state senate. When the Civil War began he resigned his political office and joined the military. In summer 1861 he recruited a large Union force of infantry, cavalry, and artillery at Camp Joe Holt in Indiana. This success led to his appointment as colonel, commander of the 3d Kentucky Infantry, and subsequent promotion to brigadier general in October. He commanded a brigade in the Army of the Ohio and fought at Shiloh. Afterward he participated in the siege of Corinth and in operations against Chattanooga, during which he assumed a division command. Rousseau accompanied the army on its retreat to Louisville. At Perryville he was the senior division commander, I Corps, and he was largely responsible for the corps' deployment. During the battle his leadership and presence on the battlefield helped to prevent his division's collapse. Moreover he became one of the few Union general officers present to receive a promotion for his actions during the battle of Perryville. As a major general, he continued to perform ably at Stones River and at the subsequent Tullahoma campaign. From 1863 until 1865 Rousseau served as a district commander in Nashville, Tennessee. During this period he also led one of the more successful Union cavalry raids of the war and successfully defended Nashville during the 1864 Confederate invasion of Tennessee. After the war he resigned from the military and pursued his political career at the national level. As a congressman, however, he was forced to resign after beating another representative with a cane. Rousseau rejoined the military and served in Alaska and Louisiana before his death in 1869.

Donelson's brigade continued to advance, driving the 2d and 33d Ohio back with effective volleys. Watching the Confederates threaten to outflank Harris' brigade Webster ordered his 50th Ohio forward in support. Most of the regiment's soldiers, however, refused to move. Concerned about the poor quality of weapons and training among his other regiments Webster opted to rally the 2d Ohio (Harris' brigade) and return it to the fight.

The combined efforts of three Union brigades and supporting artillery finally broke Donelson's charge. However this location remained a focal point of Confederate interest. Donelson made two further charges over the same ground, the second occurring with elements from Stewart's brigade and his remaining fresh regiments finally recalled from their previous battery support mission. However Union firepower broke up these attacks with heavy casualties. In the forefront of each of Donelson's attacks the 16th Tennessee suffered particularly high losses: 46 killed, 170 wounded, 3 missing, or 59 percent of the unit's strength.

Union infantry weapons: Union soldiers at Perryville were not uniformly equipped with the latest rifled muskets. Instead the most newly formed regiments received an array of weapons from available stocks shortly after being mustered. Muskets varied among regiments and, in some cases, within the regiments themselves. Many weapons were smoothbore muskets or refurbished pieces whose quality varied considerably. They included Austrian, French, Belgian, and British weapons in addition to an assortment of American-made muskets, some dating from the 1840s. Calibers ranged from .577 to .71. Some weapons misfired or did not otherwise function properly. In Webster's brigade, for example, the 80th Indiana was armed with older substandard smoothbores with weak mainsprings. The tendency of new soldiers to fire their ramrods in the heat of battle or load weapons several times without firing them only compounded the problems inherent to these muskets. In the latter case the weapon might not fire at all or might explode if fired. (Note: This information was obtained from a unit data base the park manager compiled and maintained.)

Vignette: "I then returned to Harris' brigade, hearing that the enemy was close upon him, and found that the Thirty-third Ohio had been ordered farther to the front by General McCook and was then engaged with the enemy, and needed support. General McCook in person ordered the Second Ohio to its support, and sent direct to me to order up the Twenty-fourth Illinois also, Captain [August] Mauff, commanding. I led the Twenty-fourth Illinois, in line of battle, immediately forward, and it was promptly deployed as skirmishers by its commander, and went gallantly into action on the left of the Thirty-third Ohio. The Second Ohio, moving up to the support of the Thirty-third Ohio, was engaged before it arrived on the ground where the Thirty-third was fighting. The Thirty-eighth

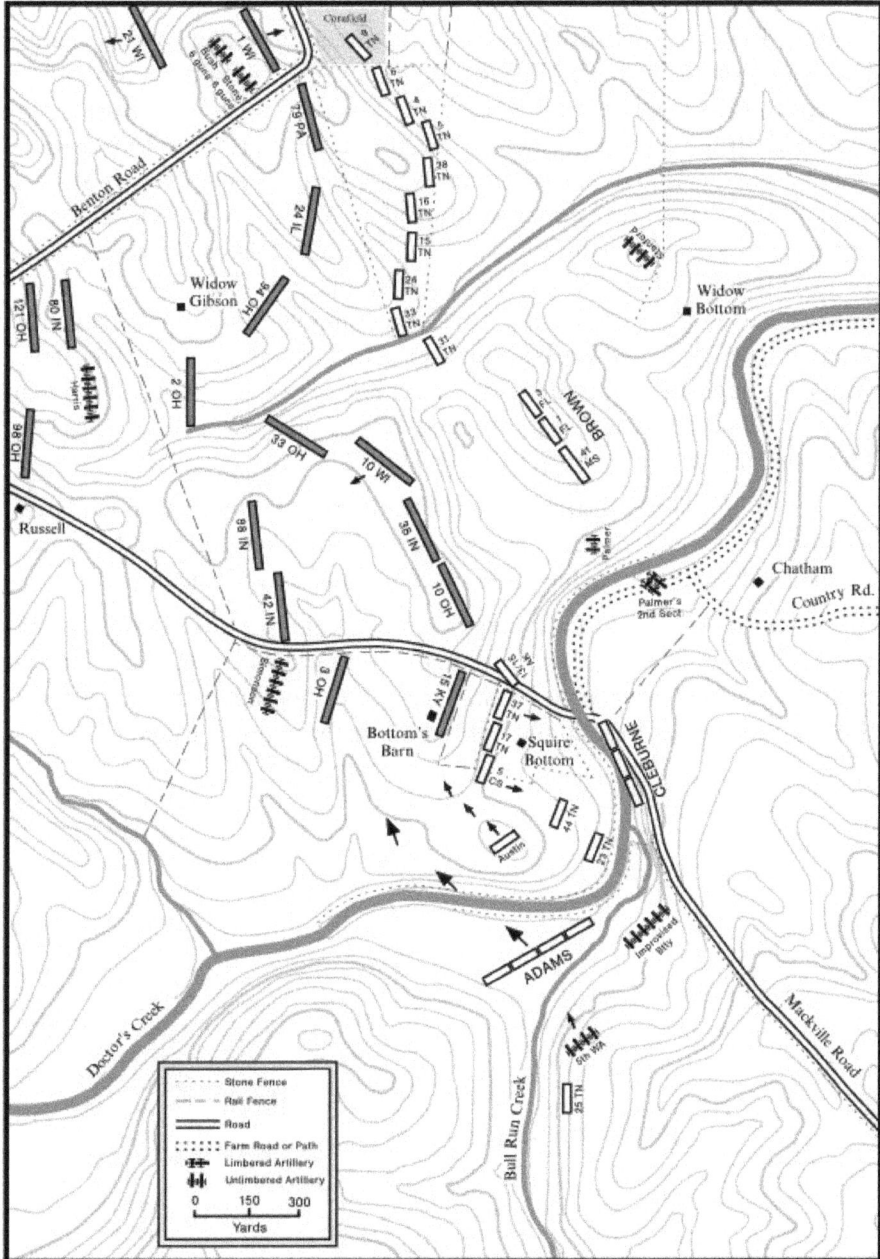

Map 9. Buckner and Anderson's attack, 1545.

155

Indiana, Col. [Benjamin] F. Scribner commanding, then went gallantly into action on the right of the Second Ohio. Then followed in support the Ninety-fourth Ohio (Colonel [Joseph W.] Frizell). I wish here to say of this regiment on the left and center by the continuous and persistent assaults of the enemy, and knowing if our left was turned our position was lost and a total rout of the army corps would follow, I felt the importance of my presence there, and could not look after the interests of the Seventeenth Brigade [COL William H. Lytle's brigade]; but the whole division fought under the eye of Major-General McCook, commanding First Army Corps, Army of the Ohio, and I felt no fear that anything necessary for its safety would be neglected; and, besides, Lieut. F.J. Jones, my assistant adjutant general, was often sent to learn its condition." (BG Lovell H. Rousseau, 3d Division, *OR*, series I, vol. XVI, *Part I*, 1046-47.)

Teaching points: Terrain analysis, troop deployment, unit boundaries, situational awareness/understanding, battle command, commander's place on the battlefield, unit behavior under fire, soldier equipment.

Route to Stand 10: Follow the path heading east toward the park entrance. Before reaching Park Informational Marker 12 (Stand 2), a gravel pathway leads south across a small creek. Follow this path until it forks. Take the left (east) fork up the hill to Park Informational Marker 13.

Buckner and Anderson's Attack

Stand 10
Lumsden's Battery

Location: Park Informational Marker 13 (hill—UTM grid 7920 7114).

Situation: Shortly after Donelson's initial attack ended at 1430 COL Thomas M. Jones' brigade advanced toward COL Leonard A. Harris' 9th Brigade (Stand 12). In support Captain Charles L. Lumsden led his Alabama battery across Doctor's Creek onto this hill. From here Lumsden commenced firing in support of his parent brigade on Harris' line. Indeed Jones' brigade was the first Confederate unit to launch an attack supported from the outset with its artillery. Lumsden provided counterbattery fire against the 5th Battery, Indiana Light Artillery, commanded by Captain Peter Simonson. He tried to suppress the Union cannon firing into the ranks of COL Jones' brigade. Initially much of this fire had little effect. Although the terrain between this position and that of Harris' brigade appears level, there are two depressions. Moreover the nature of the terrain made the Union battery appear much closer than its actual distance. This optical illusion resulted in Lumsden's canister falling short with little effect. When Jones' brigade withdrew Lumsden accompanied it.

Unit note: Lumsden's battery formed in 1861. By the battle of Perryville its personnel had become an efficient team through continuous service together. However Perryville marked the first major engagement for the battery. Its principal weaponry comprised four Napoleons. These 12-pound smoothbore cannon had a bore diameter of 4.62 inches and weighed 1 ton. At 5-degree elevation they could fire solid shot to 1,600 meters, case shot to 1,100 meters at 3.4 degrees, or common shell to 1,300 meters at 3.45 degrees. Despite these ranges this cannon more commonly engaged targets at 1,000 meters or less. It also employed canister against personnel targets under 500 meters. A trained crew could achieve a rate of fire of two aimed shots per minute or up to four canister rounds in the same time. The Napoleon proved to be one of the most common cannon used by either side during the Civil War. Compared to the rifled artillery the smoothbore fired a heavier shot with greater destructive power against linear formations. Rifled pieces had better accuracy and longer range but less killing power, and their performance with canister rounds was not as effective as the smoothbore. These qualities made the Napoleon more effective as a defensive weapon.

Teaching points: Terrain analysis, fire support.

Route to Stand 11: Follow the park path past the Widow Bottom Site (Park Informational Marker 14) along the Doctor's Creek Trail to Park Informational Marker 15. This site identifies where Jones' brigade crossed the creek and formed for battle. Turn right and follow the path up the hill toward Jones Ridge (Park Informational Marker 16). This route traces the movement of Jones' brigade as it advanced to contact. Note how the hill provides cover to an attacking force and also restricts what can be seen forward.

En route discussion point: Mobility obstacle represented by Doctor's Creek on linear formations.

Stand 11
Jones' Brigade/Brown's Brigade/Wood's Brigade

Location: Park Informational Marker 16 (hill—UTM grid 7902 7089).

Situation 1: Bragg's battle plan envisioned an attack by echelon from the Confederate right to left starting with Cheatham's division. The firing that surrounded Donelson's and then Maney's advance triggered the advance of Jones' brigade shortly after 1430, although neither the division or wing commander directly ordered it. Initially deployed on the heights west of Doctor's Creek the brigade crossed the creek (Park Informational Marker 15), formed its three untested regiments in a single line, and advanced. Before reaching this position, however, the brigade did not know the Union forces' disposition. Nor could the brigade commanders see the enemy until they reached this hill. At this point Jones' brigade abruptly encountered elements of Harris' and Lytle's brigades and Simonson's battery at less than 300 meters' distance, separated from the Confederates by the deep depression and sinkhole. Receiving infantry and artillery fire as soon as they became visible, Jones' regiments made repeated efforts to advance into the depression. Union firepower shattered each attempt and finally forced the Confederates to retire. Jones' brigade did no more fighting for the day, suffering an estimated 50-percent casualties. The 34th Mississippi, for example, entered the fight with 300 men and lost 24 killed, 125 wounded—including its commander—and one missing.

Situation 2: BG John C. Brown's brigade initially formed on the heights west of Doctor's Creek behind Jones' brigade. While Jones attacked Brown's regiments lay on the ground enduring intermittent Union artillery fire. Following Jones' withdrawal Brown ordered his brigade forward at about 1530. He advanced his three regiments over the same path as Jones' brigade and attacked Harris' line from this position. Only the 1st Florida had any battle experience. Upon reaching this position, Brown's men came under intense Union musket fire from the 10th Wisconsin and 38th Indiana. An attempt was made to bring a section of cannon forward and deploy to the left of this location. It quickly became the Union infantry's principal target, and many of the gunners and horses became casualties after firing only a few rounds. Other battery personnel advanced and withdrew the cannon. Brown's regiments then engaged the Union line in a prolonged firefight, amid dwindling ammunition supplies. Unlike Jones' earlier experience, however, Brown's brigade did not experience close-range artillery fire. Simonson's battery had withdrawn after the prior

Confederate attack, having run short of ammunition and losing significant casualties among its gunners.

Brown ultimately succeeded against Harris. As the firefight continued both sides ran low on ammunition. Brown, however, was able to resupply his regiments, while Harris could not find additional supplies forward of the Russell House. The Union line also faced new threats from other Confederate forces to its front and flanks. Unable to hold his position Harris withdrew, and Brown's regiments advanced through the depression forward of this position. Brown and his successor as brigade commander, however, lay wounded.

Vignette: "The 1st Brigade marched out and Oh Lord. Shells soon came tumbling amongst us. Many knocking men out of their places, wounded several. Rifle firing began in front . . . we could see for miles in front of us, men getting enough of this, no way to hit back. Soon we saw our line advance and with the wild yells they cleared the field and crossed the dry creek bed. 'Attention' rang along our line; up jumped the 1st Brigade. Gen'l Brown lined us up as if on Drill. Drew his sword and with the command 'Forward, Guide right, March' we started from a march to trot and yelling like the others. We were soon at a run, cut into the brambles, high as our heads, and in terrible bad order. Gen'l Brown stopped to get the Third Fla in line. *Cussed* us from being too quick. 'Dress up or you will be cut to pieces in such order;' the men and officers soon were in line.

"We again started, and bullets began to whistle, men to fall fast. 'Close up.' . . . We relieved ... [a] Brigade who cheered us as they moved to the right. . . . We now lay down fire engaging the enemy, firing steady. Gen'l Brown hit, also Col. Church. It hit his shoulder, collarbone broken. The groans of dying and the cries for water of the wounded were terrible. I am nearly killed enemy giving way on all sides." (Lieutenant John L. Inglis, 3d Florida, quoted in "El Escribano," *The St. Augustine Journal of History*, vol. 23, Saint Augustine Historical Society, 1986, 85-86.)

Confederate command issue: BG J. Patton Anderson's division comprised COL Jones', BG Brown's, BG Daniel W. Adams', and COL Samuel Powell's brigades. At Perryville this formation did not fight as a single command. When Bragg arrived on the battlefield in the morning of 8 October he found the Confederate forces in a defensive deployment. Determined to attack he directed the redeployment of the three Southern divisions on hand. Cheatham moved toward Walker's Bend, and MG Simon B. Buckner moved behind the Chatham Heights east of Doctor's Creek. Anderson's division, however, was split. Brown's and Jones' brigades assumed positions between Buckner and Cheatham while Adams and Powell remained forward of the town of Perryville. This curious disposition ensured a continuous line stretching from the town to Walker's Bend, but it broke the divisional integrity of Anderson's formation. He remained throughout the battle with Adams and Powell. Separated from their division commander, Jones and Brown became by default independent commands and acted independently of their parent division and wing. As the Confederate echelon attack plan unfolded neither brigade commander had a clear sense of when or where to attack. MG William J. Hardee intended for BG Bushrod R. Johnson's larger veteran brigade to lead his wing's advance. Instead Jones advanced first on his own initiative, apparently in response to the sounds of battle from Donelson's attack. Brown similarly attacked without orders after Jones withdrew.

Situation 3: During Brown's engagement with Harris MG Simon B. Buckner decided to commit BG Sterling A.M. Wood's brigade. Buckner sensed an opportunity to carry the ridgeline that Lytle and Harris held through a concerted attack on it. With Confederate forces already engaging the Union position's center and right Buckner directed Wood's regiments to advance and threaten its left. Wood's regiments were well placed to execute this movement. During the earlier redeployment of Confederate forces from Perryville onto the heights overlooking Doctor's Creek, Wood had moved farther north than his parent formation to occupy a hill between Cheatham's division and Jones' and Brown's brigades (see map 6).

There he remained under an intermittent bombardment during the subsequent artillery duel, during which he received an injury that left him unable to command. COL Mark Lowrey, commander, 32d Mississippi, assumed brigade leadership. When ordered forward Lowrey advanced the brigade between Brown's and Donelson's brigades. However, the crowded battlespace afforded sufficient room for barely two regiments to advance abreast. The 32d Mississippi and the 33d Alabama accordingly led the brigade.

The appearance of this new Confederate forced contributed to Harris' decision to withdraw. As the Union infantry retired from the ridgeline Lowrey advanced on the position that Webster's brigade and battery held (Stand 17). However, enemy artillery and infantry fire soon forced his temporary retreat, just as it had Donelson's previous attacks on the same position. Lowrey rallied his regiments and launched another attack supported by elements of Donelson's and Stewart's brigades. This concerted effort finally triggered the collapse of Webster's position.

Teaching points: Situational awareness, chain of command, mass, strength of defense, catastrophic loss, nature of the infantry firefight.

Route to Stand 12: Follow the park path into the depression, past the sinkhole, and up the heights to Park Informational Marker 17.

Stand 12
Harris's Brigade

Location: Park Informational Marker 17 (hill—UTM grid 7884 7076).

Situation: Harris's brigade deployed along the northern end of this ridge, his right flank anchored by COL William H. Lytle's brigade and his left stretching toward the low ground between this position and Stand 9. Simonson's battery provided immediate fire support from this location while the 10th Wisconsin deployed to its left. The initial Confederate attack by Donelson's brigade threatened Harris's left flank. He responded by pushing forces toward the low ground over which Donelson tried to advance. The fire of Harris's infantry and Simonson's cannon helped to repel the attack.

A new threat soon appeared without warning on the ridge directly in front of this location (Stand 11). There Jones' brigade tried to advance across the depression and assault the Union line. With support from Lytle's 10th Ohio and Simonson's battery, the 10th Wisconsin stopped every Confederate attempt to advance. The combination of close-range canister fire and repeated volleys of musket fire shattered Jones' brigade. The encounter, however, left Simonson short of ammunition. His cannon withdrew to a new position astride the Mackville Road (now Hayes May Road) on the next ridgeline. The 38th Indiana moved forward and deployed where the battery had been. The 10th Wisconsin, however, had little ammunition and resorted to taking what could be found from the dead and wounded.

Despite the repulse of Jones' brigade, the Confederates launched a second attack over the same ground. Brown's brigade, too, remained concealed until its regiments appeared on the ridgeline forward of this position (Stand 11). Two cannon that unlimbered along the southern end of the ridge supported them. These guns fired only a few rounds before Harris' muskets felled most of their crews and silenced them. Union firepower, however, proved insufficient to drive back this second Confederate attack. The 38th Indiana and 10th Wisconsin began to run short of ammunition, and the 10th Ohio refused to open fire in their support. Instead the 10th Ohio followed its brigade commander's orders to lie down and conserve fire. When the 10th Wisconsin exhausted its ammunition Harris withdrew it from the ridge. The 38th Indiana subsequently ran out of ammunition and remained in line and under fire with bayonets fixed until it was finally withdrawn. These regiments' retrograde movements uncovered the left flank of this ridgeline, and Brown's Confederate regiments advanced to seize this position.

Vignette: "I saw the necessity of holding my position, with or without support, until the right was successful or compelled to retire, and I determined to do so. If I had been driven back, the Seventeenth Brigade would have been cut off from the main body and in my judgment irretrievably lost. During this part of the engagement Colonel Scribner informed me that the regiment on the right was not firing. I sent Lieutenant [H.E.] Spencer, my aide, to inquire the cause and to ascertain what regiment it was. On his return he informed me that it was the Tenth Ohio, and that Colonel Lytle said that they were reserving their fire. Half an hour afterward I sent to Colonel Lytle, informing him that I had been compelled to withdraw the Tenth Wisconsin for want of ammunition. The withdrawal of this regiment left an interval of 200 yards on the left of the Thirty-eighth Indiana. In the meantime the Fifteenth Kentucky and Third Ohio, which were on the extreme right, were compelled to retire. Colonel Scribner now informed me that they had exhausted their ammunition and were using the ammunition of the dead and wounded. My aide that I sent after support and ammunition informed me that no support could be had and that ammunition was some distance to the rear. The only aide I now had with me having had his horse shot under him, I rode over to Colonel Lytle and informed him of the condition of things. Upon my return to the Thirty-eighth Indiana, I found they had exhausted the cartridges of the dead and wounded. Colonel Scribner then directed his men to fix bayonets and hold the position, which was promptly done. Without a round of ammunition, under a heavy fire in front and an enfilading fire from the artillery, they held their position for twenty-five minutes. Seeing the hopelessness of longer attempting to hold the position I gave the order to retire, which was done in perfect order. I had not fallen back more than 100 yards when a tremendous fire from a column of infantry, which had turned the right flank of the Tenth Ohio, was poured in upon their left and my retiring column." (Excerpt from Harris' report of the battle, quoted in Henry Fales Perry, *History of the Thirty-Eighth Regiment Indiana Volunteer Infantry*, Palo Alto, CA: F.A. Stuart, 1906, 29-30.)

Teaching points: Terrain use, situational awareness, fire support, combat supply, unit coordination.

Route to Stand 13: From Stand 12 walk along the gravel roadway toward the Hayes May Road to Park Informational Marker 19.

Stand 13—Part I
Loomis' Battery

Location: Park Informational Marker 19 (hill—UTM grid 7891 7056).

Situation 1: On the morning of 8 October III Corps attacked BG St. John R. Liddell's Confederate brigade on Peters Hill, which lies south of this position on the Springfield Pike (now Route 150). Union infantry captured and occupied the hill mass while the opposing artillery continued to exchange fire. Captain William Hotchkiss' battery participated from this position. Hotchkiss' cannon belonged to III Corps' cavalry brigade whose skirmishers screened the corps' left flank from this ridgeline. As Rousseau's division of I Corps began to arrive between 1000 and 1100 near the Russell House, Hotchkiss requested support. Rousseau responded by dispatching the 42d Indiana and Captain Cyrus O. Loomis' battery forward to this hill. Both units belonged to COL Lytle's brigade. The Confederates, however, withdrew toward the town of Perryville and the firing ceased. Hotchkiss and the cavalry with him rejoined their parent brigade west of Peters Hill.

Rousseau and his staff rode forward and from this position saw no Confederate forces. They did, however, see dust clouds from the direction of Harrodsburg Pike (now Route 68). Rousseau concluded that the Confederates were retreating from Perryville. He issued orders for his division to obtain water from Doctor's Creek one unit at a time. Lytle's entire brigade now moved forward from the Russell House while the 42d Indiana entered the creek bed, stacked arms, and began refilling canteens. Skirmishers from the 10th Ohio crossed the creek and advanced up the Chatham Heights visible to the east. They continued to move vigorously and spread out along the high ground. The Confederates, however, were not withdrawing. Instead, following Bragg's orders, they were redeploying in preparation for an attack. Moving into position the regiments of Buckner and Anderson's divisions soon encountered Lytle's still-advancing skirmishers. The skirmishers quickly retreated back across the creek and rejoined their regiment.

The appearance of Confederate infantry surprised Rousseau. He hastily began to deploy his division, and Lytle's brigade assumed battle positions along this high ground. Loomis' battery occupied this location with the 10th Ohio directly behind as support. The 3d Ohio extended the line south across the road to the end of the ridgeline where a barn (no longer present) stood. Behind it lay the 15th Kentucky. The 88th Indiana deployed farther to the rear near the Russell House. The 42d Indiana, however, remained in the creek bed.

The Confederate artillery bombardment commenced at 1230, shortly after these dispositions were completed. Several batteries east of Doctor's Creek opened fire. I Corps artillery responded and an artillery duel ensued for nearly an hour. During this engagement Loomis' battery engaged at least two Confederate batteries (Carnes' and Stanford's), forcing one to retire. In this fight the battery demonstrated its ability to conduct rapid and effective fire. However it did so without regard for its ammunition supply. Indeed Loomis continued to fire at suspected targets long after every other battery had ceased fire. Finally having exhausted much of his ammunition, Loomis withdrew his cannon back toward the Russell House. He received orders from the corps commander to conserve his fire exclusively for short-range targets. Unfortunately Loomis' failure to control his fire left Lytle without fire support when faced with the more serious, subsequent threats that the Confederate infantry posed.

*Unit Profile (**Battery A, 1st Michigan Light Artillery Regiment**):* The 1st Michigan Light Artillery comprised 12 batteries, each equipped with six cannon. The regiment, however, served administrative rather than tactical purposes. The regiment's batteries did not serve together as a single unit. Instead they were attached to various infantry formations operating in the west. Battery A mustered into US service in May 1861 under the command of Captain Loomis. During its initial operations in western Virginia the battery gained a reputation for efficiency and discipline. It also received a new issue of six 10-pound Parrott rifled cannon to replace its original brass six-pounders. In December, following the campaign in West Virginia, the battery transferred to Kentucky, joining Buell's Army of the Ohio. When this force moved on Bowling Green in February 1862 Battery A was in the van. Outside the city the battery disrupted Confederate preparations to withdraw with accurate, long-range fire that earned praise from its division commander. Their rapid movement to Bowling Green also prompted a commendatory order from the War Department. Battery A moved to Nashville and remained there into the summer while Buell undertook operations against Chattanooga. The battery often divided into detachments to perform a variety of duties in eastern Tennessee and northern Alabama, including railroad security and participating in efforts to pursue raiding Confederate cavalry. The battery rejoined Buell's command during his retreat to Louisville. In the course of these operations Battery A had become a well-trained veteran unit. Its gun crews were noted for their proficiency.

Route to Stand 14: Walk eastward down the path toward the bridge over Doctor's Creek. Stop in the field immediately across from the H.P. Bottom House, close enough to the water to see the ravine to your left.

Stand 14
42d Indiana/Johnson's Brigade

Location: Open field north of Hayes May Road opposite the H.P. Bottom House (unnumbered Park Informational Markers—UTM grid 7906 7042).

Situation 1: The 42d Indiana moved down from the heights (Stand 13) to the creek bed here to obtain water. The regiment was the first to do so because of its forward position in support of Loomis' battery. It reached the water covered by a skirmish line from the 10th Ohio that moved up the sloping ground east of the creek. The 42d Indiana's 10 companies entered the creek bed north and south of the Mackville Road (now the Hayes May Road). The ravine-like nature of Doctor's Creek north of the road, however, required the soldiers to climb down a steep gradient to reach the water. The entire regiment then stacked arms and began to refill its canteens.

The 10th Ohio skirmishers encountered Confederate infantry on the wooded hills east of this position and withdrew behind Loomis' battery. Shortly thereafter Confederate artillery began their 1230 bombardment, and Union artillery answered. Throughout the duel of cannon that followed the 42d Indiana remained in the creek bed. Upon its conclusion, with no further evidence of combat other than Loomis' sporadic shots, the regiment resumed its efforts to obtain water. It stacked arms and some soldiers began to eat. In this condition of repose the regiment was ill prepared to receive an attack, particularly since there were no friendly troops between the Indiana soldiers and the Confederates.

After 1400 the Union soldiers began to hear nearby infantry forming into line of battle. They believed a friendly regiment was taking position on their left. In fact the sounds emanated from Confederate units preparing to attack, probably Jones' brigade advancing to attack Harris' line (Stand 11). The ground to the 42d Indiana's front inclined gently into a wooded ridgeline. Here BG Bushrod R. Johnson's brigade deployed to attack. To the right of the Union regiment, on the high ground overlooking the H.P. Bottom House and road bridge, another Confederate brigade deployed in preparation for an attack. BG Daniel W. Adams commanded this unit that included Captain Cuthbert H. Slocomb's six-gun battery.

The Indiana soldiers did not notice these developments until a small party seeking water wandered south and drew fire from sharpshooters in Adams' brigade. This encounter triggered flanking fire from Slocomb's battery into the ravine. Johnson's brigade began to advance down the slope toward the creek with fire support from its brigade artillery. The 42d Indiana soldiers retrieved their arms and attempted to form a battle line amid great confusion. Resistance proved short, especially in the absence of Loomis' battery, which withdrew after expending much of its ammunition during the artillery duel. The 42d Indiana broke, its soldiers seeking refuge behind the ridgeline where Loomis had been. Those companies trapped in the ravine, however, first faced a steep climb up the creek's bank before moving across the open slope to their rear. They did so under fire and suffered considerable casualties. The regiment rallied behind the shelter of the ridge before assuming a position farther to the rear.

Note: The Confederate soldiers who initially fired on the 42d Indiana belonged to the 14th Battalion, Louisiana Sharpshooters. The unit commander believed his target to be Union, but the brigade commander, BG Adams, remained unconvinced until the 42d Indiana returned fire. This uncertainty regarding the location of Union and other Confederate forces led to the subsequent fratricide against Johnson's brigade.

Vignette: "The men were lying around with their guns stacked in perfect confidence when suddenly a few stray shots from some of the enemy whose impatience to go at their game got ahead of the word of command, came whizzing by us. Colonel [James G.] Jones immediately called 'attention' and the men sprang to their arms. The enemy immediately poured down a volley of musketry, and the cannon which we had thought silenced commenced sweeping the ravine with a terrible shower of grape. They did not get our range for the first three or four rounds, and consequently, although the shot struck the ground all around us, but few were struck.

"It was a most terrible position in which any regiment could be placed. In front of us an enemy concealed, firing volley after volley; on our right a battery of artillery throwing grape with little accuracy to be sure but all the time getting nearer the range; behind us a steep precipice up which the men must climb exposed all the time to the fire of the enemy's sharpshooters; when was a regiment in a closer place." (James Maynard Shanklin, *"Dearest Lizzie": The Civil War as Seen Through the Eyes of Lieutenant Colonel James Maynard Shanklin of Southwest Indiana's Own 42nd Regiment, Indiana Volunteer Infantry*, Kenneth P. McCutchan, ed., Evansville, IN: Friends of Willard Library Press, 1988, 228-29. Note: Shanklin held the rank of major at Perryville.)

Situation 2: Shortly after 1430 Johnson prepared to advance as part of the echelon attack that General Bragg adopted. Deployed onto the heights east of this position Johnson's six regiments had not yet begun to move when division commander MG Simon B. Buckner intervened.

He removed the 17th Tennessee to support the brigade's battery. He also changed the direction of the brigade's advance from straight ahead to a left oblique. Instead of the brigade crossing Doctor's Creek and attacking the Union line on Jones' immediate left Buckner intended to attack farther south, exploiting the low ground and trees along Doctor's Creek to minimize the troops' exposure to Union cannon.

The new orders, however, were not well understood and were poorly executed. Confusion resulted. The 37th Tennessee followed its original orders and marched straight ahead. It soon encountered the 42d Indiana trapped in the ravine. The 25th Tennessee, 44th Tennessee, and 5th Confederate Regiments quickly became disorganized and separated from one another as they navigated rolling terrain and fences. They advanced across the front of Adams' brigade and Slocomb's battery, moving in the same general direction as the retreating 42d Indiana and the previously withdrawn 10th Ohio skirmishers. The Confederate gunners opened fire on Johnson's regiments, believing them to be more Union soldiers. The three regiments responded by charging the cannon. The firing stopped, but Adams ordered the 25th and 44th Tennessee to remain with the battery. Neither unit belonged to his brigade or parent division.

Johnson remained in the rear, unaware of the breakdown of his brigade's attack. He now ordered his remaining two regiments forward. These additional forces became intermingled with the original attackers. The steep banks of Doctor's Creek channeled the entire mass farther south toward this point where the Mackville Road crossed the creek and there was a gentler gradient. The Confederates advanced in a disorganized state toward Lytle's brigade that was deployed on the high ground astride and south of the road. Although at least two batteries fired in support of Johnson his regiments nevertheless became pinned along a stone fence halfway up the hill near the H.P. Bottom House. There they remained, exchanging fire with the Union line until, having exhausted their ammunition, they withdrew.

Vignette 1: "We advanced about 200 yards, when from the brow of a hill we had reached we saw the enemy in line below and received a heavy volley from them; simultaneously my men fired upon the enemy, who immediately fell back. Several of my men were wounded on the first fire by the small arms of the enemy, shells and grape from their batteries, which swept around us in perfect showers. I commanded my men to reload immediately, and they continued to load and fire until we discovered that we were separated from the brigade, which was to us a matter of no little surprise, as we had received no command but forward. A house, outhouses, and orchard were situated immediately to our right, which

170

obstructed the view and prevented us from observing the movements of the left of the brigade. Ascertaining that it had moved in the direction of the woods to the left, I commanded my men to march by the left flank in that direction. After passing the orchard we discovered a regiment emerging from the woods in the rear in the direction from which the brigade first moved; we wheeled into line on the right of what turned out to be the Seventeenth Tennessee and advanced to a stone wall in the hollow below, which inclosed a house, several hundred yards to the left of the house first alluded to. Colonel [Albert S.] Marks took his position behind a wall running parallel with the hollow. I filed right and took my position behind a post and rail fence running diagonally to the wall; here we were met with an almost overwhelming storm of lead from a corn or cane field near by. I commanded my men to mount the fence and take position behind a stone wall which separated the yard from the field, running parallel with and about 50 yards distant from the wall behind which the Seventeenth was stationed. They promptly and cheerfully obeyed the order and immediately opened upon the enemy, I hope with some effect. The fire raged with unabated fury for about one hour and a half, when, our ammunition being exhausted, we were compelled to cease firing, but were soon relieved by General [Patrick R.] Cleburne, but not until the enemy had almost ceased to fire." (COL Moses White, 37th Tennessee, *OR*, series 1, vol. XVI, *Part I*, 1131-32.)

Vignette 2: "We were again ordered forward and occupied a ravine, and there remained until General Cheatham's division on our right made a charge, when we were ordered to advance upon the enemy and oblique to the left of our then present position.

"The regiment was promptly in motion and charged rapidly over the hill and forward through a corn field and over a large meadow, where we were exposed to an enfilading fire coming from the enemy on our right and a battery upon our left. Obliquing to the left here we suffered terribly from the fire of the batteries right and left of us and the sharpshooters of the enemy posted in the orchard and behind the rock fence on our right. We charged rapidly up the hill with fixed bayonets to silence and take the battery on our left, and having gained the top of the hill we found it to be the Washington Artillery, and immediately reported to them that they had been playing upon their own men, when the firing ceased. This battery was supported by Brigadier General Adams' brigade, who ordered the Forty-fourth and Twenty-fifth Tennessee Regiments to remain there to assist him, as the enemy was reported to be advancing on him to the left in heavy force." (COL John S. Fulton, 44th Tennessee Infantry, *OR*, series 1,

Situation 3: As Johnson's regiments began to exhaust their ammunition the brigade commander requested permission to withdraw. Buckner agreed and committed BG Cleburne's brigade to assume the position that Johnson's regiments soon would vacate. Moving down from the heights east of Doctor's Creek, Cleburne crossed the creek. He assumed a position behind Johnson and extending to the Mackville Road (now Hayes May Road). The 15th Kentucky occupied the heights east of this location and south of the road. The 10th Ohio occupied the heights north of the road (Stand 13), but at the time of Cleburne's advance this regiment lay face down just behind the crest. The 15th Kentucky's position thus became Cleburne's principal target. He deployed the 13th/15th Arkansas at right angles to Johnson's line. From this position it could engage the 15th Kentucky while Johnson's regiments maneuvered to the rear. As they did so Cleburne's remaining regiments moved into their vacated positions. With this movement under way Slocomb's battery deployed forward to engage the 15th Kentucky's right flank. The 15th Kentucky finally retired under this pressure. Cleburne prepared for a further advance up the hill.

Vignette: "The enemy lined the ridges west and south of the creek. They were strongly posted behind stone walls and were keeping up a rapid fire on the brigade of General Johnson, which was trying to ascend the ridges in the face of this galling fire. We now received the order to advance quickly to his support. We advanced down the open ground into the creek bottom exposed to a heavy fire of artillery and small arms. I ordered the brigade to advance in double time and we were soon in the rocky bed of the creek so immediately under the enemy that their fire passed harmlessly over us. General Johnson's brigade was still on the side of the acclivity in our front, exchanging a rapid fire with the enemy. By moving the Fifteenth Arkansas Regiment a short distance farther to the right of my line, and then changing front forward on the left company, I placed this regiment against a stonewall lining the Mackville road. This movement placed the Fifteenth Arkansas on the hillside with its line at right angle to that of General Johnson and the enemy, and so situated as to give me a flank fire on the enemy's left without being myself exposed at the same time. General Buckner got a battery into such a position to the left of General Johnson's line of battle as to enfilade the stonewall from behind which the enemy were firing. About this time General Johnson's brigade had exhausted their ammunition and fell back into the bed of the creek; at the same time I moved forward and occupied the position previously occupied by his brigade. On examination I found the enemy had been driven back from the stone wall near the crest of the ridge and were now sheltering themselves behind the crest. I ordered the Fifteenth Arkansas back to their position on the right of my line and sent forward skirmishers to reconnoiter the enemy's line preparatory to an advance." (BG Patrick R. Cleburne, *OR*, series I, vol. LII, *Part I*, 51-52.)

Teaching points: Situational awareness, force protection, retreat under fire, coordination, fratricide, maneuver, command responsibilities, chain of command, passage of lines

Route back to Stand 13: Return up the path you descended to Park Informational Marker 19.

Stand 13—Part II
Lytle's Brigade

Location: Park Informational Marker 19 (hill—UTM grid 7891 7056).

Situation: Lytle's position marked the right flank of I Corps. There was no direct link with the III Corps elements on Peters Hill. However, the high ground made Lytle's position a strong one. When Jones' brigade attacked (Stand 11), the 10th Ohio supported Harris' brigade and helped shatter the Confederate ranks. The attack of Johnson's regiments, however, focused Lytle's attention on his right. There the 3d Ohio pinned the Confederates along a stone fence but at the cost of considerable casualties. In addition to Johnson's infantry regiment firing up the hill from stone walls near the Bottom House Lytle received two batteries' attention. Captain Putnam Darden's battery (Johnson's brigade) deployed in sections on the heights north of the Mackville Road and overlooking the bridge. The high ground to Lytle's front right where a white cement building now stands marks the location where Slocomb's battery (Adams' brigade) deployed.

When the 3d Ohio's ammunition began to run short it retired and the 15th Kentucky assumed its position. A new threat soon emerged on the regiment's open right flank. Adams' brigade used the low ground south of the Bottom House to outflank and enfilade the Union line. Artillery fire ignited the barn that marked the southern edge of this ridgeline. The 15th Kentucky retreated amid smoke and spreading grass fires. It refused its right flank to face Adams. Lytle's attention quickly shifted to his collapsing right flank. The 10th Ohio linked his brigade with Harris'. While focused on Adams' attack he ordered the Ohio unit to lie down and conserve its fire. Hence the 10th Ohio refused to support Harris' brigade in its confrontation with Brown's Confederates.

Lytle's position finally collapsed when Adams attacked into his right flank and Cleburne's newly committed brigade advanced on his front. Lytle withdrew into the low ground to the rear of this position. The 10th Ohio, however, remained in position with no additional orders. When Brown's brigade also began to approach Lieutenant Colonel Joseph W. Burke, commanding the regiment, ordered a charge on his own initiative. He attacked Brown's brigade, halted its advance, and retired in good order to this location (his original position). Deploying skirmishers to cover its movement the 10th Ohio then retreated up the Mackville Road under fire.

Vignette: "About two o'clock the rebel infantry was seen advancing across the valley, and I ordered the Third to ascend the hill and take position on the crest. The enemy's batteries now reopened with redoubled fury,

174

and the air seemed filled with shot and exploding shells. Finding the rebels were still too far away to make our muskets effective, I ordered the boys to lie down and await their nearer approach. They advanced under cover of a house on the side hill and, having reached a point one hundred and fifty yards distant, deployed behind a stone fence that was hidden from us by standing corn. At this time the left of my regiment rested on the Maxville [sic] and Perryville road, the line extending along the crest of the hill, and the right passing somewhat behind a barn filled with hay. In this position, with the enemy's batteries pouring upon us a most destructive fire, the Third arose and delivered its first volley. For a time, I do not know how long thereafter, it seemed as if all hell had broken loose; the air was filled with hissing balls; shells were exploding continuously and the noise of the guns was deafening; finally the barn on the right took fire, and the flames, bursting from roof, windows, doors, and interstices between the logs, threw the right of the regiment into disorder; the confusion, however, was but temporary. The boys closed up to the left, steadied themselves on the colors, and stood bravely to the work. Nearly two hundred of my five hundred men now lay dead and wounded on the little strip of ground over which we fought." (Experience of the 3d Ohio recounted by the regiment's commander in John Beatty, *Memoirs of a Volunteer 1861-1863*, New York: W.W. Norton & Co. Inc., 1946, 136-37.)

Teaching points: Fire discipline, unit behavior under fire, unit cohesion, battlefield confusion, flank security, retreat under fire.

Route to Stand 15: Follow the path toward Park Informational Marker 20. Stop on the path about 100 meters behind Loomis Heights (Stand 13) looking east toward the ridgeline just vacated.

Stand 15
Cleburne's Brigade

Location: Between Park Informational Markers 19 and 20 (low ground—UTM grid 7875 7056).

Situation: Following the retreat of his and Harris' brigade from the high ground astride the Mackville Road Lytle tried to re-form a line in this low ground. Grass fires created a smoky, confused atmosphere that did little to discourage soldiers from continuing their rearward motion. Meanwhile Cleburne's brigade began advancing up the recently abandoned heights (Stands 12 and 13). Confederate artillery mistakenly fired into them and temporarily stalled the ascent until aides from Johnson and Cleburne informed the gunners of their error. Cleburne's regiments reformed and advanced up the hill, preceded by a skirmish line bearing the unit battle flags. As Cleburne's men came into view Lytle's makeshift line assumed the presence of the colors marked the Confederate line of battle and prematurely fired. While the Union soldiers reloaded the mass of Cleburne's brigade appeared on the crest and fired into them at close range. Lytle's line broke and retreated toward the Russell House (see map 5, point R) with Cleburne in pursuit. Lytle fell wounded and was captured. Cleburne continued his advance toward the Russell House, his left flank on the Mackville Road.

Vignette: "I received great assistance from Captain [G.] Dixon, of the Fifteenth Arkansas. He advanced alone to within thirty steps of the enemy's line, and gave me much information and made some useful suggestions which were afterward turned to good account. . . . I now advanced in line of battle, my skirmishers ten paces in front of the line and carrying the battle-flags of the regiments. As we ascended the hill we were fired into by our own artillery in the rear. Several of our men were killed and wounded, and we had to fall back. I sent an aide to stop this battery. I can only account for this blunder from the fact that most of our men had on blue Federal pants. We again advanced in the same order. The moment our flags, carried by the line of skirmishers, appeared above the crest of the hill, the enemy, supposing our line of battle was in view, emptied their guns at the line of skirmishers. Before they could reload our true line of battle was upon them; they instantly broke and fled, exposed to a deadly fire. Their brigade commander, Colonel Lytle, rallied about 100, but they were routed in a moment with heavy loss. We continued to advance through a cornfield, and became so scattered in the pursuit I found it necessary to halt the brigade and reform line of battle. This I did, my left resting on the Mackville road, my line at right angles to this road." (BG Patrick R. Cleburne, *OR*, series I, vol. LII, *Part I*, 52.)

Teaching points: Terrain use, combat reconnaissance, tactics, unit behavior under fire.

Route to Stand 16: Continue along the path to Park Informational Marker 20.

Stand 16
Russell House Line

Location: Park Informational Marker 20 (high ground—UTM grid 7852 7070).

Situation: At dusk the Confederates continued to advance toward the Russell House in the wake of Lytle's retreating brigade. The Mackville Road served as a unit boundary between Cleburne and Adams' brigade. Cleburne moved north of the road while Adams moved south of it. Behind and to the right of Cleburne marched Brown's brigade. Behind the Confederate infantry, several batteries converged and deployed on the hill position Lytle abandoned (Stand 13). Their massed cannon provided effective support for the final Confederate attacks toward the Russell House.

Cleburne's men reached this position and found themselves facing another Union line on the higher ground immediately east of this location. This line resulted from the personal intervention of Rousseau and McCook who sought to prevent the collapse of I Corps' right flank. Elements of Harris' and Lytle's brigades, including the resupplied 3d Ohio and 15th Kentucky, prepared for a final stand. McCook also committed the 1st Michigan Engineers and Mechanics. Intended for bridge building this regiment had been split to provide support for I and II Corps. Three companies were assigned to Rousseau's 3d Division. They now found themselves thrust into an infantry battle that was reaching its climax. Loomis' battery, positioned on the higher elevation just south of the Mackville Road, provided fire support.

Cleburne approached the Russell House to find Union resistance stiffening and becoming more desperate. Faced with canister fire from Loomis' guns and intensified musket fire, Cleburne's brigade ran short of ammunition and lost its momentum. On its left Adams' brigade also faltered. It proved unable to break the resistance near the Russell House and became the target for enfilading artillery fire from Peters Hill. This fire marked III Corps' belated effort to support the collapsing I Corps. It surprised and disorganized the Confederates who had assumed only a token Union force occupied Peters Hill. Adams withdrew amid considerable confusion. Without additional forces and more ammunition neither Adams nor Cleburne had enough combat power to sustain their advance. With their withdrawal the Confederate attack on this portion of the battlefield effectively ended.

Note on Loomis' engagement criteria: When Loomis retired toward the Russell House he received orders from the I Corps commander to

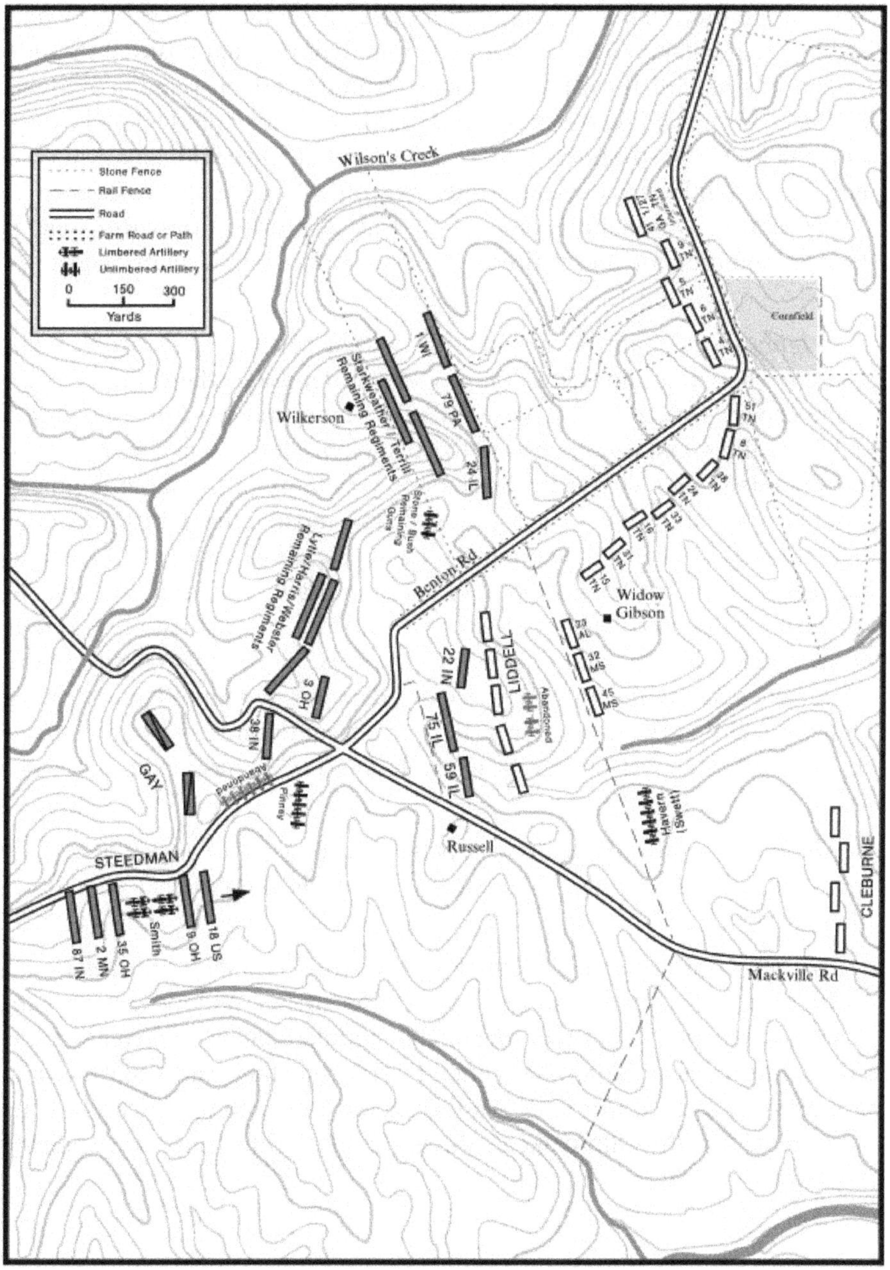

Map 10. Liddell's attack, 1745.

University Press of Kentucky

179

conserve ammunition and fire only on close-range targets. As Lytle's and Harris' regiments fell back in disorder from their original position (Stands 12 and 13) toward the Russell House Loomis' cannon remained silent. While Cleburne and Adams advanced on I Corps' headquarters and Rousseau and McCook struggled to form a coherent defense with any available unit, Loomis did not believe his orders permitted him to engage the enemy. With Cleburne within 200 meters of the Russell House it took Rousseau's personal intervention and a direct order before Loomis' cannon began firing.

Vignette: "I again advanced until within seventy-five yards of the position known as the white house [Russell House], where a fresh line of the enemy were strongly posted, flanked by artillery. At this juncture I had no artillery and no supporting force upon my left. I sent Captain Carlton, commanding a few sharpshooters, to watch my left. A large regiment posted in the valley to my right gave way, and most of them, in spite of my entreaties, fled to the rear, leaving my small brigade of not over 800 men in the center of the battle, unsupported on either flank. A furious cannonade between our own artillery, posted on the hill we first carried on the right of the Mackville road, and the enemy's artillery, posted on the right of the white house before mentioned, was carried on our own line. This, together with the fact that [we] were almost out of ammunition, prevented us from advancing farther." (BG Patrick R. Cleburne, *OR*, series I, vol. LII, *Part I*, 52.)

Teaching points: Battlefield momentum, situational awareness, unit behavior under fire, flank security, fire power in the defense, fire discipline.

Route to Stand 17: Follow the path west past Park Informational Marker 22. This sign identifies the location of the Widow Gibson site. During the battle the civilian inhabitants huddled under the cabin's floor. The cabin stands at the southern end of a ridgeline that marks Starkweather's second position. Continue west along the park path up the hill to your front. Note that the path makes a 90-degree turn, following the boundary of private property.

Stand 17
The Last Act

Location: Hill west of Park Informational Marker 22 (UTM grid 7821 7100).

Visibility note: This location marks the original position of Harris' battery. However the tree line to the south that identifies the boundary between park and private property also obscures visibility toward the park entrance and the open field over which Donelson's, Stewart's, and Wood's Confederate brigades attacked. The tree line did not exist in 1862. Also note that Harris' battery would have occupied much of the entire hill mass the tree line and property boundary now separate. Looking east to your front you will see another hill nearby. This hill is the southern tip of the ridge upon which Starkweather established his second position. Starkweather's forces, however, were concentrated closer to the northern end where the stone wall marking the extreme left flank was.

Situation 1: On the morning of 8 October Jackson's division marched from Mackville toward Perryville. As it neared the Russell House the sounds of the Peters Hill fighting led the formation to advance slowly behind a screen of skirmishers. Webster's brigade arrived near the Dixville Crossroads (close to the current intersection of the Hayes May and Whites Roads) and the Russell House before Terrill. There McCook directed the brigade to form south of the Mackville Road, effectively forming a second line behind the one Rousseau already formed along the heights overlooking Doctor's Creek (Stands 12-13). McCook then left to oversee the arrival of Terrill's brigade.

Webster placed Harris' battery on this hill. The 98th Ohio advanced to provide support. It deployed behind this hill between the Mackville and Benton Roads (now Hayes May and Whites Roads). The limited space, however, prevented the brigade's extension into a full-length line. Instead the regiment split into two halves that formed in tandem, effectively creating a shorter, four-rank line. Most of the brigade subsequently formed behind the battery north of the Mackville Road rather than south as McCook intended. Instead of a second line behind Rousseau Webster formed his brigade in a rough line that angled forward. This position protected the Dixville Crossroads and covered the I Corps headquarters at the Russell House. From these heights Harris' battery had a broad field of fire that supported Rousseau's line and helped cover the gap between the positions that Starkweather's and Harris' brigades had assumed.

During the successive attacks of Donelson, Stewart, and finally

181

Wood, Webster's brigade and battery helped to anchor the Union line. The infantry regiments maneuvered on and forward of this hill to block the Confederates as they advanced over the low ground toward and finally past the Widow Gibson site (Park Informational Marker 22). In response to Maney's attack on Parsons' battery (Stand 5), the 98th and 121st Ohio were separately ordered forward to support the battery, but the position fell before Webster's regiments arrived.

Shortly before 1630 Rousseau's brigades on Loomis Heights withdrew under pressure from Adams', Cleburne's, and Brown's Confederate brigades. Their advance threatened Webster's right flank. By that time Starkweather had already abandoned his initial position (Stand 7), and he was struggling to hold I Corps' left flank (see map 8). In between, Webster noted the friendly forces' retrograde movements on both flanks while facing a powerful thrust by Wood's newly committed brigade together with elements of Donelson's and Stewart's commands.

With its ammunition nearly exhausted and becoming the target of growing Confederate infantry fire, Harris' battery withdrew. Due to losses among its horses only two cannon and several caissons retired, but they did so by driving straight through the 80th Indiana.

Panic and exhaustion began to afflict Webster's brigade. He ordered the 80th Indiana to retire. The 50th Ohio fled after them, leaving only the 98th and 121st Ohio to face the Confederate attack. With little training, without fire support, and subjected to intensifying Confederate fire these regiments collapsed when Webster received a mortal wound. Elements of the 121st Ohio, however, rallied and returned to fight. They joined the collection of units fighting under Starkweather's control on I Corps' left flank.

Vignette 1: "About fifteen minutes of two P.M., the 34th Brigade, commanded by Col. Webster, was ordered to take its position. Col. [William P.] Reid, of the 121st Ohio, received orders to march his regiment. When the order was given the regiment to march on the field of battle, many of them were astounded that they should be compelled to go and support a battery, when they knew that their guns could not be used. I would remark here that the guns had been inspected a few days before this, and it was fully known to the commander of the brigade that more than four hundred of those guns were totally useless. But the men marched and took their position." (*Cincinnati Daily Commercial*, 8 November 1862. Photocopy in Dr. Kenneth A. Noe's collection in files of Perryville Battlefield Preservation Association, Perryville, Kentucky.)

Vignette 2: "I do not know how the other boys felt while we were lying there with the shot and shell and musket balls singing and whistling o'er us, but I know I began to think we were up against the real thing this time, and no mistake. No Fort Mitchell or Camp King foolishness about this, and though there was a big dust arising out in front, it was not caused by a drove of government mules, but by real live 'Johnnie Rebs,' very much alive too, from the way they sent their leaden and iron messages over among us; to say it was demoralizing would be putting it very mild indeed. I felt like there might be safer places to lie down than where we were just at that time." (Erastus Winters, *In the 50th Ohio Serving Uncle Sam: Memoirs of One Who Wore the Blue*, Privately Printed, East Walnut Hills, OH, 1905, 20.)

Unit note (*19th Battery, Indiana Light Artillery*): Commanded by Captain Samuel J. Harris, this battery included four 12-pound smooth-bores and two 3-inch rifles. The battery participated in the artillery duel that commenced at 1230 when the Confederates opened a preliminary bombardment in preparation for their attack. During the later fighting this battery remained in continuous operation, firing over 900 rounds at both infantry and artillery formations. The physical exhaustion of many of the gunners finally resulted in soldiers from the 98th Ohio assisting in work-ing the guns. When it finally retreated the battery had suffered nearly 13-percent casualties. Harris' battery proved to be significant for the support it rendered throughout much of the battle. The Confederates also launched their initial attack in the mistaken belief that Harris' cannon marked the left flank of the Union line.

Situation 2: The collapse of Webster's brigade permitted Wood's bri-gade to advance onto this hill. The Confederates moved into and through the position that Harris' battery previously occupied amid considerable disorder. The attacks on Webster had been costly, particularly among the 32d Mississippi and 33d Alabama. These regiments led the brigade at-tack and finally overran the Union position, but many of their officers lay dead or wounded, including acting brigade commander COL Lowrey. Consequently unit cohesion began to break down, and a high state of dis-organization characterized the Confederate regiments. Nevertheless they continued to advance toward the Dixville Crossroads (near the current intersection of the Hayes May and White Roads). As dusk fell they sensed the collapse of Union resistance.

The arrival and counterattack of a fresh Union brigade, however, checked the Confederate advance. The Union force appeared at the Dix-ville Crossroads as a result of MG McCook's belated efforts to secure sup-port for his beleaguered corps. At 1430 he had sent an aide to BG Philip

H. Sheridan, whose division held Peters Hill, requesting that he secure I Corps' right flank. McCook dispatched a second staff officer at 1500 to obtain assistance from the nearest III Corps unit. The officer encountered BG Albin Schoepf, commanding the III Corps' reserve division. Unwilling to act on his own authority Schoepf referred the staff officer to the III Corps commander who in turn referred him to Buell's headquarters more than 2 miles away.

McCook's staff officer finally reported directly to Buell at about 1600 indicating I Corps' status and its need for reinforcements. His arrival surprised the army commander who found it difficult to believe that a major Confederate attack had been under way for some time. The headquarters had received no prior reports of enemy action, and acoustic shadow had masked the sounds of battle (see Battlefield Orientation [Army of the Ohio]). Nevertheless Buell ordered the immediate dispatch of two brigades from Schoepf's division to support I Corps.

In the meantime McCook had sent yet another staff officer to III Corps for reinforcement. Unfortunately the timing of this request coincided with a Confederate attack directly on III Corps. In response to Sheridan's enfilade fire on Adams' brigade as it neared the Russell House Bragg ordered COL Samuel Powell to attack Peters Hill and silence the Union artillery. Bragg was unaware of the true size of the Union formation on the hill mass. Powell's single brigade dutifully advanced from its position just west of the town of Perryville to engage an entire corps on high ground with eight batteries of supporting artillery. The attack had no chance of success, but it fixed the III Corps commander's attention on his front and dampened enthusiasm for sending troops to help I Corps. In response to McCook's request for support Gilbert directed a single brigade from BG Robert B. Mitchell's division to move to his assistance. The subsequent receipt of Buell's orders to support I Corps resulted in the dispatch of a second brigade from Schoepf's division. Hence total III Corps assistance comprised intermittent artillery fire and two infantry brigades from separate divisions.

COL Michael Gooding's brigade (Mitchell's division) moved quickly in column toward the Dixville Crossroads. There, elements of Rousseau's division were withdrawing. As Gooding approached via the Benton Road (now Whites Road), McCook oversaw his brigade's deployment. The 22d Indiana formed on the right, the 75th Illinois in the center, and the 59th Illinois on the left. These units formed a single line near the Russell House stretching from the Mackville Road to the Benton Road (now Hayes May and Whites Roads). McCook also guided Captain Oscar F. Pinney's battery into position where it soon began firing at the muzzle flashes of Confederate cannon. As Wood's disorganized regiments advanced toward the Dixville Crossroads against diminishing resistance they suddenly found themselves engaged in a firefight with Gooding's solid line of formed infantry. This engagement continued until the 22d Indiana launched a bayonet charge. The already disordered Confederates collapsed and retreated in confusion. The Indiana regiment then advanced in pursuit toward Webster's original position, and Gooding readjusted his line along the crest and reverse slope of this hill (see map 10).

Unit notes (30th Brigade, 9th Division): The 30th Brigade was formed at Louisville as part of Buell's reorganized army. The brigade included the 59th, 74th, and 75th Illinois Infantry Regiments; the 22d Indiana infantry; and the 5th Battery, Wisconsin Light Artillery. The brigade's composition reflected Buell's efforts to mix veteran and new regiments together in the same brigade. The 74th and 75th Illinois mustered into federal service in September 1862. The 59th Illinois and 22d Indiana, however, previously served with the Army of the Southwest. They fought with distinction at Pea Ridge in March 1862. They constituted part of the reinforcements sent in response to Buell's request for assistance during the summer operations against Chattanooga. They accompanied the Army of the Ohio during its retreat to Louisville where it was reorganized. The 30th Brigade's strength at Perryville included 1,423 soldiers of all ranks. Although it included four regiments there is no record that the 74th Illinois actively participated in the brigade's engagement with Liddell. Indeed official reports of the brigade's role at Perryville do not mention this regiment, and no losses were listed for it. Before its commitment to the fight, the 75th Illinois underwent a change of command. Upon learning that the regiment lacked sufficient ammunition and had not reported this condition, the corps commander ordered the unit commander's arrest. The unit commander, however, fought in the ranks as a common soldier. He fought well during the ensuing combat, and his command was restored after the battle.

Situation 3: Before Gooding's regiments could further exploit the retreat of Wood's brigade, BG St. John R. Liddell's brigade engaged them. Following its action on Peters Hill in the early morning this brigade had been withdrawn from the fight. Now as the Union I Corps appeared on the verge of collapse, MG Hardee committed Liddell's brigade to sustain the momentum of the Confederate attack. The wing commander did so without consulting Buckner whose division included Liddell's brigade. In fact, Buckner feared that the Union position near the Russell House had been reinforced. He therefore desired Liddell to remain in reserve, and he tried to warn Hardee of the potential danger.

Hardee believed one more significant push would shatter Union resistance. Thus Liddell advanced, but he did so with minimal guidance as to his objective. Told only to enter the fight where it seemed most intense, Liddell followed the path of Wood's brigade toward the sound of fighting. He soon encountered Gooding's brigade in the gathering darkness. Despite a full moon both Union and Confederate infantry became wary of firing into their own troops. Neither force had any clear sense of the other's exact location or disposition. Gooding rearranged his line in response to the undefined threat that Liddell posed. The veteran 22d Indiana moved to the left flank of the line, which placed it directly in the path of the Confederates poised to attack.

Into this confusion rode MG Polk. He rode forward alone to ascertain the identity of the troops facing Liddell, believing a friendly unit was about to be attacked. Instead he discovered the 22d Indiana and fled back to Confederate lines. At close range Liddell's regiments delivered massed volleys into the Union regiment and shattered it. The survivors fled, and Confederate fire shifted to the other units of Gooding's brigade. The Union regiments withdrew beyond the Dixville Crossroads, accompanied by Pinney's battery.

Note on firefight: The brief firefight between Liddell's and Gooding's brigades marked some of the most deadly musket fighting of the entire battle. Gooding was captured and the commander of the 22d Indiana killed. Below is a breakdown of the known Union casualties from this engagement with initial strength indicated in parenthesis. It is likely that the darkness and uncertainty of friendly and enemy locations resulted in Liddell engaging Gooding from very close range.

59th Illinios	(325)	29 killed	55 wounded	29 missing
75th Illinois	(730)	44 killed	169 wounded	12 missing
22d Indiana	(300)	59 killed	119 wounded	17 missing

Liddell consolidated his position and advanced his brigade's battery for fire support. Upon completion his force moved into the Dixville Crossroads and prepared to continue the fight. Opposing him lay the other brigade dispatched from III Corps: BG James B. Steedman's five infantry regiments, which included the regulars of the 18th US Infantry and an artillery battery. Further fighting ended, however, when Polk ordered a cessation to combat over Liddell's objections. The battle thus ended with I Corps finished as an effective fighting force. Both sides began the difficult task of finding and collecting their wounded.

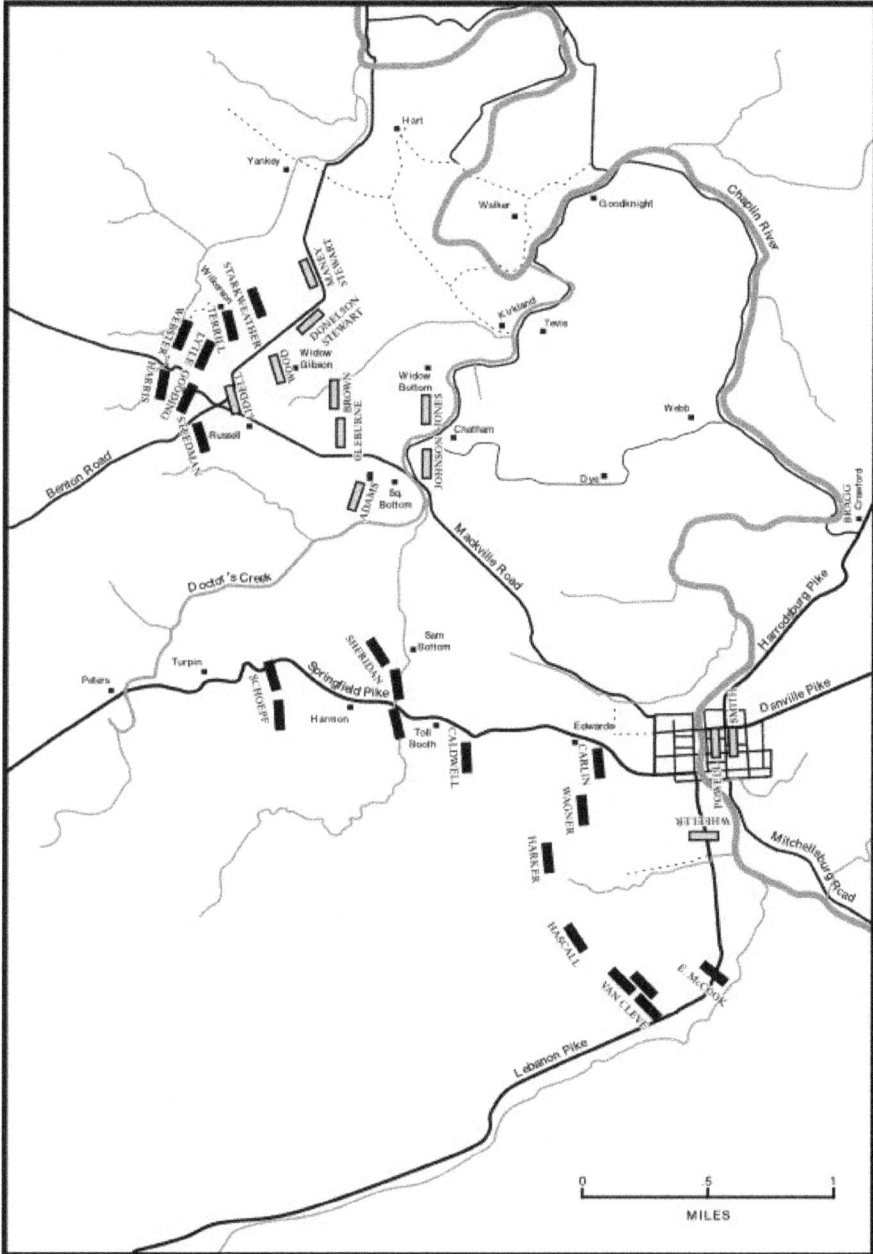

Map 11. Final positions, 2000.

187

Russell House and Dixville Crossroads significance: The final fighting around the Russell House and Dixville Crossroads constituted more than another fight for a piece of terrain. The former housed the I Corps headquarters and served as a hospital. Along the Mackville Road (now Hayes May Road) leading to the Dixville Crossroads lay I Corps' baggage and ammunition wagons. The nature of the terrain prevented these vehicles from being parked off the road. The Dixville Crossroads represented the principal hub in the road net connecting I and III Corps. Its loss complicated communication and movement between the two corps. Hence losing both the Russell House and the Dixville Crossroads to Liddell placed I Corps in danger of complete collapse and separation from III Corps. Nightfall, the last-minute arrival of III Corps reinforcements, and the absence of additional Confederate forces to sustain the fight helped to prevent this outcome.

Vignette: "I waited no longer. The news was circulated loudly, 'Yankees!' The trumpet sounded to 'fire.' A tremendous flash of musketry for the whole extent of the line for nearly one quarter of a mile in length followed. It continued for some fifteen minutes. I discovered that the return fire had ceased and therefore directed the trumpeter to signal the cessation on our part. The smoke soon cleared up, which enabled General Polk to ride forward with me and see the result.

"The Federal force had disappeared everywhere. The ground before my line of battle was literally covered with the dead and dying. I returned to the line and announced the cheering fact that the field was ours. It was answered with repeated cheers and then followed loud cheering *far to our left*, which we supposed to be from Anderson's Division. But it turned out to be the enemy, who had driven in our left wing, as we had done their left." (St. John Richardson Liddell, *Liddell's Record: St. John Richardson Liddell*, Nathaniel Cheairs Hughes, Jr., ed., Dayton, OH: Morningside, 1985, 93.)

Teaching points: Fire support, unit cohesion, unit behavior under fire, flank security, battle command, commander's intent, fratricide, effects of mass casualties.

Route to Next Stand: Follow the park path east through Stand 9 to the vicinity of the Confederate cemetery and Union monument near the museum building.

Aftermath

Location: Confederate Cemetery (UTM grid 7895 7146).

Situation 1: During the course of the battle the wounded were largely left to fend for themselves. Many simply lay where they fell. Hospitals were established at various points, but there were few ambulances to evacuate the wounded from the battlefield. Some comrades assisted soldiers and helped them to a hospital. Others whose injuries did not prevent them from walking sought medical assistance on their own. The nature of the makeshift hospitals, however, sometimes discouraged soldiers from entering and seeking aid.

Vignette: "When my horse got shot I was lying close by him on the same side.

"I immediately called one of the boys to help take him out and run around to the near side in order to unbuckle the breast strap.

"I had it but half unbuckled when a shell from the enemy struck me on the left arm and passing on, struck the ammunition chest, exploded and caused the cartridges in the chest to explode.

"It was all done in an instant and resulted in the instant death of F. Eric who was struck in the head with a piece of shell and the wounding of four others, C. Miller, burnt; A. Farg, arm broken and badly burnt on head and face; A. Pettit, lip cut and wounded slightly in the head; and myself cut in the left arm, right arm, and face.

"When the chest blew up it took me in the air about ten feet.

"I had my thoughts during the operation and concluded I was torn to pieces, but after striking the ground and lying there about three minutes, I jumped up and saw that I was badly wounded, my clothes were all torn off, and the burn from the powder set me near crazy.

"The smoke of the explosion was so thick I could see nothing and as I remember the head surgeon passed us before the battle and told us where the hospital would be found and to come there if we got wounded, I thought it the best policy for me to reach them as soon as possible for fear the loss of blood would weaken me so I would be unable to walk.

"Leaving everything, (for I was in such pain I cared for nothing) I started in their direction.

"The balls flew around me like hail as I made my steps back but little did I heed them.

"At one time a twelve pound shell exploded within a few feet of me, tearing up the ground, in a fearful manner, and I had not gone more than a quarter of a mile when I felt so exhausted I could hardly stand.

"Here a young man gave me a canteen of water which revived me and I again started and soon reached the first hospital which was a small log house within a quarter mile of the left of our line of battle.

"Shell and shot were passing all around the house and it afterward was struck by a shell, killing two men.

"I went in and tried to have my wounds dressed, but the surgeon was so frightened that he knew nothing, as he wanted to take my arm off when there was no bone injured.

"I left him at once and found another hospital but a short distance in a farm house: here there were about 300 wounded.

"Such a sight I never beheld before and never wish to again.

"I saw there was no chance here and as I felt as though I could get a little farther, concluded to find another place; the loss of blood by this time had made me so weak I could hardly stand.

"When I reached the road (which was but a short distance from the house) I fell and could go no further.

"A few minutes passed in loneliness and I had given up to die and cared for nothing—I was almost crazy through pain.

"After I had laid here a short time, J. Countz who had been sent after water for the boys in the battery came along, recognized me at once, got off and poured some water on my head and face, gave me a drink and with some help got me on his horse and started for the hospital a half mile distant.

"We had gone but a short distance when we came to a man that has a tub full of whiskey poured out of a barrel and was giving it to the wounded.

"Countz handed me a quart basin full and I would have drunk every bit of it had they not taken it away from me; but for all that I drank near the quart and felt no effects from it any more than it gave me a new spirit.

"We pressed on and soon came to a hospital which was a farmhouse.

"I was here but a short time when Countz brought a surgeon who dressed my arm." (Private Ormond Hupp, *In the Defense of This Flag: The Civil War Diary of Pvt. Ormond Hupp, 5th Indiana Light Artillery*, Fredonia, NY: Bluehome Press, 1992, 21-22.)

Situation 2: Darkness effectively ended the battle. Bragg initially determined to remain on the battlefield and renew the contest the next day. However as information arrived detailing the day's events it became clear to the Confederate commander that he had engaged only a portion of the Union Army. While he had committed all but one brigade and suffered considerable casualties doing so, Buell had two more corps that had seen little or no fighting. Realizing he faced Buell's entire army, Bragg opted to retreat during the night despite the views of many subordinates who felt a victory had been won and the fight should be continued. Orders were issued to recover weapons and replace cannon with more modern pieces that had been captured during the day. Buell did not learn that a major battle had even been fought until the evening. At first surprised he then began preparing to renew the conflict in the morning. By then the Confederates had left the field.

Bragg's army entered the battle with an estimated strength of 16,800. By day's end he had suffered at least 532 killed, 2,641 wounded, and 228 missing. Buell's forces suffered 894 killed, 2,911 wounded, and 471 missing out of a total force of 55,261. I Corps suffered most of the casualties: 700 killed, 2,235 wounded, and 384 missing from a beginning strength of 13,121. In addition to the physical casualties both armies suffered from exhaustion and leader losses that eroded the effectiveness of many of the regiments that had been engaged.

The night of 8-9 October proved to be one of misery and suffering for the wounded of both sides. Many lay where they had fallen, unable to move and without water. Soldiers from each army looked for comrades seeking to recover those who were still alive. Neither army had adequate ambulances or medical support. Buell's medical corps, in particular, suffered from insufficient ambulances and supplies. During the march toward Louisville Buell reduced the allocation of ambulances to one per brigade as part of a broader effort to reduce the army's baggage and speed its movement. At Perryville, in addition to the lack of medical supplies and ambulances, Union surgeons received little guidance on creating hospitals or organizing medical personnel. On their own initiative several brigade surgeons pooled their resources. However, the large numbers of wounded quickly overwhelmed the makeshift hospitals. Shortages of water and medical supplies of all types soon became manifest. Confederate medical support proved to be no more effective.

Vignette: "We found our poor major dead and stripped. Oh, I loved him! What a loss to us! Others were dead, and many wounded; I helped carry off four and then gave out from exhaustion. This is a strange word for me, but no other express it. The moon shone full upon the scene; it is utterly useless to describe the sight—men and horses dead and wounded, wagon-wheels, army caissons scattered, and the moans and shrieks of the wounded. Oh, may you never see such a sight! I helped carry off one poor fellow with his mouth and lower jaw shot off—stop, stop! I can't say more. We slept till sunrise; I expected to see it rise for the last time, for I supposed at daylight we should pitch in till death or victory were ours; but no, the rebels had fled. We moved on two or three miles, and rest yet. Thank God, we have water! Of our squad only two remain well; Company C, on our left, has no officers left. This morning the loss averaged thirty-five—quite a reduction. Our colonel has an arm broken, and a wound in the neck. Many were the hairbreadth escapes. The poor horses have had nothing all day except a little water." (Account of Sergeant Mead Holmes, Jr., Company K, 21st Wisconsin, quoted in *A Soldier of the Cumberland: Memoir of Mead Holmes, Jr., Boston, MA: American Tract Society, 1864, 92-96.)*

Situation 3: After the armies departed, the local community contin-ued to cope with the human debris of battle. Many of the buildings in and around Perryville served as temporary hospitals. The armies had largely taken the available food, leaving little for the civilians or wounded in the battle's wake. To help care for the wounded the US Sanitary Commission ultimately sent more than 10 tons of supplies to Perryville.

Vignette: "From this place [Mackville] to Perryville, some ten miles, nearly every house was a hospital. At one log cabin, we found 20 of the 10th Ohio, including the Major and two Captains. At another house were several of the 92d Ohio; and the occupants were very poor, but doing all in their power for those in their charge. The mother of the family promised to continue to do so, but said, with tears in her eyes, she feared that she and her children must starve when the winter came. As at the other houses on this road, the sick had no regular medical attendance. . . . We reached Perryville after dark.

"On our arrival we learned that we were the first to bring relief where help was needed more than tongue can tell. Instead of 700, as first report-ed, at least 2,500 Union and rebel soldiers were at that time lying in great suffering and destitution about Perryville and Harrodsburg. In addition to these, many had already been removed, and we had met numbers of those whose wounds were less severe walking and begging their way to Louis-ville, 85 miles distant. To these we frequently gave help and comfort by sharing with them the slender stock of food and spirits we had taken with

Chapter 4. Administrative Support

Information and Assistance

Armor Historian. On Fort Knox the Office of the Armor Historian has a wealth of background information and an overview presentation of the battle and related campaign. This office can also provide advice on structuring the staff ride to meet training objectives. This office may be contacted at—

Cavalry and Armor Proponency Office
ATTN: ATZK-CAH (Historian)
Fort Knox, KY 40121-5000
DSN: 464-1495
Commercial: 502-624-1495

Armor School Library. The Armor School Library is the principal repository of published and primary sources on Fort Knox. Its holdings include several works and articles related to the battle of Perryville. It can also be used to secure additional sources via interlibrary loan, and it has onsite Internet access for military personnel. The library may be contacted via DSN 464-6231 or commercial 502-624-6231.

Perryville Battlefield State Historic Site. The park manager has a wealth of information about the battle. This office can provide advice on conducting a staff ride and using the park. An onsite museum also includes exhibits and information about the battle, and the gift shop has a collection of Civil War publications focused on the war in the west. Contact the park at—

Park Manager
Perryville Battlefield State Historic Site
P.O. Box 296
1825 Battlefield Road
Perryville, KY 40468-0296
Commercial: 859-332-8631

Note on Using the Topographic Map

The map coordinates referenced throughout this handbook correspond to a topographic map of the Perryville Quadrangle published by the US Department of the Interior Geological Survey in cooperation with the Kentucky Geological Survey. The map uses a 1:24,000 scale and the 1927 North American data. The coordinates provided permit plotting points and measuring distances. The map uses the Universal Transverse Mercator (UTM) grid system. This system is **not** interchangeable with the

Military Grid Reference System (MGRS-New). To plot points and measure distances on this map, users need to secure a protractor or measuring device with a 1:24,000 scale. This item is generally available in military bookstores and shopettes. Global Positioning Systems (GPS) users must set their units to read the appropriate data, or their positions will not match the map's grid system. The data required is indicated in the GPS as NA27CONUS. All UTM grid coordinates indicated are in zone 16.

The Kentucky Geological Survey will furnish copies of this map for a nominal copy and shipping fee. To order one or more copies of the map, identify it as a topographic map of the Perryville Quadrangle, which is part of the 7.5-Minute Quadrangle Series. Contact the Kentucky Geological Survey at—

Kentucky Geological Survey
Publication Sales
228 Mining and Mineral Resources Building
University of Kentucky
Lexington, KY 40506-0107
(606) 257-3896

Driving Instructions From Fort Knox

Driving time from Fort Knox is approximately 1.5 hours. For planning purposes, allow 2 hours to accommodate slower-moving traffic on local, two-lane roadways closer to the park.

- Route 31W south to Route 313
- East on Route 313 to Interstate 65
- Interstate 65 south to Bluegrass Parkway
- East on Bluegrass Parkway toward Lexington
- Exit onto US 150
- Take US 150 through Springfield to Perryville
- In Perryville turn left onto KY 1920 and follow to park entrance

Food and Lodging

Staff ride groups need to plan to bring their own food and use the picnic facilities at the park. There are no restaurants in the immediate vicinity of the park that will support a large group of 40 to 60 people. En route to the park Springfield hosts several small eateries and fast food restaurants. Two convenience stores within the town of Perryville offer sandwiches and light foods. Danville and Bardstown offer a variety of restaurants and should be considered for any possible post-event reception or dinner.

These places vary in price and quality from fast food to formal dining. Should a group desire to remain overnight in the area Danville offers an array of lodging. For more information contact—

Danville-Boyle County Convention and Visitors Bureau
1-800-755-0076

Appendix A
Army of the Ohio Order of Battle

Army of the Ohio

I Corps

II Corps

III Corps

Army of the Ohio

Strength: 55,261 men and 147 cannon

Commander
MG Don Carlos Buell

Escort
Anderson Troop, Pennsylvania Cavalry
4th US Cavalry (six companies)

I Corps
MG Alexander M. McCook

3d Division
BG Lovell H. Rousseau
10th Division
BG James S. Jackson

II Corps
MG Thomas L. Crittenden

4th Division
BG William Sooy Smith
5th Division
BG Horatio P. Van Cleve
6th Division
BG Thomas J. Wood
1st Cavalry Brigade
COL Edward M. McCook

III Corps
MG Charles C. Gilbert

1st Division
BG Albin Schoepf
9th Division
BG Robert B. Mitchell
11th Division
BG Philip H. Sheridan
3d Cavalry Brigade
Captain Ebenezer Gay

I Corps

Commander
MG Alexander McDowell McCook
Strength: 13,121 men and 38 cannon

10th Division
BG James S. Jackson

33d Brigade
BG William R. Terrill
80th Illinois, COL Thomas G. Allen
123d Illinois, COL James Monroe
Garrard's Detachment, COL Theophilus Garrard
105th Ohio, COL Albert S. Hall
Parsons' Battery, Lieutenant Charles C. Parsons

34th Brigade
COL George Webster
80th Indiana, COL Jonah R. Taylor
50th Ohio, LTC Silas A. Strickland
98th Ohio, LTC Christian L. Poorman
121st Ohio, COL William P. Reid
19th Battery, Indiana Light Artillery,
Captain Samuel J. Harris

3d Division
BG Lovell H. Rousseau

17th Brigade
COL William H. Lytle
42d Indiana, COL James G. Jones
88th Indiana, COL George Humphrey
15th Kentucky, COL Curran Pope
3d Ohio, LTC John Beatty
10th Ohio, LTC Joseph W. Burke
Battery A, 1st Michigan Light Artillery,
Captain Cyrus O. Loomis

Unattached
2d Kentucky Cavalry (six companies),
COL Buckner Board
1st Michigan Engineers and Mechanics
(three companies), MAJ Enos Hopkins

9th Brigade
COL Leonard A. Harris
38th Indiana, COL Benjamin F. Scribner
2d Ohio, COL John Kell
33d Ohio, LTC Oscar F. Moore
94th Ohio, COL Joseph W. Frizell
10th Wisconsin, COL Alfred R. Chapin
5th Battery, Indiana Light Artillery,
Captain Peter Simonson

28th Brigade
COL John C. Starkweather
24th Illinois, Captain August Mauff
79th Pennsylvania, COL Henry A. Hambright
1st Wisconsin, LTC George E. Bingham
21st Wisconsin, COL Benjamin J. Sweet
4th Battery, Indiana Light Artillery,
Captain Asahel K. Bush
Battery A, Kentucky Light Artillery,
Captain David C. Stone

II Corps

Commander
MG Thomas L. Crittenden
Strength: 20,000 men and 65 cannon

6th Division
BG Thomas J. Wood

15th Brigade
BG Milo S. Hascall
100th Illinois, COL Frederick A. Bartleson
17th Indiana, LTC George W. Gorman
58th Indiana, COL George P. Buell
3d Kentucky, LTC William T. Scott
26th Ohio, Major Chris M. Degenfeld
8th Battery, Indiana Light Artillery,
  Lieutenant George Estep

20th Brigade
COL Charles G. Harker
51st Indiana, COL Abel D. Streight
73d Indiana, COL Gilbert Hathaway
13th Michigan, LTC Frederick W. Gordon
64th Ohio, COL John Ferguson
65th Ohio, LTC William P. Young
6th Battery, Ohio Light Artillery,
  Captain Cullen Bradley

21st Brigade
COL George D. Wagner
15th Indiana, LTC Gustavus A. Wood
40th Indiana, COL John W. Blake
57th Indiana, COL Cyrus C. Hines
24th Kentucky, COL Louis B. Grisby
97th Ohio, COL John Q. Lane
10th Battery, Indiana Light Artillery,
  Captain Jerome B. Cox

Unattached
1st Michigan Engineers and Mechanics
  (four companies), COL William P. Innes
1st Ohio Cavalry (four companies),
  Major James Laughlin
3d Ohio Cavalry (four companies),
  Major John H. Foster

5th Division
BG Horatio P. Van Cleve

11th Brigade
COL Samuel Beatty
79th Indiana, COL Frederick Knefler
9th Kentucky, LTC George H. Cram
13th Kentucky, LTC J.B. Carlile
19th Ohio, LTC E.W. Hollingsworth
59th Ohio, COL James P. Fyffe
7th Battery, Indiana Light Artillery,
  Captain George Swallow

14th Brigade
COL Pierce B. Hawkins
44th Indiana, COL Hugh B. Reed
86th Indiana, COL Orville S. Hamilton
11th Kentucky, LTC S.P. Love
26th Kentucky, COL Cicero Maxwell
13th Ohio, COL Joseph C. Hawkins
Battery B, Pennsylvania Light
  Artillery, Lieutenant Alanson Stevens

23d Brigade
COL Stanley Mathews
35th Indiana, COL Bernard F. Mullen
8th Kentucky, COL Sidney M. Barnes
21st Kentucky, COL Samuel W. Price
51 Ohio, LTC Richard W. McClain
99th Ohio, LTC John E. Cummins
3d Battery, Wisconsin Light Artillery,
  Captain Lucius Drury

4th Division
BG William Sooy Smith

10th Brigade
COL William Grose
84th Illinois, COL Louis H. Waters
36th Indiana, LTC Oliver H.P. Carey
23d Kentucky, LTC J.P. Jackson
6th Ohio, COL Nicholas L. Anderson
24th Ohio, LTC Frederick C. Jones
Battery H, 4th U.S Artillery,
  Lieutenant Samuel Canby
Battery M, 4th US Artillery,
  Captain John Mendenhall

19th Brigade
COL William B. Hazen
110th Illinois, COL Thomas S. Casey
9th Indiana, COL William H. Blake
6th Kentucky, COL Walter C. Whitaker
27th Kentucky, COL C.D. Pennebaker
41st Ohio, LTC George S. Mygatt
Battery F, 1st Ohio Light Artillery,
  Captain Daniel T. Cockerill

22d Brigade
BG Charles Cruft
31st Indiana, LTC John Osborn
1st Kentucky, LTC David A. Enyart
22d Kentucky, COL Thomas D. Sedgewick
20th Kentucky, LTC Charles S. Hanson
90th Ohio, COL Isaac N. Ross
Battery B, 1st Ohio Light Artillery,
  Captain William E. Standart

Cavalry
2d Kentucky (four companies),
  LTC Thomas B. Cochran

1st Cavalry Brigade
COL Edward M. McCook
2d Indiana Cavalry, LTC Robert Stewart
3d Kentucky Cavalry, COL Eli Murray
Battery M, 4th US Light Artillery (one section), Lieutenant Henry A. Huntington
1st Kentucky Cavalry, COL Frank Wolford
7th Pennsylvania Cavalry (one battalion), MAJ John E. Wynkoop

III Corps

Commander
MG Charles C. Gilbert
Strength: 22,000 men and 44 cannon

11th Division
BG Philip H. Sheridan

35th Brigade
LTC Bernard Laibold
44th Illinois, Captain Wallace W. Barrett
73d Illinois, COL James F. Jaques
2d Missouri, Captain Walter Hoppe
15th Missouri, Major John Weber

36th Brigade
COL Daniel McCook
85th Illinois, COL Robert S. Moore
86th Illinois, COL David D. Irons
125th Illinois, COL Oscar F. Harmon
52d Ohio, LTC Daniel D. T. Cowen

37th Brigade
COL Nicholas Greusel
36th Illinois, Captain Silas Miller
88th Illinois, COL Francis T. Sherman
21st Michigan, COL Ambrose A. Stevens
24th Wisconsin, COL Charles H. Larrabee

Artillery
Battery I, 2d Illinois Light Artillery,
Captain Charles M. Barnett
Battery G, 1st Missouri Light Artillery,
Captain Henry Hescock

3d Cavalry Brigade
Captain Ebenezer Gay
9th Kentucky Cavalry (eight companies), LTC John Boyle
2d Michigan Cavalry, LTC Archibald P. Campbell
9th Pennsylvania Cavalry, LTC Thomas C. James
2d Battery, Minnesota Light Artillery (one section),
Captain William A. Hotchkiss

9th Division
BG Robert B. Mitchell

13th Brigade
COL Michael Gooding
59th Illinois, Major Joshua C. Winters
74th Illinois, COL James B. Kerr
75th Illinois, LTC John E. Bennett
22d Indiana, LTC Squire I. Keith
5th Battery, Wisconsin Light Artillery,
Captain Oscar F. Pinney

31st Brigade
COL William P. Carlin
21st Illinois, COL John Alexander
38th Illinois, Major Daniel H. Gilmer
101st Ohio, COL Leander Stem
15th Wisconsin, COL Hans C. Heg
2d Minnesota Battery (two sections),
Lieutenant Richard L. Dawley

32d Brigade
COL William W. Caldwell
25th Illinois, LTC James S. McClelland
35th Illinois, LTC William P. Chandler
81st Indiana, LTC John Timberlake
8th Kansas (Battalion), LTC John A. Martin
8th Battery, Wisconsin Light Artillery,
Captain Stephen J. Carpenter

Unattached
36th Illinois Infantry (one mounted company),
Captain Samuel B. Sherer

1st Division
BG Albin Schoepf

1st Brigade
COL Moses B. Walker
82d Indiana, COL Morton C. Hunter
12th Kentucky, COL William A. Hoskins
17th Ohio, COL John M. Connell
31st Ohio, LTC Frederick W. Lister
38th Ohio, LTC William A. Choate
Battery D, 1st Michigan Light Artillery,
Captain J.W. Church

2d Brigade
BG Speed S. Fry
10th Indiana, COL William C. Kise
74th Indiana, COL Charles W. Chapman
4th Kentucky, COL John T. Croxton
10th Kentucky, LTC William H. Hays
14th Ohio, LTC George P. Este
Battery C, 1s Ohio Light Artillery,
Captain D.K. Southwick

3d Brigade
BG James B. Steedman
87th Indiana, COL Kline G. Shyrock
2d Minnesota, COL James George
9th Ohio, LTC Charles Joseph
35th Ohio, COL Ferdinand Van Derveer
18th US, Major Frederick Townsend
Battery I, 4th US Light Artillery,
Lieutenant Frank G. Smith

Unattached
1st Ohio Cavalry (six companies),
COL Minor Milliken

Appendix B
Army of the Mississippi Order of Battle

Army of the Mississippi

Left Wing

Right Wing

Army of the Mississippi

Strength: 16,800 men and 56 cannon

Commander
General Braxton Bragg
Escort
3d Tennessee Cavalry (four companies)
13th Tennessee Cavalry Battalion (one company)

Left Wing
MG William J. Hardee
Anderson's Division
BG J. Patton Anderson
Buckner's Division
MG Simon Bolivar Buckner
Wheeler's Cavalry Brigade
COL Joseph Wheeler

Right Wing
MG Leonidas Polk
Cheatham's Division
MG Benjamin Franklin Cheatham
Wharton's Cavalry Brigade
COL John A. Warton

Left Wing

Commander
MG William J. Hardee
Strength: 9,451 men and 40 cannon

Buckner's Division
MG Simon Bolivar Buckner

Cleburne's Brigade
Brigadier General Patrick R. Cleburne
13/15th Arkansas, Col. Lucius E. Polk
2nd Tennessee, Capt. C. P. Moore
35th Tennessee, Col. Benjamin J. Hill
48th Tennessee, Col. George H. Nixon
Lt. Thomas Key's Section, Calverts Arkansas Battery

Liddell's Brigade
BG St. John R. Liddell
2d Arkansas, COL John Graibot
5th Arkansas, COL Lucius P. Featherston
6th Arkansas, COL Alexander T. Hawthorne
7th Arkansas, COL D. A. Gillespie
8th Arkansas, COL John H. Kelly
Captain Charles Swett's Mississippi Battery

Johnson's Brigade
BG Bushrod R. Johnson
5th Confederate, COL James A. Smith
17th Tennessee, COL Albert S. Marks
23d Tennessee, LTC Richard H. Keeble
25th Tennessee, COL John M. Hughs
37th Tennessee, COL Moses White
44th Tennessee, COL John S. Fulton
Captain Putnam Darden's Mississippi Battery

Wood's Brigade
BG Sterling A.M. Wood
16th Alabama, COL William B. Wood
33d Alabama, COL Samuel Adams
3d Confederate, LTC Henry V. Keep
32d Mississippi, COL Mark P. Lowrey
45th Mississippi, COL Aaron B. Hardcastle
15th Battalion, Mississippi Sharp-shooters, Major A.T. Hawkins
Captain Henry C. Semple's Alabama Battery

Anderson's Division
BG J. Patton Anderson

Adams' Brigade
BG Daniel W. Adams
13th Louisiana, COL Randall L. Gibson
16th Louisiana, COL Daniel C. Gober
20th Louisiana, COL August Reichard
25th Louisiana, COL Stewart W. Fisk
14th Battalion, Louisiana Sharp-shooters, Maj. John E. Austin
5th Company, Washington Artillery, Captain Cuthbert H. Slocomb

Jones' Brigade
COL Thomas Marshall Jones
27th Mississippi, LTC James L. Autry
30th Mississippi, COL G. F. Neill
34th Mississippi, COL Samuel Benton
Battery F, 2d Alabama Light Artillery, Captain Charles L. Lumsden

Brown's Brigade
BG John C. Brown
1st Florida, COL William Miller
3d Florida, COL Daniel B. Bird
41st Mississippi, COL William F. Tucker
Battery A, 14th Battalion, Georgia Light Artillery, Captain Joseph Palmer

Powell's Brigade
COL Samuel Powell
45th Alabama, COL James G. Gilchrist
1st Arkansas, COL John W. Colquitt
24th Mississippi, COL William F. Dowd
29th Tennessee, LTC Horace Rice
Captain Overton W. Barrets Missouri Battery

Wheeler's Cavalry Brigade
COL Joseph Wheeler
1st Alabama Cavalry, COL William W. Allen
3d Alabama Cavalry, COL James Hagan
6th Confederate Cavalry, LTC James A. Pell
8th Confederate Cavalry, COL W. B. Wade
2d Georgia Cavalry (five companies) Major C. A. Whaley
Smith's Georgia Cavalry Battalion, COL John R. Hart
1st Kentucky Cavalry (five companies), Major John W. Caldwell
6th Kentucky Cavalry (three companies), J. Warren Grigsby
9th Tennessee Cavalry, James D Bennett
12th Tennessee Cavalry Battalion (four companies), LTC T. W. Adrian
Lieutenant S.G. Hanley's Section, Calverts Arkansas Battery

205

Right Wing

Commander
MG Leonidas Polk
Strength: 7,349 men and 16 cannon

First Division
MG Benjamin Cheatam

Donelson's Brigade
BG Daniel S Donelson
8th Tennessee, COL William L. Moore
15th Tennessee, COL Robert C. Tyler
16th Tennessee, COL John H. Savage
38th Tennessee, COL John C. Carter
51st Tennessee, COL John Chester
Captain William W. Carnes's
Tennessee Battery

Stewart's Brigade
BG Alexander P. Stewart
4th Tennessee, COL Otho F. Strahl
5th Tennessee, COL Calvin D. Venable
24th Tennessee, LTC Hugh L.W. Bratton
31st Tennessee, COL Egbert E. Tansil
33d Tennessee, COL Warner P. Jones
Captain Thomas J. Stanford's Mississippi Battery

Maney's Brigade
BG George Maney
41st Georgia, COL Charles A. McDaniel
1st Tennessee, COL Hume R. Field
6th Tennessee, COL George C. Porter
9th Tennessee, LTC John W. Buford
27th Tennessee, LTC William Frierson
Captain Melancthon Smith's Mississippi Battery
(Lieutenant William B. Turner)

Smith's Brigade
BG Preston Smith
12th Tennessee, COL Tyree H. Bell
13th Tennessee, COL Alfred J. Vaughan, Jr.
47th Tennessee, COL Munson R. Hill
154th Tennessee, COL Michael Magevney
9th Texas, COL William H. Young
Captain William L. Scott's Tennessee Battery

Wharton's Cavalry Brigade
COL John A. Wharton
2d Georgia Cavalry (four companies), LTC Arthur Hood
1st Kentucky Cavalry (four companies), Captain Thomas A. Ireland
4th Tennessee Cavalry (five companies), Major Baxter Smith
Major John Davis' Tennessee Cavalry Battalion (four companies)
8th Texas Cavalry, LTC Thomas Harrison

Appendix C
Medal of Honor Recipients

John S. Durham

Background: Born in New York, New York in 1843
Entered service in Malone, St. Croix County, Wisconsin

Rank at Perryville: Sergeant

Company: F

Regiment: 1st Wisconsin Infantry

Meritorious action: Seized the flag of his regiment when the color sergeant was shot and advanced with the flag midway between the lines amid a shower of shot, shell, and bullets until stopped by his commanding officer.

Date of Issue: 20 November 1896

William H. Surles

Background: Born on 24 February 1845 in Steubenville, Ohio

Rank at Perryville: Private

Company: G

Regiment: 2d Ohio Infantry

Meritorious action: In the hottest part of the fire he stepped in front of his colonel to shield him from the enemy's fire.

Appendix D
Meteorological Data

❖ North central Kentucky suffered from severe drought conditions in fall 1862. No appreciable rain fell in the days immediately before the battle on 8 October. Consequently water levels in the Chaplin River and Doctors Creek were very low.

❖ A steady wind blew from the south-southwest and contributed to the acoustic shadow experienced at MG Buell's headquarters.

❖ Weather conditions during the battle were unseasonably hot and dry, aggravating the dehydration most soldiers experienced.

❖ A burning barn and grass in the vicinity of Stand 15 marred the clear skies and excellent visibility that predominated during actual combat.

❖ The area experienced a full moon the night of 7 October.

❖ On 8 October sunrise occurred at 0504 and sunset at 1733. Evening twilight ended at 1759.

Appendix E
Cavalry Operations in the Kentucky Campaign

Cavalry significantly influenced the course and outcome of the Kentucky campaign. Mounted forces set the stage for the campaign, proved to be the principal source of intelligence for all armies involved, and were responsible for the poor situational awareness demonstrated at Perryville. The campaign witnessed the Confederate cavalry's steady decline in effectiveness through overuse. Conversely Union mounted forces became more aggressive and increasingly capable of performing a wide range of missions. These trends foreshadowed similar later developments throughout the Union and Confederate armies.

Following the siege and Confederate withdrawal from Corinth in May 1862 Southern fortunes in the west reached a nadir. The overwhelming concentration of Union forces in and around Corinth temporarily stifled Confederate offensive operations. The Army of the Mississippi constituted the principal Southern army in the region, but it lay in a demoralized state at Tupelo, its strength dissipated through disease and desertions. When MG Don Carlos Buell's Union Army of the Ohio undertook operations east toward Chattanooga and eastern Tennessee it faced little opposition. A weak garrison held Chattanooga, but it could not hope to hold the town against a sustained attack. Indeed, an earlier foray by BG Ormsby M. Mitchel's division quickly came within striking distance of the town.

Despite the lack of organized resistance, however, Buell needed to overcome significant logistics obstacles. His supply source was in Louisville, Kentucky, necessitating the maintenance of a supply line more than 300 miles long. Rail transport permitted rapid supply movement only from Louisville to Nashville. Wagon train shuttles had to carry the supplies from central Tennessee to his field forces in northern Alabama. Nor was Buell permitted simply to march on Chattanooga. His mission included repairing and securing the Memphis and Charleston Railroad that connected Chattanooga and Corinth. The railroad required extensive track repair and the rebuilding of trestles and bridges destroyed during previous operations. Simultaneously Buell sought to improve his logistics infrastructure by establishing rail links between Nashville and forward depots in northern Alabama. He tried to transform his supply line from a collection of wagons, trains, and ferries into an efficient rail-based one that could sustain his army once it entered Chattanooga.

These efforts required time, and they occupied Buell's army throughout much of June and July. The Confederates lacked sufficient strength at

Chattanooga to confront Buell directly in battle. Instead they seized the initiative by using cavalry and partisan groups to interfere with Union operations. In June while Buell's army repaired railroads Confederate raiders began to strike at small concentrations of Union troops in eastern Tennessee and northeastern Alabama. These operations did not jeopardize Northern campaign plans, but they raised concerns about central Tennessee's security. Moreover additional Confederate cavalry forces were being raised to conduct larger-scale expeditions. At Chattanooga two new cavalry brigades formed—one commanded by COL John H. Morgan, the other by newly promoted BG Nathan B. Forrest. By month's end the Confederate mounted force in eastern Tennessee amounted to four brigades commanded by Morgan, Forrest, Colonel John Scott, and Colonel Benjamin Allston.

In July Morgan embarked upon a raid into Kentucky intended to strike at the vulnerable Louisville and Nashville Railroad. Near Tompkinsville, Kentucky, Morgan attacked and routed a Union force moving to intercept him. He then destroyed supplies gathered at Glasgow and Lebanon, moved along the Louisville and Nashville Railroad, and headed east. He crossed the Kentucky River near Lawrence and entered the Bluegrass region of north central Kentucky. There he roamed freely, defeating several small garrisons and destroying Union military supplies. He evaded pursuit and arrived safely back in eastern Tennessee convinced that a large segment of the Kentucky population would support a Confederate invasion of the Commonwealth.

While Morgan spread panic and mayhem in Kentucky, Forrest launched his new command into central Tennessee. He made several attacks in the vicinity of Nashville against Union outposts, destroying stores and burning bridges. On 13 July Forrest struck at Murfreesboro, defended by Union infantry and cavalry. He captured the garrison and a cache of supplies before moving down the Nashville and Chattanooga Railroad destroying track and bridges. This line had only just been opened to Union rail traffic the previous day, and Buell relied on it to create a forward depot at Stevenson to sustain his army in its final advance on Chattanooga. Forrest's attack constituted a major blow against Buell's emerging rail-based supply line.

However, additional threats to the Union rear area materialized in northern Mississippi and Alabama. Partisan bands launched continuous strikes against the Memphis and Charleston Railroad between Tuscumbia and Decatur. Indeed the barren, inhospitable region through which the railroad ran proved to be an ideal haven for these irregular elements. Much of the populace proved to be pro-Confederate. In late July BG Frank Armstrong led a cavalry brigade against the railroad near Decatur. In a series of actions he defeated one Union garrison, destroyed track and bridges, and seized temporary control of portions of the line. When General Bragg prepared to move the Army of the Mississippi to Chattanooga, he also dispatched a cavalry force under COL Joseph Wheeler into western Tennessee to shift attention from his army's movement. Through his actions Wheeler tried to create the impression of a pending Confederate advance into the same area. By attaching a small force of infantry he tried to reinforce the impression that his actions were more than just a cavalry raid. He also waged a campaign of disinformation, leaking false information concerning the movements of Bragg's army. After initial forays against Union positions he dispersed his command and commenced a series of raids as if to foreshadow a major offensive.

Collectively the activities of Confederate cavalry and partisans in June and July underscored the vulnerability of Buell's supply line and indeed the entire Department of the Ohio's rear area. While his principal objective was to capture Chattanooga, as a department commander Buell retained responsibility for much of Tennessee and Kentucky. In addition to maintaining sufficient combat power for an attack on Chattanooga he also had to repair the rail net over which his supplies flowed and provide security for the entire departmental area. The Confederate raids threatened all three primary responsibilities.

Buell faced the dilemma of how best to allocate his forces among rear area security, railroad maintenance, and direct operations against Chattanooga. He resisted the temptation to dilute his forward combat power too much to secure his lines of communication. Instead he resorted to establishing fortified outposts at critical points. These he garrisoned to check against roving cavalry and partisans. He could not entirely leave his forward dispositions unaltered, however, in the face of increasingly effective Confederate cavalry attacks. Political pressure for protection in Kentucky and Tennessee rose dramatically in the wake of Morgan and Forrest's activities, and the temporary disruption to Union supplies their raids caused helped to slow the pace of operations against Chattanooga. Buell was forced to respond by shifting some of his infantry from northern Alabama into central Tennessee to protect the approaches to Nashville and the capital. He left Kentucky to fend for itself with the forces that were on hand.

The Confederate cavalry's successes and their mobility encouraged changes in the Union cavalry's organization and use. At the start of the

Chattanooga campaign much of Buell's cavalry did not operate in large concentrations. Instead regiments found their companies dispersed among multiple infantry divisions where they served under an infantry commander performing reconnaissance and administrative activities. Alternatively regiments were split into detachments and scattered over a broad area to provide security to railroads and supplies. A brigade organization did not exist. Cavalry equipment varied considerably from regiment to regiment. Some units had few firearms, making even small-scale skirmishes with their Confederate counterparts' hazardous undertakings.

Others benefited from much better weaponry. The 2d Michigan, for example, carried Colt revolving rifles that gave it a considerable firepower advantage in combat. Similarly the quality of mounts also varied widely. Most units discovered that their best horses were those initially issued to the unit. Afterward the likelihood of receiving quality mounts declined sharply because of a scarcity of animals suitable for military use and the Army's growing demand for horses. Dispersion, inadequate equipment, and the status of their mounts inhibited the Union cavalry's effective training. As a result their employment tended to be much more conservative and less effective than Confederate cavalry regiments.

At the end of June the Army of the Ohio included nearly 5,000 cavalry soldiers. However, the climate in northern Alabama took its toll of men and animals. With the army focused on movement along and repair of the Memphis and Charleston Railroad, railroad security and repair constituted the Union cavalry's principal activities. Some cavalry soldiers functioned in work gangs, laying and repairing track, although such work did little to hone their effectiveness as mounted soldiers. Against the Confederate raids of June and July the Union cavalry proved only marginally effective. It certainly did not stop or discourage similar future endeavors. Indeed the frequency of such raids created the impression of swarms of Confederate cavalry roaming at will throughout Tennessee and Kentucky.

Buell attempted several measures to cope with the raiders. He sought additional mounted units. In late July the War Department authorized the creation of six new regiments in Kentucky, but the time needed to raise and train cavalry limited their influence in both the Chattanooga campaign and the subsequent Confederate invasion of Kentucky. Infantry commanders found themselves encouraged to act aggressively against enemy mounted threats, but they could not match the enemy cavalry's mobility. Buell also attempted to create a larger cavalry organization. On 24 July, responding to Forrest's and Morgan's actions, he directed BG Richard W. Johnson to assume command of several cavalry and infantry regiments with artillery and operate against the Confederate raiders in central Tennessee. Johnson was to build a combined arms brigade to fight as a concentrated mass. However, the infantry assigned to it was soon reassigned, and Johnson's command became a pure cavalry organization.

August marked the end of Buell's attempt to take Chattanooga. Bragg's Army of the Mississippi arrived in the town before undertaking its own offensive while MG Edmund Kirby Smith's Army of Eastern Tennessee prepared to invade Kentucky. Smith's preparations included dispatching John Hunt Morgan on another raid toward Gallatin, Tennessee, to divert Union attention away from his intended movements near the Cumberland Gap. On 11 August Morgan left Sparta, Tennessee, passed through Hartsville, and arrived at Gallatin on the 12th. The same day he attacked the town and captured its garrison of nearly 400 Union soldiers. The Louisville and Nashville Railroad ran through a tunnel near Gallatin. Morgan destroyed the tunnel by running several burning freight cars into it. This action effectively cut Buell's link with his base in Louisville and stopped all traffic on the railroad for the 98 days it took to repair the tunnel. Morgan remained in the vicinity for several days, destroying additional track and a railroad trestle.

Buell responded by ordering BG Johnson to gather all available cavalry in central Tennessee and pursue Morgan. Johnson gave chase with elements drawn from four different cavalry regiments. Catching Morgan near Gallatin Johnson attacked on 21 August. In the ensuing battle, however, Morgan's men outfought Johnson and forced him to surrender along with much of his command. The Confederate cavalry then retired to Hartsville and rested. Morgan had cut the Louisville and Nashville Railroad and destroyed Buell's only effort to date at creating a brigade-size cavalry organization.

Morgan's raid focused Union attention on the Louisville and Nashville Railroad while Smith's Army of Eastern Tennessee crossed the Cumberland Mountains into Kentucky. Smith bypassed the Union position astride the Cumberland Gap, instead moving quickly toward Lexington. Scott's cavalry brigade screened the movement of Smith's columns into Kentucky. Once the Army had concentrated on the principal road heading toward Lexington Scott's cavalry probed ahead, giving Smith a clear sense of Union dispositions across his path. This information encouraged the army commander to act aggressively and move quickly to cross the Kentucky River before its banks could become part of a naturally strong defensive line. Warned of a Union force south of the Kentucky River, Smith advanced and attacked. Fought on 30 August, the ensuing battle of Richmond resulted in a decisive Confederate victory. Scott's cavalry developed the situation before the battle and blocked the Union retreat afterward, ensuring that most of those enemy soldiers not killed or wounded became prisoners.

Conversely a lack of information hampered Union movements in the days before the battle of Richmond. In the wake of Morgan's severance of the Louisville and Nashville Railroad, Buell dispatched MG William Nelson and several other officers to Louisville to organize Kentucky's defenses and repair the railroad. Upon arriving in Louisville, however, Nelson became the commander of the Army of Kentucky that was formed in response to Smith invading the state. Nelson gathered newly formed regiments in the Danville-Lancaster region of Kentucky. From this central position he tried to protect the Louisville and Nashville Railroad and Buell's open northern flank. He could also move to relieve the Union forces trapped at the Cumberland Gap. However, Nelson's dispositions were made without accurate information regarding Smith's army. Three new cavalry regiments had been raised and placed under BG James S. Jackson's overall command. Their mission included determining the strength and location of Smith's army. Ironically they accomplished this objective, but the information failed to reach Nelson in time to avert the disaster at Richmond. There, two Union infantry brigades without orders suddenly found themselves confronting Smith's Confederates. Jackson's cavalry provided only limited support and did not effectively cover the Union infantry's retreat.

After the battle of Richmond Smith's cavalry moved quickly to secure a crossing site over the Kentucky River and prevent the creation of a Union defensive line along this natural barrier. Scott's Confederate cavalry brigade brushed aside the meager opposition it encountered, crossed the Kentucky River, and quickly seized Lexington and Frankfort. His rapid thrust increased the confusion and panic among the Union command structure. Smith exploited this situation to consolidate his hold on the state capital and the Bluegrass region. A mixed cavalry and infantry force also marched toward Cincinnati, threatening a Union force holding Covington, Kentucky, directly across the Ohio River from Cincinnati. Cavalry probes moved toward Louisville.

The remnants of the Union Army of Kentucky retired on Louisville. Jackson's cavalry and a second makeshift mounted force commanded by Captain Ebenezer Gay provided a rear guard to cover this retreat. Upon reaching Louisville the army remained there and began to fortify the city in expectation of a Confederate attack. With much of central Kentucky cleared of a Northern military presence Smith dispersed his army. In actuality too weak to either attack Louisville or Cincinnati, he contented himself with securing his gains, capitalizing on Union fears of further offensive operations by his army. Such actions, however, were largely limited to cavalry raids against portions of the Louisville and Nashville Railroad. Morgan rejoined the army at Lexington on 4 September. While most of his command moved north to Covington, a small party attacked Shepherdsville. There it overcame the garrison and burned the railroad bridge over the Salt River. Although the bridge was not entirely destroyed it suffered sufficient damage to render it inoperable. Scott similarly moved west to attack the rail line, targeting the large span across the Green River at Munfordville. There he met advance elements of Bragg's Army of the Mississippi and participated in the failed attack on the town on 14 September.

These activities underscored the cavalry's highly visible role. Consequently many of the few Kentuckians who volunteered to fight for the Confederacy during the campaign did so in newly raised cavalry regiments. However, aside from raids Smith's army remained in the Lexington-Frankfort area for much of the remainder of the Kentucky campaign. Lacking sufficient strength to mount a major attack on its own, Smith's army did not try to coordinate its efforts with Bragg's Army of the Mississippi. He did agree to return the two infantry brigades he borrowed from Bragg at the start of his own invasion of Kentucky. This move reduced Smith's infantry strength further and did little to encourage him to play a more aggressive role.

Smith's Army of Eastern Tennessee began its move through the Cumberland Mountains into Kentucky on 13 August. Bragg's Army of the Mississippi did not commence operations until the 28th. It spent the interim waiting on its artillery and wagon train to arrive and making final preparations. During this period Forrest's cavalry brigade launched another raid into central Tennessee. For several days he tracked a large Union wagon train moving from McMinnville to Murfreesboro. The train included nearly 400 wagons and a powerful escort. Forrest planned his attack and struck on 27 August. Unable to overcome the escort he retired to begin a series of attacks on select Union positions. However, unlike his earlier spectacular success at Murfreesboro, these actions ended in a string of defeats and considerable casualties to his command. Moreover, engaged in these operations, Forrest was unable to support Bragg's army as it began to move through the Sequatchie Valley and Cumberland Mountains on the 28th.

Instead Bragg relied on Wheeler's cavalry brigade and two additional mounted regiments commanded by COL John Lay. These elements screened the advancing infantry columns and provided intelligence regarding what lay along their line of march. Wheeler's brigade also undertook a series of offensive movements intended to divert Union attention away from Bragg's army and its northward movement toward Sparta. These deception operations included spreading disinformation. Collectively the Confederate cavalry's efforts proved successful. With one exception Buell's cavalry failed to pinpoint the location of Bragg's infantry columns. On 29 August the 3d Ohio Cavalry penetrated the Confederate screen and identified Bragg's headquarters and three of his infantry brigades. In general, however, Buell and his commanders did not acquire a clear sense of Confederate intentions or their dispositions. Thanks to Wheeler's actions Bragg's army seemed to be everywhere and nowhere. Amid this confusion Forrest rejoined the Army of the Mississippi by moving through the rear of Buell's army and creating further uncertainty regarding Confederate intent.

Buell responded by withdrawing his army first to Murfreesboro and then to Nashville. Lacking timely and accurate information on Bragg's movements he fell back on the main route to Nashville, which he feared might be the Confederate objective. Later Buell would be accused of "suffering Kentucky to be invaded by rebels under General Bragg." Poor situational awareness and the lack of accurate information on Bragg's movements certainly influenced Buell's decision to withdraw. This retrograde movement marked the success of screening and deception efforts by the Confederate cavalry.

Having negotiated the Cumberland Mountains and evaded Buell, the Army of the Mississippi headed north toward Kentucky. Bragg initially considered striking at Nashville and recovering central Tennessee. However, apprised by his cavalry of the city's fortifications and Buell's obvious preparations to march his army north, Bragg opted for Kentucky. He tried to draw Buell's forces out of Tennessee and keep between them and Smith's army in the Bluegrass region. While the infantry columns marched toward Glasgow, Kentucky, Forrest's and Wheeler's cavalry brigades tracked and reported Buell's movements directly to Bragg. The cavalry also attempted to delay the Union march, but it had little success in doing so.

Buell's rapid march from Nashville resulted in the Confederate cavalry getting astride the Union line of march only after numerous elements had already passed safely toward Bowling Green. However, several skirmishes with Wheeler and Forrest did occur, and in one of these Confederate cavalry captured dispatches for the Army of the Ohio that clearly indicated Buell's intentions. Armed with this information Bragg moved his army quickly north. His infantry began to arrive in Glasgow on 12 September with elements of Chalmers' brigade sent forward to Cave City to break the Louisville and Nashville Railroad.

At Glasgow Bragg reorganized his cavalry. He subordinated Wheeler's and Forrest's brigades to his left and right wing commanders, respectively. This change effectively ended the direct communications link between the army commander and his cavalry. Instead the cavalry's reports were now to be channeled through the wing commanders. Wheeler remained responsible for maintaining a rear guard and delaying the Union march. Forrest, however, received the task of reconnoitering and screening the army's northward march. With his army north of Buell's, Bragg also reshuffled his mounted strength. He placed most of his cavalry strength under Wheeler, leaving Forrest two regiments and one squadron with which to conduct his tasks. These adjustments were not implemented until after the battle of Munfordville.

Munfordville attracted the attention of Scott's cavalry. Scott had been sent to attack bridges along the Louisville and Nashville Railroad. One of the largest lay at Munfordville on the Green River. When Scott arrived he found the town too heavily garrisoned to attack alone. However, he soon encountered Chalmers' brigade embarked on its mission to Cave City. Together Chalmers and Scott determined to attack Munfordville on 14 September. This attempt failed and the bridge remained intact, securely in Union hands. Bragg responded by marching his entire army to Munfordville and forcing the garrison's surrender on the 15th. The Army of the Mississippi then spent several days at the town prepared to give battle should Buell attempt to force the Green River line.

The Union commander, however, resolved to attack Glasgow under the mistaken understanding that Bragg's army still remained there. This inaccurate intelligence reflected Buell's poorer situational awareness during the march from Nashville to Bowling Green. While Bragg received regular reports on the Union army's status and location, Buell received minimal information regarding Confederate movements. Bragg correspondingly sought to maneuver himself onto Buell's supply line ahead of the Union army while Buell simply continued his march north unsure of Confederate intentions or location. On 16 September Union forces advanced on Glasgow against the limited opposition that Wheeler's rear guard actions offered. Unknown to the Union attackers Bragg's wagon train remained in Glasgow. Wheeler took it upon himself to protect the train and move it north. Fighting a series of delaying actions he rejoined

Bragg at Munfordville with the train intact on 18 September. Learning of Munfordville's capture and the prior Confederate movement from Glasgow, Buell moved to Cave City just over 10 miles from Munfordville.

During these movements the Union cavalry began to demonstrate a new aggressiveness and effectiveness. On the eve of the Confederate advance from Chattanooga Buell authorized the creation of a light brigade, comprising four cavalry and two infantry regiments. Tasked with countering Morgan's and Forrest's actions in the Nashville and Murfreesboro areas this brigade marked the latest in a string of actions intended to combat the roving Confederate cavalry. On 5 September Buell also established a cavalry division. Commanded by COL John Kennett, it comprised two brigades led by COL Edward McCook and COL Lewis Zahm. However, this formation lacked an effective organization, and many of its soldiers had little sufficient training. Consequently the brigades were employed separately, and the division remained such in name only.

The abortive attack on Glasgow marked the first aggressive use of these brigades. They led Buell's infantry columns and engaged Wheeler's rear guard in a series of skirmishes. Forced to maneuver to avoid envelopment by the Union cavalry and still trying to cover the escape of the Confederate wagon train Wheeler's ability to conduct reconnaissance diminished. Consequently Bragg learned belatedly of the arrival of Buell's army at Cave City. The news came as an unpleasant surprise for the Confederate commander, and it forced him to decide quickly whether to risk a fight on the Green River line. The Union cavalry had effectively screened Buell's advance.

Bragg opted to retire on Bardstown. The army arrived there on 23 September where it remained until early October. During this period Wheeler and Forrest dispersed their brigades to cover the principal approaches to Bardstown from west and north. Wheeler covered a line stretching along the Rolling Fork River from New Haven to Lebanon Junction while Forrest's smaller force deployed along the Salt River from Taylorsville toward Shepherdsville. Despite the broad frontage over which the brigades assumed responsibility, the imbalance of forces between them remained unchanged. Most of Bragg's cavalry assets remained with Wheeler. Those elements unattached to either brigade served in detachments performing a variety of administrative and escort duties, particularly with respect to the wagon train. Neither brigade had sufficient strength to contest any serious advance on them. The Confederate cavalry was vulnerable to defeat in detail by sudden attack.

Such an attack materialized from elements of Buell's increasingly aggressive cavalry. Bragg's retreat to Bardstown provided Buell with an unobstructed path to Louisville where his army began to arrive on 25 September. However, McCook's cavalry brigade of Kennett's division remained at Elizabethtown where it guarded the flank of the army's march route north. It also lay poised to act against further attacks on the Louisville and Nashville Railroad or strike at Wheeler's line along the Rolling Fork River. Zahm's brigade escorted Buell's wagon train toward Louisville. Since the abortive attack on Glasgow both brigades became seasoned through continuous skirmishes with Wheeler's rear guard. Unlike many of Buell's cavalry regiments these mounted elements had not compromised their effectiveness through detachments to infantry divisions. Consequently they became more capable. Nevertheless McCook and Zahm's brigades generally operated independently rather than as integral parts of a division structure. Yet their aggressiveness and emerging prowess soon began to tell on their Confederate counterparts.

On 29 September elements of McCook's brigade struck Wheeler's line at New Haven. There they surprised the 3d Georgia Cavalry and captured most of that regiment without loss. This action symbolized the shift in relative effectiveness between the Union and Confederate cavalry in the Kentucky campaign. While the former began to shed its inefficiency through better organization and aggressive leadership the latter lost its tactical edge. The Confederate cavalry's declining effectiveness stemmed partly from exhaustion and attrition. It had remained in continuous action and in close contact with the enemy since Bragg's departure from Chattanooga. Now with the army resting at Bardstown the cavalry remained in the field.

Although the Confederates raised some new cavalry regiments in Kentucky, these units lacked training and equipment. Moreover, they predominantly served in Smith's army, leaving Bragg's mounted arm without any reliable source of replacements. The loss of the 3d Georgia at New Haven was compounded by the temporary loss of the 6th Confederate Cavalry. This unit was undergoing reorganization and in the midst of selecting new officers through a contentious election process. Moreover those chosen had still to stand before a formal board that would determine their military competency to lead. Hence the regiment remained in disarray and largely ineffective pending the confirmation of its leadership. A third cavalry regiment, the 2d Georgia, had been effectively dissolved to provide detachments for a variety of administrative and escort functions for the army.

Leadership loss also undermined the Confederate cavalry's performance. The commander of the 3d Georgia had been captured at New Haven, and the commander of the 2d Georgia resigned for personal reasons. Elections in the 6th Confederate resulted in ousting an experienced cavalry leader in favor of another officer who was still in Mississippi. In his absence yet another commander assumed temporary command of the regiment. Continuous operations and skirmishing with Union forces also resulted in the combat loss of many junior officers, including company commanders. Centrally coordinating the cavalry's actions might have offset the effects of leader loss at the regimental level, but Bragg's army had no chief of cavalry. Nor did it continue to benefit from Forrest's presence as a brigade commander. On 25 September Bragg ordered him to return to Tennessee and assume command of a new force intended to operate against Nashville and prevent additional forces reaching Buell from western Tennessee. In Kentucky COL John A. Wharton replaced Forrest as brigade commander.

The mounted units serving with Smith's army shared the problems that faced Bragg's cavalry. Overuse and attrition, too, sapped their effectiveness. The willingness of some Kentuckians to volunteer to fight for the Confederacy resulted in the creation of several additional cavalry regiments. Organized into two brigades, one commanded by Morgan and the other by BG Abraham Buford, these units lacked equipment, experienced leaders, and training. Nor did they have sufficient time to address these deficiencies before being thrust into active operations. On 16 September the Union force isolated at the Cumberland Gap began its march through eastern Kentucky toward Ohio and safety. The move surprised Smith. He directed Morgan to harass and delay the Union retreat while he sent his infantry eastward—away from Bragg's army—to an anticipated interception. Morgan, however, could only harass but not delay the Union column. His cavalry proved too weak and green to obstruct the movements of a powerful infantry force resolutely led. On 2 October as the Union force neared the Ohio River, Morgan abandoned his efforts to interfere with its movement.

While focused on eastern Kentucky Smith relied on two other cavalry forces to warn of hostile movements from Cincinnati and Louisville. The 2d Kentucky Regiment was responsible for the region in Kentucky across the Ohio River from Cincinnati. This veteran regiment had been under Morgan's leadership during his summer raids, but it was now led by COL Basil Duke who secured the Confederate northern flank through continuous attacks on outposts and small groups of Union soldiers. In late

September Duke embarked on a more ambitious raid intended to carry these attacks across the Ohio River. On the 27th he attacked the river town of Augusta, Kentucky. Instead of quick victory Duke's command became embroiled in a protracted fight inside the town with the local militia. He defeated this force but at considerable cost in casualties. Abandoning his raid into Ohio Duke retired, barely escaping from a hastily assembled Union pursuit force.

West of Frankfort and the Kentucky River Scott's cavalry brigade maintained a presence across the major routes heading toward the state capital. While Duke embarked on his ill-fated raid, Scott received instructions to advance toward Louisville. By 28 September forward elements lay within 10 miles of the city. Their proximity prompted a concentration of Union cavalry that forced Scott to withdraw several miles or risk a sustained engagement with a larger, aggressive enemy. Captain Ebenezer Gay commanded the Union cavalry in these encounters. Previously he had organized a mounted screen line to cover the principal approaches to Louisville should the Confederates attack.

When Buell arrived in the city he reorganized the Army of the Ohio into three corps. He intended to advance on Bardstown with each of his corps following a different route converging on the town. He also prepared a fourth column to march directly on Frankfort to convince the Confederates that the state capital rather than Bragg's army constituted the Union objective. Buell also restructured his cavalry assets to support these movements. He assigned Gay to command a new brigade formed largely from those cavalry assets already active in the Louisville vicinity. Several other cavalry regiments functioned as collections of detachments assigned to various infantry divisions. Collectively these forces would screen the advance of those columns headed toward Bardstown.

The two brigades of Buell's cavalry division were also available to support operations. McCook's brigade lay at Elizabethtown from where it launched its successful attack on the 3d Georgia at New Haven. Zahm's brigade escorted the Army of the Ohio's wagon train into Louisville. Much of this unit then became assigned to support the feint toward Frankfort. With its component elements operating independently the division commander had little influence over their operations. Moreover, dispersing the formation's brigades effectively nullified the potential tactical value of the division organization. However, Buell's overall cavalry structure marked a significant improvement over the earlier complete dispersal of mounted regiments. The organization and employment of cavalry brigades encouraged improvements in the Union cavalry's effectiveness.

The Confederate cavalry spent the final days of September moving closer to Louisville. In the north Scott advanced a screen line toward the city until his nearness prompted a counterstrike by Union cavalry. Wharton also began to move his cavalry north of the Salt River, maintaining loose contact with Scott on his right and Wheeler on his left. These movements resulted in a weak screen line investing Louisville that might warn Bragg and Smith early of any Union movement out of the city.

On 1 October Buell's army left Louisville. His three corps followed separate but converging roads toward Bardstown while a smaller force feinted toward Frankfort. Cavalry preceded each force, quickly driving back the Confederate screen line. By the evening of 3 October Buell's corps columns had breached Wharton's original line along the Salt River. His feint arrived at Shelbyville, covering more than half the distance between Louisville and Frankfort. Confederate cavalry proved unable to inflict significant delays on any of these movements. Buell's cavalry effectively screened his infantry columns and aggressively sought out Confederate cavalry. The latter retired without being able to determine Buell's location or his army's strength and disposition.

This lack of information hindered Bragg's ability to react. Since he subordinated the cavalry to his wing commanders there was no longer a direct communications link between the army commander and his principal sources of information regarding enemy activities. Instead he relied on reports from his wing commanders. However, Bragg had not remained at Bardstown with his army. He had gone to Frankfort to oversee preparations for the inauguration of a Confederate governor there. This geographic separation lengthened considerably the time lag between the initial acquisition of key information and its receipt by Bragg. Moreover the cavalry's inability to determine the Union columns' strengths resulted in the army commander planning operations without access to either timely or accurate intelligence.

Bragg assumed that Buell sought to recover the state capital. He therefore sought to concentrate his army with Smith's and strike the Union column moving directly on Frankfort. He directed Smith to concentrate his scattered infantry for an attack west. He also ordered the Army of the Mississippi north. Bragg sought to attack the Union column approaching Frankfort from both front and flank. In effect he was belatedly concentrating his forces to strike at Buell's feint. Union forces were already moving east between Bardstown and Frankfort.

In Bragg's absence MG Leonidas Polk commanded the Army of the

Mississippi at Bardstown. Faced with the advance of several enemy columns of unknown strength Polk opted not to follow Bragg's instructions. Instead on 4 October the Confederate Army abandoned the town and retreated toward Danville. It moved in two columns, one led by MG William J. Hardee and the other led by Polk. Cavalry screened these moves. Wheeler's brigade abandoned its line along the Rolling Fork River to protect Hardee's northern flank. Wharton remained in position north of Bardstown until the infantry had cleared the town. Buell, however, attacked. With all three Union corps approaching Bardstown, Buell employed his cavalry with infantry support to envelop Wharton's flanks. The move nearly succeeded, but Wharton drove away the Union cavalry and fought his way out of the trap. Once clear he positioned his brigade to cover the retiring Confederate infantry columns' rear.

By evening Buell's columns had reached Bloomfield and Bardstown, but neither Bragg, Polk, nor Hardee understood the Union army's strength or disposition. Indeed while the Confederates retreated from Bardstown the inauguration ceremony in Frankfort was prematurely ended following the sound of distant artillery fire. Assuming that the capital was soon to be attacked, Bragg and Smith abandoned the town and debated whether to burn the bridges over the Kentucky River. The threat comprised a Union cavalry force that skirmished with elements of Scott's cavalry some 10 miles west of Frankfort. Supporting Union infantry lay too far to the rear to be able to attack the capital as Bragg feared. However, with only vague estimates of the approaching Union force Bragg now planned to concentrate Smith's army and his own at Harrodsburg.

Lack of accurate intelligence continued to generate confusion among the Confederate leadership. On 5 October Union cavalry entered Frankfort. Bragg transferred his headquarters to Harrodsburg, and arrangements were made for Smith to cross the Kentucky River. Smith, however, demurred, arguing that early reports overestimated the enemy's strength in Frankfort. He preferred to remain east of the Kentucky River, retaining control of the Bluegrass region. Polk's column began to march toward Harrodsburg, but Hardee's force encountered several difficulties. The road selected for his march from Bardstown proved to be too rocky and hilly for rapid progress. He moved his column on to the better road that Polk had followed through Springfield and Perryville. Doing so required time, during which Buell's III Corps closed on the Confederate column.

Wheeler's cavalry assumed the responsibility for screening the move and delaying the Union advance. He soon found himself engaged in a series of skirmishes with Union cavalry intent on overwhelming his brigade.

Indeed Buell had gained additional mounted strength through the addition of McCook's cavalry brigade. This unit had comprised part of the cavalry division left at Elizabethtown. With the withdrawal of Wheeler's screen along the Rolling Fork River, McCook advanced and rejoined the army at Bardstown. This reinforcement added to the pressure on Wheeler who focused his efforts on delaying Buell's columns and survival. No serious attempt was made to determine the Union forces' strength or to track their movements. No assistance came from Wharton's brigade that, after a series of conflicting orders from Bragg, Polk, and Hardee, had been dispatched to Lebanon to guard Hardee's southern flank against a nonexistent threat. While Wharton remained idle Wheeler's lone brigade was left to block the advance of three Union corps.

Events on 6-7 October did not improve Bragg's situational awareness. Scott's cavalry sent a stream of confusing reports on the Union force at Frankfort, alternating between suggestions of an imminent advance by up to 20,000 men and inaction by unsupported cavalry. Hardee's column continued its march through Springfield to Perryville closely pursued by a force of unknown size. Reports of other Union columns also reached Bragg, but these represented impressions of enemy activity, unconfirmed and offering few details. Despite several days of contact with elements of Buell's army, Bragg had no sense of the Union commander's intent, strength, or dispositions. Consequently Confederate forces remained on both sides of the Kentucky River dispersed between Perryville and Frankfort. This scattering reflected both a desire to cover several of Buell's potential actions and uncertainty regarding the best consolidation point.

On the evening of 7 October Bragg resolved upon a two-point plan. Hardee's column had reached Perryville closely pursued by an unknown enemy force. Bragg further dispatched an additional infantry division and directed Polk to assume command of the Confederate forces gathering at Perryville. Wharton also marched to the town, although he received no clear instructions to do so. Bragg ordered Polk to attack at Perryville on the 8th. Afterward he was to march north where Bragg intended to join his army with Smith's and march on Frankfort. These dispositions represented an attempt to wrest the initiative from Buell and recapture the state capital, which was still believed to be the principal Union objective.

However, Bragg's plan owed more to guesswork than accurate knowledge of the enemy's intent. It also highlighted the Confederate cavalry's failure to conduct effective reconnaissance. Both Bragg's and Smith's mounted forces were responsible for screening Confederate troop movements, performing rear guard actions, delaying Buell's movements, and determining the strength and locations of his columns. The last mission, however, did not receive sufficient emphasis. Wheeler, Wharton, and Scott all focused more on their delay and rear guard functions, thus excluding reconnaissance. Too often these commanders became immersed in fighting Union cavalry. Scott's aggressiveness encouraged this focus, forcing Confederate cavalry to fight for its survival rather than gather information. Consequently Buell's cavalry successfully screened the Union infantry columns and kept the Confederate leadership confused as to Union intentions.

The Confederate cavalry brigades operated independently of one another. Each belonged to a different command chain. Although the brigade commanders sometimes determined their own ad hoc means of coordinating actions, no formal mechanism existed to do so. There was no central coordination of cavalry operations at the army command level. Even the simple expedients adopted among unit commanders quickly collapsed under the strain of reacting to Buell's advance and continuous encounters with Union cavalry. Neither Bragg nor Smith had a chief of cavalry to centrally coordinate cavalry activities and establish mission priorities. Bragg especially required information upon which to base his plans, but his cavalry reported to their respective wing commanders. Thus he did not directly influence cavalry operations.

Polk and Hardee did, but their focus was on the security of their respective commands, not in providing a clear picture of the enemy's activities. Hence, during the retreat from Bardstown, they employed their cavalry to screen their infantry columns and delay the Union advance. In turn Wheeler and Wharton largely neglected reconnaissance, limiting their assessments of the enemy to the reception they received in battle. What intelligence they did obtain was often outdated by the time it passed through the wing commanders and reached Bragg. Scott's cavalry proved no better at keeping Smith informed during its operations around Frankfort.

By 8 October nearly 17,000 Confederates had massed at Perryville to execute Bragg's orders to attack. They remained unaware that they faced three Union corps, numbering more than 55,000 men. Apprised of Hardee's deployment the previous day Buell intended to attack with his entire army. However, delays in concentrating his forces resulted in the planned assault being delayed one day. On the 8th, while Buell's corps arrived and deployed, the Confederates attacked. In the confused battle that followed most of the Confederate force fought only a single Union corps. The other two corps provided only minimal support while Buell remained unaware of the battle until it had nearly ended.

Cavalry played a minor role in the engagement. Wheeler and Wharton largely screened the left and right flanks of the Confederate line, respectively. Wharton helped clear skirmishers from the path of the initial assault. Later he helped position an artillery battery that enfiladed the Union line. Without infantry support Wheeler helped secure the Confederate left flank by demonstrating against the Union II Corps throughout the day. This formation played little role in the battle largely because of command issues, but Wheeler's presence contributed to its inaction. Neither cavalry brigade, however, significantly contributed to Confederate situational awareness on the battlefield. Bragg and his commanders only learned that they had fought Buell's entire army from prisoner interrogations after the battle. When the fight began they had intended to envelop the Union left flank. Instead they struck the center of I Corps, and the first committed regiments found themselves caught in an unexpected crossfire. With little sense of what lay in front of them the Confederate infantry simply continued to attack until exhaustion and nightfall ended the fight.

The Union cavalry's accomplishments proved little better. Gay's cavalry participated in some skirmishing early in the day and occupied a forward position that proved important during the battle. McCook's brigade skirmished with Wheeler in advance of II Corps. However, no serious effort was made to reconnoiter the Confederate lines or determine the strength of the force poised to attack. Buell remained uncertain as to the true strength of Bragg's force until after the battle's conclusion. Nor did he learn of the Confederate retreat from the battlefield until his infantry advanced the following morning.

Through battle Bragg had finally determined Buell's location. Outnumbered Bragg opted to retreat from Perryville, falling back toward Smith's army. During the night of 8-9 October the Confederate Army began to march toward Harrodsburg. Wharton's brigade served as a rear guard while Wheeler moved to cover the approaches to Danville. Smith also began to concentrate his forces, following several skirmishes near Lawrenceburg. His cavalry brigades covered this move and continued to watch for a sudden Union advance from either Frankfort or Cincinnati. After a belated juncture with Bragg, the combined armies continued to retreat, arriving at Bryantsville by 11 October. There and at Camp Dick Robinson supply depots had been established. Unfortunately they had supplies for only a few days' operations. Bragg now determined to leave Kentucky before inclement weather or Union actions blocked his path of retreat through the Cumberland Gap into Tennessee.

The Confederate forces left Bryantsville on 13 October and marched to Lancaster. There they split into two columns, one commanded by Bragg, the other by Smith. The former comprised the Army of the Mississippi, and the latter included elements of both Smith's and Humphrey Marshall's original invasion forces. Smith's column also included the Confederate wagon train carrying the military equipment captured during the course of the campaign. From Lancaster it continued east to Big Hill before turning south toward the Rockcastle River. Unencumbered by wagons Bragg's column marched rapidly south along the east bank of the Dick's River, then west to Crab Orchard and the Wilderness Road. It then followed this road south across the Rockcastle River to London. There the two columns intended to reunite before the final move through the Cumberland Gap and into Tennessee while Marshall detached himself and returned to western Virginia.

Bragg's principal concern during these movements was in the security of the two columns. Smith's wagon train, however, slowed his progress and increased his vulnerability. Therefore Bragg selected march routes that kept his own army between Buell and Smith's column. He also relied on his cavalry to escort the wagons, screen each column, and delay pursuing Union forces sufficiently for each column to avoid being attacked. These missions necessitated the careful coordination of the cavalry assets available to Smith and Bragg. They also demanded the precise correlation of cavalry movements with those of the columns to ensure the latter's continuous security and to prevent the isolation and piecemeal destruction of the cavalry rear guards. Bragg therefore appointed Wheeler as the chief of cavalry for both his own and Smith's army. All Confederate cavalry was subject to Wheeler's orders and reported directly to him. In this manner a mechanism to centrally control and track cavalry activities finally emerged within the Confederate command structure. Moreover Bragg supported Wheeler's actions and gave him clear guidance regarding his priorities as the armies moved toward London. At least one cavalry commander found himself under arrest for ignoring orders the new chief of cavalry had issued.

These new arrangements helped the cavalry ensure the successful extraction of the Confederate armies in Kentucky. Moreover the emphasis on rear guard and delaying actions played to the cavalry's strength. Throughout the campaign Confederate mounted units had performed these functions, developing considerable expertise in their execution. Indeed they represented a distinguishing characteristic of Wheeler's leadership, exemplified by his actions before and during the battle of Perryville. His success in covering the Confederate retreat also stemmed from continuous updates regarding the progress of Bragg's and Smith's columns. This information permitted him to make accurate determinations regarding the location and duration of the cavalry's delaying actions.

Wheeler's task, however, was complicated by the emergence of a gap between the two retreating columns. Unencumbered by a wagon train Bragg's force quickly reached Crab Orchard and marched down the Wilderness Road, the principal roadway connecting Danville with the Cumberland Gap. By 15 October he had crossed the Rockcastle River. Smith, however, made slower progress and had only reached Big Hill. A distance of 30 miles separated the two columns. A Union thrust into this gap threatened to isolate and possibly destroy Smith's force with its vulnerable wagon train. Inserting strong cavalry assets into the gap averted the danger. They conducted aggressive rear guard actions and obstructed the roads over which Union cavalry and infantry struggled to pass. Their actions effectively sealed the gap long enough for Smith's column to reach the relative safety of the Rockcastle River by the 18th.

Wheeler's task became simplified with both columns across the river. As the latter moved through London and Barboursville toward the Cumberland Gap Confederate cavalry lay between them and their pursuers. Moreover the Union threat now remained entirely to the north, permitting Wheeler to focus on a single direction and block the principal roads leading south toward the Cumberland Gap. The rocky and hilly terrain of southeastern Kentucky proved ideal for a mobile delaying force. Forced to clear felled trees from their path and deploy into line of battle upon contact with Wheeler's cavalry, the Union pursuit quickly slowed. As the Confederate columns neared the Tennessee border Morgan embarked upon another raid across Kentucky to threaten Buell's line of supply.

On 18 October Morgan began a series of attacks that carried him to Lexington, Ashland, Bardstown, and Elizabethtown. Although this raid proved far less destructive than his summer forays it distracted Buell. Already concerned about his ability to sustain his army in the rugged terrain of southeastern Kentucky, Morgan's newest attack reinforced his caution. Outside Chattanooga similar raids had had a crippling effect on operations. Therefore he diverted two cavalry brigades from pursuing the Confederate armies to chasing Morgan. The latter, however, evaded capture and retired into Tennessee.

Buell's concern for his line of supply influenced his overall conduct of operations after Perryville. Following the battle there he intended to thrust toward Danville to place his army between the Confederate armies and their path to Tennessee. Only Wheeler's cavalry brigade stood in his path. Learning of Bragg's retreat toward Harrodsburg, however, he feared the possibility of the combined Confederate armies striking his northern flank and supply line. Therefore he divided his forces and advanced on both Danville and Harrodsburg. The movement began slowly, however, and all three corps remained in the vicinity of Perryville throughout 9 October.

While the Confederate armies retired toward Bryantsville, Buell advanced cautiously. His infantry corps moved along different routes behind a cavalry screen similar to the manner in which they had marched from Louisville. Then the cavalry's primary role lay in keeping the Confederate cavalry away from the marching columns. Now with the Confederate armies in retreat the Union cavalry's mission changed. It needed to provide accurate, timely information on the location of the Confederate columns and to interfere with their movements. However, the limited road net and rugged terrain of southeastern Kentucky left Buell few options for maneuver. To intercept the Confederate armies required overwhelming Wheeler's rear guard and moving quickly against the retiring infantry and wagons. Alternatively a blocking force astride the Confederate line of march could delay the retreat long enough for Buell's corps to close and attack.

These types of actions became standard missions for Union cavalry later in the war. However, they proved beyond the capability of Buell's cavalry, which lacked the necessary concentrated combat power and capacity for independent operations. In the days following Perryville Buell increased the nominal size of his cavalry division. Gay's, Zahm's, and McCook's brigades were assigned to it. COL Minor Milliken assumed command of a newly created fourth brigade. However, these units continued to be employed independently of one another, often providing support for Buell's three corps. Dispersing its assets made the division little more than an administrative grouping. It did not constitute a cohesive mass of cavalry that might have been able to race ahead of the Confederate columns and delay them. Additional cavalry regiments continued to function as collections of detachments supporting specific infantry divisions.

Cavalry led the advance of Buell's corps, but it did not aggressively seek out the enemy and its weak points. Instead it remained close to supporting but slower-moving infantry. Against their tenacious and well-led Confederate counterparts operating in terrain that favored the defense, the Union cavalry became timid. Upon encountering determined opposition it tended to await the arrival of infantry and artillery rather than attacking independently. These tactics resulted in time-consuming deployments and invariably failed to penetrate Wheeler's cavalry screen. Moreover they slowed the pace of pursuit and surrendered the tactical initiative to Confederate cavalry commanders. They determined when and where they would fight with little interference from the Union cavalry.

This caution on the part of Buell's mounted force stemmed partially from deficiencies in training, equipment, and leadership. Some regiments had been in service only since the Confederates invaded Kentucky. They lacked experience in basic cavalry operations and had yet to become familiar with sustained, independent operations. Yet such missions were not likely to occur as long as the cavalry remained subordinate to infantry formations. Corps and division commanders preferred to keep their mounted assets close to their infantry. Nor were the restraints on cavalry operations likely to disappear since Buell encouraged them. Consequently the infantry step rather than the cavalry trot determined the army's pace.

While Bragg and Smith concentrated at Bryantsville and began their march toward the Cumberland Gap, Buell's columns followed in their wake. The Union cavalry's prior aggressiveness became blunted during repeat encounters with well-sited Confederate rear guards. Their resistance often forced the Union cavalry to await infantry support. This timidity precluded exploiting opportunities that arose to interfere with the Confederate retreat. On 16 October Union cavalry reached the Rockcastle River before Smith's force and prepared to block his movement. The timely intervention of Wheeler's cavalry, supported by infantry from Bragg's column, prevented this threat from being realized. After Smith crossed the Rockcastle River Buell's pursuit continued. It consisted of little more than marching after the Confederates amid the continuous delays that Wheeler's cavalry incurred.

Any possibility of catching Bragg or Smith before they reached the Cumberland Gap ended when two cavalry brigades dispersed to counter Morgan's raid into central Kentucky. Buell had little interest in mounting or sustaining an operation into eastern Tennessee. He did not believe the mountainous terrain, time of year, or logistics challenges inherent to such a move justified it. Instead he left one corps to observe the Confederate armies and ensure their return to Tennessee. The rest of the army marched toward Nashville via Bowling Green. With the Confederate invasion of Kentucky ending Buell planned to return to central Tennessee. From there he would restart his failed offensive toward Chattanooga.

The Lincoln administration thought otherwise and relieved him. MG William Rosecrans replaced Buell and inherited the mission of liberating eastern Tennessee. One of his first actions was to reorganize the cavalry.

Rosecrans requested additional cavalry from the War Department. He also sought to make his available mounted units more effective by eliminating equipment deficiencies, providing training, and improving their organization. Buell's contribution was creating the basis for a viable cavalry force. He had begun to concentrate regiments in mounted brigades and used them with success during his march to Perryville. However, during the pursuit of the Confederate armies, Union cavalry experienced limitations in its capabilities. Rosecrans sought to build a mounted arm capable of sustained and independent operations on a larger scale.

By 24 October Bragg's and Smith's Confederate armies had left Kentucky via the Cumberland Gap. Thanks to the efforts of Wheeler's cavalry the principal dangers to the marching infantry and wagon train did not come from Buell's army. Hunger and terrain made the passage memorable. For the Confederate cavalry, however, the final movements into Tennessee marked their success. For two weeks it shielded the retreating armies despite their movements along different routes that sometimes separated them by 30 or more miles. This accomplishment occurred despite persistent Union efforts to penetrate the rear guard the Confederate cavalry maintained. In these operations the mounted arm's success came from a clear mission, central coordination, favorable terrain, good tactical leadership, and familiarity with rear guard and delaying actions.

Appendix F
Combat Reconnaissance at Perryville

While on campaign an army commander had a variety of potential intelligence sources from which he could assess the enemy's intent and dispositions. Information received from other commands, delivered via courier or telegraph when available, provided a sense of operational understanding. He might also use spies or sympathetic civilians. In both cases, however, the accuracy of the information received depended on the individual's experience and background. Buell received numerous accounts of Confederate strength in Chattanooga before Bragg's advance into central Tennessee, but the reports exaggerated the troop numbers actually present by between two and three times the actual effective strength. Nor were friendly civilians always available or willing to assist.

The most direct means of determining enemy strength was using cavalry in a reconnaissance mode. Cavalry often operated close to the enemy. It therefore could better track the enemy's movements and over time more accurately assess troop strength. Whether this information reached the army commander quickly depended on the relation between the army commander and his cavalry in the chain of command. Bragg received direct reports from his cavalry commanders during his initial advance into Kentucky. He subsequently realigned his mounted regiments under the wing commanders. To receive intelligence he depended on the wing commander's assessments, which did not always arrive in time and reflected the wing commanders' separate biases. Reconnaissance also had to be made a priority mission for the cavalry, or it would become subordinate to other mounted functions such as screen and delay. As the campaign progressed Confederate cavalry increasingly became engaged in a series of minor engagements that interfered with its ability to gather information.

Once the armies deployed for battle the means of gathering information about the enemy became more limited. Personal reconnaissance by commanders at all echelons proved common, allowing them to assess terrain and nearby enemy forces. Skirmishers and picket lines provided early warnings of enemy attacks, but their ability to gather information was limited to their immediate environment. Similarly, only the parent organization generally benefited from this information, perhaps encouraging a timely formation change. Division and corps dispositions, however, were not likely to be altered by reports from skirmishers since an enemy attack was probably well developed before such formations could respond. Once a battle began skirmishers and leader recons at best offered a limited ability to see over the next hill and provided regiment and brigade commanders with some additional response time to enemy action.

At the tactical and grand tactical levels mounted units offered the best means of gathering information on the enemy's disposition. Once battle began, however, they generally retired to the flanks to perform security missions. At Perryville Wheeler's cavalry performed an important screening action against II Corps, but the value of the action to Bragg was nullified by the absence of any report from Wheeler until well after the battle had begun. Wharton successfully swept away Union skirmishers facing the advance of Cheatham's infantry, but he failed to observe the deployment of Terrill's brigade on the flank of the intended axis of advance. Confederate understanding of the Union deployment was thus limited to Bragg's prebattle reconnaissance and what unit commanders could see once the battle was joined. The Perryville battlefield's rolling terrain ensured that such situational awareness extended only to the next ridgeline.

Union awareness of Confederate dispositions proved to be just as limited. The eruption of Cheatham's infantry division from Walker's Bend came as an unpleasant surprise. Conversely the weakness of Confederate forces facing II and III Corps remained hidden. Buell remained unaware that a battle raged until late in the day. Signal Corps stations connected his headquarters with I and III Corps'. Although the signal operators informally shared information about battle progress among themselves, no formal message was ever sent via this medium from I Corps to the army commander. Situational awareness thus remained limited to what the regiment, brigade, division, and corps commanders could see amid the smoke of battle and the battlefield's topography.

Appendix G
Passage of Lines at Perryville

A critical command decision for brigade, division, and corps/wing commanders was determining when to commit fresh troops to sustain an attack's momentum. Civil War commanders often developed viable plans to assault enemy positions only to watch their regiments become mired by a combination of terrain, enemy fire, losses, and morale erosion that collectively sapped their ability to advance. Those regiments that became engaged in firefights with the enemy often quickly consumed much of the basic ammunition load, necessitating a temporary withdrawal to resupply. To prevent these commonplace battlefield developments from extinguishing offensive action, commanders worked to introduce fresh troops into battle at the proper place and time. However, simply pushing uncommitted regiments forward often created more confusion without appreciable gain. An attacking force that became pinned by an obstacle or enemy fire degenerated into a formless mass if more troops simply surged forward. To sustain momentum fresh troops needed to move through those in front of them without losing their formation or organizational integrity. Such a passage of lines, however, required skill since enemy fire added to the confusion inherent when one mass of soldiers moved through another. Not all commanders or units were able to perform this action successfully in combat.

At Perryville the Confederates repeatedly tried to keep their attack moving by pushing fresh troops forward regardless of the conditions in the front ranks. Johnson sent his second line of regiments into battle while his first had not yet untangled itself from its early disorientation. The result was a mass of soldiers that drifted toward the Bottom House where it went to ground and fired at the enemy until its ammunition expired. Earlier in the battle Maney's brigade made a similar miscalculation along the fence line. However, inspired leadership and effective artillery support finally helped the veteran regiments to restart their stalled attack and seize the Open Hill. Cleburne's passage through Johnson's brigade demonstrates a clear grasp of the problem together with some prior planning and careful execution.

Appendix H
Formation and Drill

On the Civil War battlefield drill instruction determined how maneuvers and formation changes would be performed. It identified the precise location and movements required of each soldier, noncommissioned officer, and officer at every command echelon up to the brigade level. Training provided the section, platoon, company, and regiment with a shared experience that helped to preserve order amid the sensory chaos of the battlefield. Mastery of drill, however, required continuous practice to master the different movements and formations. Units that received insufficient training risked a rapid loss of cohesion once in combat or when required to undertake the more complex movements and formation changes.

For the private soldier drill provided him with the skills necessary to function in battle. Training focused on mastering the basic body movements and positioning that were part of a formation. He then learned the manual of arms and the sequential motions to load and fire his weapon. Finally he focused on the movements necessary to retain his alignment within a formation as it maneuvered. From this training a soldier knew where he should be in relation to his comrades in all formations and movements. He came to understand how his immediate surroundings should be organized, particularly which soldiers should be to his right, left, and rear. Through repetition his understanding of drill became second nature, and he could be relied upon to respond efficiently to the commands his unit received.

Noncommissioned officers oversaw training at the soldier level. They required a thorough understanding of the drill manual being used and the ability to explain its contents clearly. Within the company the noncommissioned officers were primarily responsible for overseeing discipline and efficiency. They directly interfaced with the soldiers and embodied the link between orders given at the unit level and their execution. In combat they ensured the soldiers under them maintained their alignment and moved correctly when executing maneuvers and formation changes.

The company commander was responsible for operating his company in accordance with the regimental commander's orders. He issued orders directly to his men and with his noncommissioned officers' assistance oversaw their execution. During regimental movements and formation changes company commanders indicated the location and direction in which their soldiers should move.

At the regimental level drill focused on the entire unit's actions. All brigade elements needed to understand the same set of movements to operate in a coordinated manner on the battlefield. Much of the instruction addressed the formation change from line to column and vice versa and the operation of the line of battle. Within these broad topical areas were included more precise actions such as defile actions, movement by the flank, passage of lines, and advance/retreat movements. The regimental commander needed to understand these actions intimately because in battle he was responsible for their execution. He bore the burden of implementing movements, changing formations, and establishing firing patterns. The brigade commander issued general guidance for the regiments under his command but rarely assumed direct control of them. Instead he normally issued verbal instructions to regimental commanders who then issued the requisite orders to execute in accordance with the drill manual used.

Regiments invariably deviated from the precise letter of their drill manuals, especially after they had become proficient in their maneuvers. Experience frequently determined the nature of these changes. However, such deviation did not fundamentally alter the essence of the drill manual. The latter provided uniformity to operating linear formations that was otherwise absent.

At Perryville both armies benefited from William J. Hardee's work. Serving in Bragg's army as a wing commander, before the war Hardee had written a manual for the US Army that sought to offset the longer range of the rifled musket. The most significant development was the requirement for a faster pace on the battlefield. Faster movements in combat were thought to quicken the rate at which a formation closed with the enemy and consequently reduced its exposure to enemy fire.

Failure to master the drill manual often resulted in negative consequences for units and soldiers on the battlefield. At Perryville, however, many Union regiments entered combat for the first time with only limited drill practice. Several had never drilled at the regimental level. These units quickly lost their cohesion when subjected to enemy fire. Under the stress of combat soldiers became confused about their proper action and location within the unit. Platoon and company dislocation followed. The ensuing disorganization directly impaired the noncommissioned officers' and company commanders' ability to lead. When committed into action against veteran formations, their combat effectiveness rapidly diminished.

The 123d Illinois and 105th Ohio comprised part of Terrill's brigade. Neither unit had much prior training and had never been in combat. Deployed against Maney's Confederate brigade these regiments found themselves thrust into battle and issued complex orders that they had not practiced. The ensuing confusion resulted in them entering into combat with their rear ranks in front. Soldiers suddenly found themselves in unfamiliar environments because their section members' positions had completely changed. Soldiers became disoriented, and unit cohesion broke down. Confederate musketry accelerated their disintegration, and they were routed.

The following excerpt is taken from BG Silas Casey, *Infantry Tactics for the Instruction, Exercise, and Manoeuvres of the Soldier, A Company, Line of Skirmishers, Battalion, Brigade, or Corps D'Armée*, reprint, Dayton, OH: Morningside House, Inc., 1985, School of the Company, 130-31 and School of the Battalion, 186. The US Army adopted this manual for use in August 1862. The excerpt pertains to the command the 123d Illinois and 105th Ohio received in response to the approach of Maney's Confederates. The units were directed to "on the right, by file into line" and advance in line of battle. For units with limited drill instruction this type of maneuver proved nearly impossible to execute properly under fire.

Command (company level): "1. On the right, by file into line. 2. March."

Execution: "At the command *march*, the rear-rank men doubled, will mark time; the captain and the covering sergeant will turn to the right, march straight-forward, and be halted by the instructor when they shall have passed at least six paces beyond the rank of file closers; the captain will place himself correctly on the line of battle, and will direct the alignment as the men of the front rank successively arrive; the covering sergeant will place himself behind the captain at the distance of the rear-rank; the two men on the right of the front rank doubled, will continue to march, and passing beyond the covering sergeant and the captain, will turn to the right; after turning, they will continue to march elbow to elbow, and direct themselves toward the line of battle, but when they shall arrive at two paces from this line, the even number will shorten the step so that the odd number may precede him on the line, the odd number placing himself by the side and on the left of the captain; the even number will afterward oblique to the left, and place himself on the left of the odd number; the next two men of the front rank doubled, will pass in the same manner behind the two first, turn then to the right, and place themselves, according to the means just explained, to the left, and by the side of, the two men already established on the line; the remaining files of this rank will follow in succession, and be formed to the left in the same manner. The rear rank doubled will execute the movement in the manner already explained for the front rank, taking care not to commence the movement until four men of the front rank are established on the line of battle; the rear-rank men, as they arrive on the line, will cover accurately their file leaders."

Remarks (battalion level): "As marching by the flank in the presence of the enemy is a very objectionable movement, it will not be executed except for the purpose of moving the battalion to the right or left for a short distance, or when the narrowness of the way will not permit a company front."

If this instruction sounds complex, it was. But remember, a unit that had practiced the entire manual for a period of time would have understood the meaning of each movement. New units, however, simply floundered when they tried to execute this maneuver. Note, too, that a simple method of identifying trained units on the Civil War battlefield was through witnessing the ease with which they performed formation changes and maneuvers.

Appendix I
Perryville Battlefield State Historic Site

In the aftermath of the fighting on 8 October the Army of the Ohio collected, identified, and buried its dead. The US government planned to establish a national cemetery west of Perryville, but difficulties in acquiring a clear land title for the prospective site resulted in the project's cancellation. Many Union casualties were initially buried on Peter's Hill until reinterred in the Camp Nelson National Cemetery after the war. In the wake of the Confederate retreat shortly after the battle local farmers assumed responsibility for burying the Southern slain. Squire Bottom, upon whose property considerable fighting had occurred, oversaw the interment of several hundred soldiers on the battlefield. A stone wall surrounded and defined the quarter-acre burial site.

The Kentucky state government purchased this land in 1901. The newly formed Perryville Battlefield Commission became responsible for the burial ground's care and administration. The commission also undertook the commemoration of the battle of the Perryville, beginning with erecting a marker honoring the Confederate soldiers killed during the fighting. In 1928 the commission purchased additional acreage around the Confederate cemetery from the Bottom family and linked the site with the local road net. By the early 1930s the commission's efforts had expanded the original quarter-acre plot to 18 acres and erected a second monument dedicated to the Union soldiers who fought and died at Perryville.

The commission, however, soon disbanded. The State Parks System became responsible for the Perryville site, and in 1936 it was designated a state park. Recreational and educational development followed. By the 1960s the park included picnic areas, restrooms, and a large pond for paddleboats. A museum and visitor center provided information about the battle, and permanent staff ran the park. The next decade saw the gift shop added, additional picnic areas added, and the paddleboat pond drained. Land purchases expanded the park by more than 60 acres. Building modernization and the addition of a maintenance barn followed in the 1980s. The publication of the first edition of Kenneth A. Hafendorfer's *Perryville: Battle for Kentucky* also raised public consciousness of Perryville's significance in the Civil War.

The park flourished in the 1990s. It grew from 98 to more than 500 acres of land either directly under the park's care or in the process of being transferred to park management. At the time of this publication the park had grown to more than 700 acres with additional acreage slated to be turned over to the park in the future. This development occurred at a time when many Civil War sites became centers of controversy between land developers and organizations committed to preserving the nation's heritage. The rolling landscape at Perryville, however, remained much the same as it had in 1862. The ability to see the battlefield as Civil War soldiers had done so, coupled with the park's expansion, stimulated interest in and study of the battle. New publications and park brochures helped visitors interpret the battlefield. Military organizations also began to use the park regularly to conduct staff rides. With support from the Kentucky Heritage Council, the University of Kentucky, and Centre College, a series of archaeological surveys on park property provided a wealth of material about the Civil War-era combatants and the local inhabitants. New interpretations and understanding of the battle stimulated more scholarly interest, symbolized by Kenneth W. Noe's *Perryville: This Grand Havoc of Battle*, published in 2001. For the general public the park frequently hosted living history displays while the annual battle reenactment allowed them to immerse themselves in the Civil War genre. The battle's heightened visibility drew tourists, and annual visitation rates reached 125,000 people.

The park's success owed much to creation of several organizations dedicated to its preservation, expansion, and interpretation. In 1990 the Perryville Battlefield Preservation Association (PBPA) was established as a nonprofit organization that helped to raise funds and secure new purchases for the park. In addition, the PBPA sought to market the town and battlefield of Perryville as a major historical landmark, highlighting the area's history as a means of boosting tourism and related economic development. The state governor provided additional funding for the park in 1993 and appointed the Perryville Battlefield Commission to oversee the use of these and other funds.

The Perryville Enhancement Project included the PBPA; the battlefield commission; and a collection of federal, state, and local organizations dedicated to developing the cultural and historical resources of the area fully. The completion of a detailed plan to realize this goal in 1999 provided a roadmap for implementation and a vehicle through which to secure additional funding and support. Initial steps were implemented in 2000-2002 to continue acquiring new land, incorporate that land into the battlefield, and enhance its historical interpretation. These efforts, however, constituted only a small portion of the overall plan, which upon completion would transform Perryville's town and battlefield into a mid-19th-century equivalent to Colonial Williamsburg, Virginia.

Bibliography

This bibliography lists the principal sources used to compile this handbook. These sources are intended to support further study of the battle and related campaign. The list, however, is not comprehensive. It is oriented toward utility and likely availability. All items can be accessed via the interlibrary loan service if local library resources do not have particular works.

Staff Ride Methodology

Robertson, William G. *The Staff Ride*. Washington, DC: US Army Center of Military History, 1987.

Kentucky Campaign

Bearss, Edwin C. "General Bragg Abandons Kentucky," *Register of the Kentucky Historical Society*, 59 (July 1861): 217-44.

Brown, Kent Masterson. "Munfordville: The Campaign and Battle Along Kentucky's Strategic Axis." In *The Civil War in Kentucky: Battle for the Bluegrass State*, ed. Kent Masterson Brown. Mason City, Ia: Savas, 2000.

Buell, General Don Carlos. "East Tennessee and the Campaign of Perryville." In *Battles and Leaders of the Civil War*, Vol. III, ed. Robert Underwood Johnson and Clarence Clough Buel. Reprint. Secaucus, NJ: Castle, 1982.

Cist, Henry M. *The Army of the Cumberland*. Reprint. Wilmington, NC: Broadfoot Publishing Co., 1989.

Connelly, Thomas Lawrence. *Army of the Heartland; The Army of Tennessee, 1861-1862*. Baton Rouge, LA: Louisiana State University Press, 1967.

Cozzens, Peter. *The Darkest Days of the War: The Battles of Iuka and Corinth*. Chapel Hill, NC: University of North Carolina Press, 1997.

_____. *No Better Place to Die: The Battle of Stones River*. Urbana, IL: University of Illinois Press, 1991.

DeBerry, J.H. "Kirby Smith's Bluegrass Invasion," *America's Civil War* (March 1997): 54-60, 88-89.

Donaldson, Gary. "'Into Africa': Kirby Smith and Braxton Bragg's Invasion of Kentucky." *Filson Club History Quarterly*. 61 (1987): 444-65.

Engerud, Colonel (Ret.) H. *The Battle of Munfordville*. Munfordville, KY: Munfordville Lions Club, 1962.

Fry, James B. *Operations of the Army Under Buell From June 10 to October 30, 1862, and the 'Buell Commission.'* New York: D. Van Nostrand, 1884.

Hafendorfer, Kenneth A. *They Died By Twos and Tens: The Confederate Cavalry in the Kentucky Campaign of 1862*. Louisville, KY: KH Press, 1995.

Hammond, Paul F. "General Kirby Smith's Campaign in Kentucky in 1862," *Southern Historical Society Papers*. 9 (1873): 247-49.

Hattaway, Herman and Archer Jones. *How the North Won: A Military History of the Civil War*. Urbana, IL: University of Illinois Press, 1983.

Hess, Earl J. *Banners to the Breeze: The Kentucky Campaign, Corinth, and Stones River*. Lincoln, NE: University of Nebraska Press, 2000.

Jones, Archer. *Confederate Strategy From Shiloh to Vicksburg*. Baton Rouge, LA: Louisiana State University Press, 1961.

Lambert, D. Warren. *When the Ripe Pears Fell: The Battle of Richmond, Kentucky*. Richmond, KY: Madison County Historical Society, 1995.

McDonough, James Lee. *War in Kentucky: From Shiloh to Perryville*. Knoxville, TN: University of Tennessee Press, 1994.

McPherson, James M. *Battle Cry of Freedom: The Civil War Era*. Oxford: Oxford University Press, 1988.

Miles, Jim. *Piercing the Heartland: A History and Tour Guide of the Fort Donelson, Shiloh, and Perryville Campaigns*. Nashville, TN: Rutledge Hill Press, 1991.

Morgan, George W. "Cumberland Gap." In *Battles and Leaders of the Civil War*, Vol. III. ed. Robert Underwood Johnson and Clarence Clough Buel, 62-69. Reprint. Secaucus, NJ: Castle, 1982.

Morris, Roy, Jr. "Battle in the Bluegrass: The 1862 Struggle Between Greenhorns and Veterans at Richmond, Kentucky." *Civil War Times Illustrated*. 27 (December 1998): 15-16, 18, 20-23.

Reid, Richard J. *The Army that Buell Built*. Fordsville, KY: Wendell Sandefur, 1994.

Shea, William L., and Earl J. Hess. *Pea Ridge: Civil War Campaign in the West*. Chapel Hill, NC: University of North Carolina Press, 1992.

Starr, Stephen Z. *The Union Cavalry in the Civil War*, Vol. III, *The War in the West*. Baton Rouge, LA: Louisiana State University Press, 1985.

Stone, Henry. "The Operations of General Buell in Kentucky and Tennessee in 1862." In *Papers of the Military Historical Society of Massachusetts*, Volume VII, *Campaigns in Kentucky and Tennessee Including the Battle of Chickamauga 1862-1864*. Boston, MA: Military Historical Society of Massachusetts, 1908.

Street, James, Jr. and the Editors of Time-Life Books. *The Civil War: The Struggle for Tennessee: Tupelo to Stones River*. Alexandria, VA: Time-Life Books, 1985.

US War Department. *The War of the Rebellion: A Compilation of the Official Records of the Union and Confederate Armies*. Series I, Vol. XVI, Parts 1 and 2. Washington, DC: US Government Printing Office, 1886. This volume contains a wealth of material related to the campaign and battle of Perryville, including correspondence, commanders' battle reports, and documentation of the Buell Commission. Part I includes battle reports and the Buell Commission documents. Part II includes Union and Confederate correspondence from the start of the campaign.

Woodworth, Steven E. *Jefferson Davis and His Generals: The Failure of Confederate Command in the West*. Lawrence, KS: University Press of Kansas, 1990.

Battle of Perryville

Crawford, Thomas C. "The Battle of Perryville." *Confederate Veteran*. 40 (1932): 262-64.

Finley, Luke W. "The Battle of Perryville." *Southern Historical Society Papers*. Vol. 30, 238-50. *Confederate view of battle*.

"The General's Tour: The Battle of Perryville." *Blue and Gray Magazine*, October-November 1983, 21-39.

Grimsley, Mark. "A Wade in the High Tide at Perryville." *Civil War Times Illustrated*. 31 (November-December 1991): 18, 22, 24, 26.

Hafendorfer, Kenneth A. "Crossed-Up Obliques: The Confederate Center at Perryville." *Virginia Country's Civil War*. Vol. 4, No. 1, 49-54.

_____. *Perryville: Battle for Kentucky*. 2d ed. Louisville, KY: K.H. Press, 1991.

Harrison, Lowell H. "Perryville: Death on a Dry River." *Civil War Times Illustrated*. (May 1979): 4-6, 8-9, 44-47.

Noe, Kenneth W. "'Grand Havoc': The Climactic Battle of Perryville." In *The Civil War in Kentucky: Battle for the Bluegrass State*, ed. Kent Masterson Brown. Mason City, IA: Savas, 2000.

_____. "Last Stand Ridge: The Other High Water Mark." *North and South*. 4, 7 (September 2001): 64-77.

_____. *Perryville: This Grand Havoc of Battle*. Lexington, KY: University Press of Kentucky, 2001.

Tapp, Hamilton. "Blood Bath at Perryville." *Virginia Country's Civil War*. Vol. 4, No. 1, 25-29.

Walsh, John P., Jr. "I Tell You, Sir, They Are Yankees." *North and South*. Vol. 5, No. 6 (September 2002): 56-69.

Unit Histories—Union

Beatty, John. *Memoirs of a Volunteer 1861-1863*. New York: W.W. Norton & Co., Inc., 1946. Beatty commanded the 3d Ohio at Perryville.

Berkley, John L. *In Defense of This Flag: The Civil War Diary of Pvt. Ormond Hupp, 5th Indiana Light Artillery*. Fredonia, NY: Bluehome Press, 1992.

Fitch, Michael H. *Echoes of the Civil War As I Hear Them*. New York: R.F. Fenno and Co., 1905. Includes detailed account of 21st Wisconsin at Perryville.

Kirkpatrick, George Morgan. *The Experiences of a Private Soldier of the Civil War*. Reprint. Indianapolis, IN: The Hoosier Bookshop, 1973. Includes the account of a soldier serving in the 42d Indiana at Perryville.

Perry, Henry Fales. *History of the Thirty-Eighth Regiment Indiana Volunteer Infantry*. Palo Alto, CA: F.A. Stuart, 1906.

Record of the Ninety-Fourth Regiment Ohio Volunteer Infantry, in the War of the Rebellion. Cincinnati, OH: Ohio Valley Press, 1896.

Rowell, John W. *Yankee Artillerymen: Through the Civil War With Eli Lilly's Indiana Battery*. Knoxville, TN: University of Tennessee Press, 1975.

Sanders, Stuart W. "Buckeye Warriors at Perryville." *America's Civil War*.

(January 2001): 38-44, 86. Details the actions of the 3d Ohio.

Scribner, B.F. *How Soldiers Were Made; Or War As I Saw It Under Buell, Rosecrans, Thomas, Grant and Sherman*. New Albany, IN: 1887. Includes an account of the 38th Indiana Regiment and its actions at Perryville.

Tourgee, Albion W. *The Story of a Thousand: Being a History of the Service of the 105th Ohio Volunteer Infantry, in the War for the Union From August 21, 1862 to June 6, 1865*. Buffalo, NY: S. McGerald and Son, 1896.

Williams, Harrison C. "Regimental History of the 79th Pennsylvania Volunteers of the Civil War: The Lancaster County Regiment." *Journal of the Lancaster County Historical Society*. 84 (1980): 17-36.

Unit Histories—Confederate

Barnhill, Floyd R. *The Fighting Fifth: Pat Cleburne's Cutting Edge: The Fifth Arkansas Infantry Regiment, C. S.A.* Jonesboro, AR: Floyd R. Barnill, 1990.

Carnes, Captain W.W. "Artillery at the Battle of Perryville." *Confederate Veteran*. 33 (1925): 8-9.

Collier, Calvin L. *First In—Last Out: The Capitol Guards, Ark. Brigade*. Little Rock, AR: Pioneer Press, 1961.

Head, Thomas A. *Campaigns and Battles of the Sixteenth Regiment, Tennessee Volunteers*. McMinnville, TN: Womack Printing Co., 1961.

Hughes, Nathaniel Cheairs, Jr. *The Pride of the Confederate Artillery: The Washington Artillery in the Army of Tennessee*. Baton Rouge, LA: Louisiana State University Press, 1997.

Lindsley, John Berrien, ed. *The Military Annals of Tennessee Confederates*. Vol. I. Nashville, TN: J.M. Lindsley and Co., 1886.

Little, George and James R. Maxwell. *A History of Lumsden's Battery C.S.A.* Reprint. Tuskaloosa, AL: Sons of Confederate Veterans, 1988.

Watkins, Sam R. *"Co. Aytch," Maury Grays, First Tennessee Regiment; or, A Side Show of the Big Show*. Reprint. New York: Collier, 1962.

Williams, L.B. *A Sketch of the 33rd Alabama Volunteer Infantry Regiment*

And its Role in Cleburne's Elite Division of The Army of Tennessee 1862-1865. Auburn, AL: The Author, 1990.

Womack, Captain J.J. *The Civil War Diary of Capt. J.J. Womack; Co. E, Sixteenth Regiment, Tennessee Volunteers.* McMinnville, TN: Womack Printing Co., 1961.

Key Personalities—Union

Engle, Stephen D. "Don Carlos Buell: Military Philosophy and Command Problems in the West." *Civil War History.* 41 (June 1995): 89-115.

_____. *Don Carlos Buell: Most Promising of All.* Chapel Hill, NC: University of North Carolina Press, 1999.

Hillard, James M. "'You Are Strangely Deluded': General William Terrill." *Civil War Times Illustrated.* 13 (February 1975): 12-18.

Jenkins, Kirk C. "A Shooting at the Galt House: The Death of General William Nelson," *Civil War History,* 43 (June 1997): 101-18.

Lane, Bryan. "She Remembered: The Dying Wish of General William Lytle." *Blue and Gray Magazine.* 16 (February 1999): 22-28.

Warner, Ezra J. *Generals in Blue: Lives of the Union Commanders.* Baton Rouge, LA: Louisiana State University Press, 1964.

Key Personalities—Confederate

Buck, Captain Irving A. *Cleburne and His Command.* Wilmington, NC: Broadfoot Publishing Co., 1991.

Chitty, Arthur Ben. "Leonidas Polk: A Mediocre General But a Great Bishop." *Civil War Times Illustrated.* 2 (October 1963): 17-20.

Cummings, Charles M. *Yankee Quaker, Confederate General: The Curious Career of Bushrod Rust Johnson.* Rutherford, NJ: Fairleigh Dickinson University Press, 1971.

Elliot, Sam Davis. *Soldier of Tennessee: General Alexander P. Stewart and the Civil War in the West.* Baton Rouge, LA: Lousiana State University Press, 1999.

Hallock, Judith Lee. *Braxton Bragg and Confederate Defeat.* Vol. 2. Tuscaloosa, AL: University of Alabama Press, 1991.

Hassler, William W. "Patrick Cleburne: 'Stonewall of the West.'" *Civil War Times Illustrated.* 10 (February 1972): 4-9, 44-47.

Hughes, Nathaniel Cheairs Jr. *General William J. Hardee: Old Reliable.* Baton Rouge, LA: Louisiana State University Press, 1965.

Liddell, St. John Richardson. *Liddell's Record: St. John Richardson Liddell*. ed. Nathaniel Cheairs Hughes, Jr. Dayton, OH: Morningside, 1985.

Losson, Christopher. *Tennessee's Forgotten Warriors: Frank Cheatham and His Confederate Division*. Knoxville, TN: University of Tennessee, 1989.

McWhiney, Grady. *Braxton Bragg and the Confederate Defeat*. Vol. I, *Field Command*. New York: Columbia University Press, 1969.

_____. "Controversy in Kentucky: Braxton Bragg's Campaign of 1862," *Civil War History*, 6 (1960): 5-42.

Parks, Joseph H. *General Edmund Kirby Smith C.S.A.* Baton Rouge, LA: Louisiana State University Press, 1954.

_____. *General Leonidas Polk C.S.A.: The Fighting Bishop*. Baton Rouge, LA: Louisiana State University Press, 1962.

Sanders, Stuart W. "Every Mother's Son of Them Are Yankees!" *Civil War Times Illustrated*. 38 (October 1999): 52-59. Details Polk's personal encounter with Union troops at Perryville.

Savage, John H. *The Life of John H. Savage: Citizen, Soldier, Lawyer, Congressman*. Nashville, TN. 1903.

Stickles, Arndt M. *Simon Bolivar Buckner: Borderland Knight*. Chapel Hill, NC: University of North Carolina Press, 1940.

Sword, Wiley. "The *Other* Stonewall." *Civil War Times Illustrated*. (February 1998): 36-44. A short article on Patrick R. Cleburne.

Symonds, Craig L. *Stonewall of the West: Patrick Cleburne and the Civil War*. Lawrence, KS: University Press of Kansas, 1997.

Warner, Ezra J. Warner. *Generals in Gray: Lives of the Confederate Commanders*. Baton Rouge, LA: Louisiana State University Press, 1959.

Wheeler, General Joseph. "Bragg's Invasion of Kentucky." In *Battles and Leaders of the Civil War*, Vol. III, ed. Robert Underwood Johnson and Clarence Clough Buel, 1-25. Reprint. Secaucus, NJ: Castle, 1982.

Civil War Weapons, Tactics, and Combat

Casey, Brigadier General Silas. *Infantry Tactics for the Instruction, Exercise, and Manoeuvres of the Soldier, a Company, Line of Skirmishers, Battalion, Brigade, or Corpd D'Armée*. 2 Vols. Reprint.

Dayton, OH: Morningside, 1985. A common drill and instruction manual for the period. It provides detailed information on linear and column formations and their operation at different command echelons. Useful for understanding the mechanics of moving large bodies of men on the Civil War battlefield.

Coggins, Jack. *Arms and Equipment of the Civil War*. Reprint. Wilmington, NC: Broadfoot Publishing Co., 1987.

Daniel, Larry J. *Cannoneers in Gray: The Field Artillery of the Army of Tennessee, 1861-1865*. Tuscaloosa, AL: University of Alabama Press, 1984.

_____. *Soldiering in the Army of Tennessee: A Portrait of Life in the Confederate Army*. Chapel Hill, NC: University of North Carolina, 1991.

Griffith, Paddy. *Battle in the Civil War*. Camberley, Surrey, UK: Fieldbooks, 1986.

_____. *Battle Tactics of the Civil War*. New Haven, CT: Yale University Press, 1989.

Jones, R. Steven. *The Right Hand of Command: Use and Disuse of Personal Staffs in the Civil War*. Mechanicsburg, PA: Stackpole Books, 2000.

McWhiney, Grady and Perry D. Jamieson. *Attack and Die: Civil War Military Tactics and the Southern Heritage*. Tuscaloosa, AL: University of Alabama Press, 1982.

Ross, Charles. "Ssh! Battle in Progress!" *Civil War Times Illustrated*. (December 1996): 56-62. Discusses acoustic shadow.

Thomas, Dean S. *Cannons: Introduction to Civil War Artillery*. Arendtsville, PA: Thomas Publications, 1985.

Combat Support and Combat Service Support

Adams, George Worthington. *Doctors in Blue: The Medical History of the Union Army in the Civil War*. New York: Henry Schuman, 1952.

Baas, William P., M.D. "Preliminary Analysis of Post-Battle Deaths at Perryville." *Action Front*. (October 1997): 3.

Gillett, Mary C. *The Army Medical Department, 1818-1865*. Army Historical Series. Washington, DC: US Army Center of Military History, 1987.

Huston, James A. *The Sinews of War: Army Logistics, 1775-1953*. Army

Historical Series. Washington, DC: Office of the Chief of Military History, US Army, 1966.

Internet Sources

Battle of Perryville Web site. <http://www.battleofperryville.com> accessed 6 March 2003.

The Civil War Artillery Page. <http://www.cwartillery.org/artillery.html> accessed 6 March 2003.

Grimsley, Mark. "How to Read a Civil War Battlefield." <http://www.cohums.ohio-state.edu/history/people/grimsley.1/tour/default.htm> accessed 6 March 2003.

Perryville Battlefield Preservation Association. <http://www.perryville.net/> accessed 6 March 2003.

Perryville Battlefield State Historic Site. <http://www.danville-ky.com/BoyleCounty/perryenh.htm> accessed 6 March 2003.

About the Author

Robert S. Cameron has served as the Armor Branch historian, Fort Knox, Kentucky, since 1996. He received a Ph.D. in modern military history from Temple University, Philadelphia, Pennsylvania, in 1994. He has published several articles on US tank development, the Armor Center's urban combat training site, and historical precedents for Army transformation. He has supported staff rides for the Perryville Battlefield since 1997.